D0778847

Painting the Landscape with Fire

Painting the

Landscape with Fire

LONGLEAF PINES AND FIRE ECOLOGY

Den Latham

FOREWORD BY SHIBU JOSE

THE UNIVERSITY OF SOUTH CAROLINA PRESS

Published by the University of South Carolina Press
Columbia, South Carolina 29208

www.sc.edu/uscpress

Manufactured in the United States of America

22 21 20 19 18 17 16 15 14 13 10 9 8 7 6 5 4 3 2 1

Library of Congress Cataloging-in-Publication Data
Latham, Den.
Painting the landscape with fire : longleaf pines and fire ecology / Den Latham.
pages cm
Includes bibliographical references and index.
ISBN 978-1-61117-242-3 (hardback) — ISBN 978-1-61117-247-8 (epub)
1. Fire ecology—South Carolina. 2. Longleaf pine—Effect of fires on.
3. Forests and forestry—Southern States. I. Title.
QH545.F5L58 2013
585'.2—dc23
2012045810

This book was printed on a recycled paper with 30 percent
postconsumer waste content.

CONTENTS

ILLUSTRATIONS

FOREWORD

I cannot contain my excitement; I finished reading a book on longleaf pine that read more like a novel. Seeing a book such as Den Latham's *Painting the Landscape with Fire* has been a dream ever since I finished an edited volume, *The Longleaf Pine Ecosystem: Ecology, Silviculture and Restoration*, back in 2006. The book that I edited along with two of my colleagues filled an important void. The idea for this book was conceived originally as a textbook for a college-level course on the ecology and restoration of the longleaf pine ecosystem. The time-tested classic of Wahlenberg's, *Longleaf Pine: Its Use, Ecology, Regeneration, Protection, Growth and Management* (1946), was out of print. Also we needed an ecosystem approach for this new course. In order to train our students effectively as future resource managers and restoration ecologists, we needed to equip them with skills and science-based principles that are transportable from one system to another.

We published the book and started receiving feedback from students, scientists, and natural-resource professionals. A colleague published a review of the book in a scientific journal and commented that we had made a glaring omission. It may seem unbelievable, but we did not include a chapter devoted to fire. We had a reason; "fire" was the common thread that bound the chapters together. However, after receiving similar feedback from many readers, we were convinced that it was nonetheless an omission. It became quickly apparent that we needed a book to serve not only students, but also practitioners, scientists, policy makers, and the general public. While the number of scientific writings about the longleaf pine ecosystem and the role of fire in restoring and maintaining it increased exponentially over the past few years, there still remained a need for a popular book to tell the public why fire is such an important tool in the arsenal of natural resource professionals. I knew the day would come when someone took his or her inspiration from "fire" to write an entire book on the topic and tell the beautiful story of the longleaf pine landscape. And the day has indeed come with Den Latham's marvelous new book!

While the backdrop of Den's painting is the Carolina Sandhills National Wildlife Refuge, I would be remiss if I did not mention the historic longleaf pine ecosystem of the Southeast that existed on a range of soils and site conditions. Longleaf pine forests were one of the most extensive ecosystems in North America prior to European settlement. The presettlement forests in the South contained more than 37 million hectares of longleaf pine–dominated stands. These forests dominated coastal plains from Virginia through central Florida to Texas, occupying a variety of sites ranging from xeric sandhills to wet, poorly drained flatwoods to the montane areas in northern Alabama. However, with the clearing of land for agriculture and logging operations without adequate regeneration efforts, the area under longleaf pine decreased considerably. For example, 27 percent of the longleaf pine land had been converted to farmland by 1900. In addition to that conversion of land into fields of more aggressive pine species such as loblolly pine and slash pine and the exclusion of fire from the landscape have resulted in further decrease in longleaf pine acreage during the last several decades. Most recent estimates show that only 4 percent of the original area remains today, making longleaf pine one of the most endangered ecosystems in North America. The fact that most of the remaining longleaf pine stands are aging without adequate regeneration and replacement poses a serious threat to the sustainability of these unique forests.

In recent years recognition of the value of the longleaf pine ecosystem has motivated widespread restoration efforts throughout the Southeast. One of the biggest obstacles to successful longleaf pine ecosystem restoration is the persistence of hardwoods in the understory even after the reintroduction of fire. In some cases fire used over a relatively long time may restore the desired canopy structure, but many factors can limit the efficacy of fire after a long period of suppression, including insufficient fine fuels, presence of ladder fuels that may cause damage to crowns, and duff accumulation that can kill overstory trees when ignited. Growth of shrub rhizomes and root systems during periods of fire suppression can be extensive, making these shrubs recalcitrant even when fire is reintroduced. Mechanical and chemical reduction of the midstory may be necessary before reintroducing fire in such instances. Furthermore social factors such as the proximity of residential areas or highways can limit the ability of land managers to use prescribed fire effectively.

I often tell the story of the fire-dependent longleaf pine ecosystem from a scientist's perspective. When you read *Painting the Landscape with Fire*, Den Latham takes you through places, people, conversations, and personal stories that often leave you with a feeling of being on site with him. You smell the smoke, you hear the roar of the Gyro-trac, and you see herpetologist Kevin Messenger in his open Jeep. The rattlesnakes and red-cockaded woodpeckers come alive and nest in your brain forever. Historically fire was a dominant force shaping vegetation communities of the southeastern coastal plain. Fires in the flatwoods and sandhills were of low intensity and occurred every one to ten years. These frequent ground fires drastically reduced the litter layer and midstory shrubs whose presence often prevents seeds and sunlight from reaching the forest floor. Species such as longleaf pine depend on regular fires to create patches of bare mineral soil to allow germination of its large seed, which cannot penetrate thick litter layers. In addition the herbaceous understory also benefits from regular fires through the reduction of understory vegetation, which creates microsites suitable for germination. The plant and animal species such as the longleaf pine and red-cockaded woodpecker present in these communities are often fire dependent. Long-term fire suppression negatively affected fire-adapted species and altered the composition and structure of these communities. With the goals of fuel reduction and conservation of fire-dependent plants and animals, fire is being reintroduced throughout the range of the longleaf pine.

As Latham points out, fire was the major tool for Native Americans to manage the forests and grasslands in North America. It took us a long time to understand and appreciate the value of fire as a management tool, though. In the late nineteenth century, most foresters thought of fire as the enemy of forest stands. It is interesting to read the warning in North Carolina during this period that "the burnings of the present and future, if not soon discontinued, will mean the final extinction of longleaf pine in the state." Science has since then taught us that a well-planned and -executed prescribed fire program is the lifeline of these forests and associated wildlife species. For example, the ability of longleaf pine seedlings to survive and emerge from the grass stage will be affected if fire does not suppress the hardwoods and shrubs in the understory. The hard work and dedication of the natural resource professionals who engage in the "prescribed burning" of our cherished longleaf pine ecosystem and similar fire-dependent ecosystems elsewhere become apparent in Latham's writing. You will appreciate the attention to details and the precautions that the prescribed burners take when executing a fire plan irrespective of whether it is miles from a town or right in the middle of a wildland-urban interface.

The reintroduction of fire can lead to the recovery of many plant and animal communities. The understory plant community of a frequently burned longleaf pine stand could contain up to 170 species per 1,000 square meters. Grasses such as wiregrass, Indiangrass, bluestem, and broomsedge along with a large number of forbs and legumes will dominate the understory. Latham's discussions with wildlife biologist Judy Barnes make us appreciate the importance of this understory's structure and diversity, without delving into scientific research. Native bunchgrasses are important not only to provide fine fuel for the fire, but also for a number of species such as quail. These grasses are sparse at the ground level, but close their canopy above providing a continuous cover. While the closed canopy provides shelter for chicks from predators, the sparseness allows them to forage and flee. Quail is a species that has recovered well as a result of reintroduction of fire in the longleaf pine range.

The return of fire with proper intensity and season alone may not lead to complete vegetation or wildlife recovery if ecosystem thresholds have been crossed. And that is where ecosystem restoration and introduction of wildlife species become important. In his powerful, yet simple style, Latham describes the example of red-cockaded woodpeckers and their translocation and reintroduction program. You will never forget the way he responds when he sees red-cockaded woodpecker chicks for the first time: "They look like tiny dinosaurs." The book is not a scientific text, but that is what makes it so special and appealing to an audience ranging from practitioners to school kids and the general public.

It is my sincere hope that *Painting the Landscape with Fire* inspires the readers to visit a longleaf leaf pine forest so that they can see through their own eyes what they experienced through Latham's while reading the book. Fire is a force that shapes nature through its overwhelming power. In the right hands it can be the best tool available to restore and maintain ecosystems. Latham definitely instills in the reader a sense of duty for supporting the management of conserved land for the benefit of the species involved and for humanity. This book is essential reading for everyone who cares not only about the longleaf pine ecosystem, but about our rich natural resources and their long-term sustainability in general. With this book Latham has accomplished an admirable task of telling a complex story in a simple, yet powerful way and from a refreshing perspective.

Shibu Jose

H. E. Garrett Endowed Professor

The University of Missouri

ACKNOWLEDGMENTS

I am a writer and not a biologist, forester, or natural scientist. I am therefore indebted to all who took me with them into the woods and who patiently answered my questions, even while they were hard at work. As any researcher knows, people who love what they do are generous with their time and knowledge. Although I will not list their names here, they walk in these pages, and my respect and admiration for each of them are evident.

I will, however, single out some others: my son Adam, a writer and my chief editor, for his good counsel; my son Aaron, a wildfire fighter and forester, for his advice and inspiration; Denny Truesdale, Graham Osteen, and the *Hartsville Messenger* for publishing my early essays on natural science and early chapters of my book; Caroline Foster and *South Carolina Wildlife* magazine for the same; Lyne Askins, Scott Lanier, Patricia McCoy, Dave Robinson, and the crew of the Carolina Sandhills National Wildlife Refuge for opening the door to the longleaf ecosystem; Alexander Moore of the University of South Carolina Press for his steadfast encouragement and enthusiasm; Linda Fogle, also of USC Press, for her guidance in publishing; Johnny Stowe and the South Carolina Prescribed Fire Council for their good work and generous help; Trish DeHond, Clemson Extension agent, for her friendship and botanical tutorials; Stephen Lyn Bales for his lifelong friendship and for leading the charge; and Dixie Goswami, John Elder, and Ken Macrorie of the Bread Loaf School of English, Middlebury College, for their instruction in the writing of nonfiction and nature literature. Most of all I wish to thank my wife, Allison, for her love and faith, and for never giving up.

After a prescribed burn, the ground is smoking. A big longleaf pine dominates the scene. The needles of younger pines are still green; the low flames never reached their crowns. The growth of young scrub oaks, which threaten the longleaf habitat, has been reduced. Though much of the understory is gone, the loss is temporary. Low-intensity burns are a boon to the forest community, preserving the habitat and promoting new growth and food sources for wildlife. Photograph by the author.

Fire Is Good

THE CAROLINA SANDHILLS are ancient. The hills are small, often just subtle risings and fallings in the land. It is easy to imagine when you drive down a dirt road or hike through a forest there that the Sandhills are the time-wasted dunes of a Paleozoic sea.

A geologist tells me that's not the case. The Sandhills are the eroded peaks of the Appalachians, the oldest chain of mountains in the world, mountains that stood as high as the Himalayas before their heights were ground to dust by wind and rain and washed down by Mesozoic rivers. As lowly as the Sandhills seem, however, they are older than the Himalayas. The geologist says that I should not be overly impressed by this as the Himalayas are not old geologically.[1] Still, it impresses me.

To an untrained eye, the pine forest of the Sandhills may look monotonous. Like an old midwestern prairie, it is "a subtle landscape, typically underwhelming for the casual observer."[2] But the Sandhills harbor a remnant of one of the rarer ecosystems on Earth—a longleaf pine forest, which is home to approximately eight hundred plant species. At first glance this southeastern woodland appears to be just pines, grass, and scrub oaks, but it is rich in species that thrive only in this ecosystem.

Carolinians don't have to trek to Alaska or the Amazon to find the wild or the rare. Sadly, they don't have to go far to find the endangered either. In the Sandhills some plant and animal species are hanging onto life with slender roots or talons.

I went to the Carolina Sandhills National Wildlife Refuge in search of a topic in 2003. Two years earlier I had started writing nature essays on reptiles, geology, raptors, botany, and so forth for local newspapers and magazines, and I was looking for a new subject, maybe cottonmouths or coyotes. I like researching and writing about natural science. It gets me out of the office and into the woods and wetlands, where I meet experts who love their

A healthy longleaf forest is open and lacks a hardwood midstory. Saplings grow with few or no lateral branches to raise their terminal buds above the next fire. The ground cover here is bracken fern. Photograph courtesy of USFWS.

work and are generous with their time. At the refuge I introduced myself to manager Scott Lanier. Scott asked me to write a news article explaining to a sometimes hostile public the need for prescribed burns in longleaf pine forests, a topic about which I knew nothing.

Scott's headquarters is a red brick building surrounded by forty-five thousand acres of tall pines, wiregrass, upland bogs called pocosins, ponds, and purple-flowered lupines. Dressed in a khaki shirt, green slacks, and boots, Scott was fit and clean shaven, with a warm smile and shock of boyish brown hair. His upper sleeve sported the badge of the U.S. Fish and Wildlife Service—a logo of sun, mountains, lake, fish, and duck. He welcomed me into his office.

I immediately noticed Scott's professionalism and respect for his staff's expertise. The Carolina Sandhills prescribed fire crew is among the most experienced in the United States in a region, the Southeast, that has more prescribed burns than any other in the nation.

Prescribed burns are a hot topic both locally and nationally. In 2000 in New Mexico a prescribed burn of nine hundred acres raged into a wildfire that burned forty-seven thousand acres and destroyed more than two hundred homes.

A letter to a local newspaper complained that prescribed burns at the refuge are set by "fire arsons" who "burn up the timber and animals in the forest." Another agreed: "The people at the Sandhills will tell you also that they burn to create vegetation for the animals. Well, when you burn up the forest and engulf the animals with the flames, where are the animals to eat the vegetation?"

Distrust of fire is inbred and widespread. Of course, it's the burn that goes bad—not the ones that prevent future conflagrations—that kindles the 6:00 news.

"Fire has been suppressed for so long that when a forest finally burns, it's catastrophic," Scott explained. "Had prescribed burns been introduced periodically, we might not have experienced those wildfires."

The Sandhills region, he said, has a history of fires, both natural and man-made. Lightning caused areas to burn occasionally. In addition Native Americans set fire to fields to clear land for crops and to drive game for hunting.

From Virginia to Texas there are huge tracts of coastal plain that have no natural firebreak, such as a river. A single lightning strike might have burned a thousand square kilometers, and "a few ignitions in each state" might have sufficed "to burn most of the landscape."[3]

"Our area suffered some real smokin' wildfires in the early 1940s," said Scott, "but as the U.S. Fish and Wildlife Service began prescribed burning, catastrophic wildfires decreased. By using fires on a controlled basis, foresters reduced wildfire potential." Scott continued, "Historically much of the Sandhills and the Southeast were savannas of old-growth longleaf pines. I've read Bartram's account of traveling through the Southeast in the 1700s. He describes an endless sea of longleaf pines and grass."

For thousands of years until the early nineteenth century, spacious longleaf pine forests covered an estimated ninety million acres of the southeastern United States from Virginia to Texas. About two million acres, or 2 percent, of longleaf pine forests remain. Few of those—about twenty thousand acres—are old growth, and none is in South Carolina.

These threatened forests are the habitats of choice for endangered species such as the red-cockaded woodpecker (RCW). In precolonial times an estimated nine hundred thousand RCWs lived in the longleaf pine forests. Now about 14,000 are left, scattered across eleven states.

"RCWs need an open pine savanna," Scott told me. Open pine savannas are habitats that are "fire-dependent. Without fire, a pine forest develops a thick midstory of oaks."

A midstory of turkey oaks, for example, allows predators such as snakes to invade the woodpeckers' nest cavities more easily. A hardwood midstory also allows wildfire to jump up into the longleaf pine canopy and kill the entire forest. Without the use of low-intensity prescribed burns to control the midstory, RCWs will leave the Sandhills. There are few places left for them to go.

"We've learned that in some places fire is good for the landscape," Scott said. "There's a host of plant species that are fire dependent and shade intolerant. They need sunlight shining through the canopy of the forest."

Playing devil's advocate, I asked why we should care about longleaf pines and woodpeckers. Species go extinct all the time.

Scott didn't skip a beat. "Personally, I believe these species and this habitat are God's creations. Why should man have the right to determine which species live and which die? The American environmentalist Aldo Leopold said that the first rule of a good mechanic is to keep all of the parts. If you rebuild something but leave out a nut here, a bolt there, a cog here, and a gear there, the thing isn't going to work. Every species, every habitat, is a piece of the puzzle. When we remove pieces—an endangered species, for example—we can't put the puzzle back together.

"Also, the Carolina Sandhills National Wildlife Refuge is charged by law to manage this habitat. We're required by the Endangered Species Act to protect these forests for the red-cockaded woodpecker. Our job is to protect, preserve, and manage wisely. It's good stewardship," Scott concluded, and he invited me to witness an upcoming prescribed burn.

Back at home I dusted off a copy of William Bartram's *Travels* and thumbed to a passage where the botanist, venturing from Savannah to Augusta in the 1780s, finds himself "on the entrance of a vast plain, generally level, which extends west sixty or seventy miles. . . . This plain is mostly a forest of great long-leaved pine (*P. palustris Linn.*) the earth covered with grass, interspersed with an infinite variety of herbaceous plants."[4]

Nearly a hundred million acres of original longleaf pine forest had been lost to America. Never having seen a stand of virgin longleaf, I was incapable of imagining what we had lost. I hoped that someday I would visit a stand of old-growth longleaf pines.

NOTES

1. Dr. Fred Edinger, interview, Coker College, Hartsville, South Carolina, March, 2006.

2. Eric Higgs, *Nature by Design: People, Natural Process, and Ecological Restoration* (Cambridge, Mass.: MIT Press, 2003), 79.

3. Cecil Frost, "History and Future of the Longleaf Pine Ecosystem," in *The Longleaf Pine Ecosystem: Ecology, Silviculture, and Restoration*, ed. Shibu Jose, Eric J. Jokela, and Deborah L. Miller (New York: Springer, 2006), 13–14.

4. William Bartram, *Travels of William Bartram* (New York: Dover, 1955), 51–52.

Fire Tour

"It's pretty intense for a short period of time."

Scott Lanier, refuge manager

ON A WEEKDAY IN EARLY APRIL at 7:30 A.M. I received a call from Scott Lanier, manager of the Carolina Sandhills National Wildlife Refuge (CSNWR). Conditions looked good for a prescribed burn, and he invited me along.

Scott had told me that the use of fire is necessary to preserve the Sandhills population of endangered red-cockaded woodpeckers (RCWs) and the longleaf pine ecosystem, but I knew little about how a forest fire could be controlled or why, if you start a fire, you don't end up with significant collateral carnage.

An hour later I was with Scott at the refuge in the cab of his 4 x 4 U.S. Fish and Wildlife Service (USFWS) truck looking at a map of Carolina Sandhills NWR Compartment 17. The refuge is divided into a number of compartments. Each one's boundaries are defined by geographical features such as creeks or roads, which provide natural or man-made firebreaks. Each compartment is subdivided into smaller burn units. "Some units are as big as five hundred or six hundred acres," Scott said. "The crew may stage two or more burns per day."

Every year the crew hopes to burn about one-third of the forty-five-thousand-acre refuge. In a good year they may burn twenty thousand acres. "The burn season lasts from February to May," Scott said. "It's pretty intense for a short period of time."

The map was small but detailed, showing dirt and paved roads, NWR boundaries, fields, and even types of trees—pine, scrub oak, bottomland hardwood, upland hardwood—as well as individual RCW cavity trees that might harbor the nests of these endangered birds. Each year the crew scouts for these trees, which must be protected during burns. Every one that's found is mapped and marked with a ring of white paint.

A prescribed burn. Using a drip torch, forestry technician Brett Craig sets fire to grass near Oxpen Lake in the Carolina Sandhills National Wildlife Refuge. Prescribed burns mimic the natural process of fire to promote healthy longleaf forests, reduce competition from woody shrubs, and maintain native grasses and herbaceous plants that benefit wildlife. Photograph courtesy of USFWS.

I studied the map. "So black dot 72 is a tree with an RCW living in it?"

"We know it's an RCW cavity tree," Scott replied, "but I can't tell by looking at a map if the cavity is active," that is, if a bird was nesting in it that year. He pointed on the map to three more clusters of cavity trees. A "cluster" of cavity trees belongs to a family of RCWs. To protect these trees from fire, before a burn the ground crew rakes away the fuel—needles, leaves, fallen branches—to a minimum twelve-foot diameter. This same technique was used over a century ago by workers harvesting oleoresin, a mixture of oil and resin, for the naval stores industry.[1]

We drove to the maintenance area, a compound of buildings and storage sheds, where Mark Parker, the ground burn boss, was briefing the crew. Parked there were more USFWS trucks, ATVs, and two diesel fire engines—not big red ones but smaller yellow brush trucks specially outfitted for rough terrain and forest fires.

Scott and I entered the briefing room at the tail end of Mark's instructions. An American flag and several posters of forest fires hung on the wall. One poster, "Northwest Rockies, Fires of 2000," pictured a mountain wildfire replete with firefighters, hovering helicopter, and fleeing elk.

Except for the helicopter pilot, who wore a green flight suit, all of the crew were dressed in green or brown pants, smoke-smudged long-sleeved yellow shirts, and lace-up boots. Everyone toted hard hats and small black backpacks.

"Before every prescribed burn there's a briefing," Scott told me. "From previous experience, the burn boss knows which units burn hotter or are prone to jump firebreaks."

Typically a crew of eight to twelve works a CSNWR prescribed burn. This crew consisted of six men and two women, firefighters from this refuge and Savannah. Of these eight, three would be in the helicopter. "Much of the burning is done with a helicopter," Scott said. The briefing reminded me of a military exercise, serious and highly organized, with specialized tasks for each member.

With bulldozers, brush trucks, and helicopters, fire crews can burn several units in a single day. When the units are large and the opportunities to burn are limited, as is the case with most national forests, this capacity is crucial. In forests near public roads and heavy urban interface, aerial ignition can generate enough convective lift to get the smoke column up into the mixing layer, the height where strong atmospheric mixing occurs, and out of harm's way.[2]

At the end of the briefing, Mark introduced me as a newspaper reporter to the crew and told them that I would be with Scott on the burn, that I could take some photos and ask some questions that he hoped they'd answer, but that they should not permit me to interfere with their work. I mumbled that I was a freelance writer researching longleaf pine habitats.

The crew left for the first burn site. Scott and I rode to the helicopter landing, a concrete pad in a grassy meadow surrounded by pine forest. The helicopter was a blue and white Bell LongRanger on lease from Skylane, Inc., of Decatur, Texas. Stationed for the burn season at the Sandhills, it was also used at other prescribed burns throughout the fire district, which included fourteen stations in the Carolinas and Georgia.

The side door of the helicopter was open. Next to it was parked a pickup truck. One of the crew was loading large red duffel bags from the bed of the truck into the rear of the aircraft.

I shook hands with Terri Jenkins, the helicopter's burn boss and fire management officer from the Savannah Coastal Refuges Complex. The helicopter crew, she told me, consisted of three people. In addition to herself and the pilot, a third crew member operated what was called a Ping-Pong ball machine, a curious steel contraption bolted to the side opening of the helicopter. Officially this device is known as the Premo Mark III Aerial Ignition Machine.

In the duffel bags, Terri said, were thousands of small white plastic balls partly filled with potassium permanganate. As the helicopter flies patterns over the burn zone, a crew member feeds these balls into the aerial ignition machine, where they are injected with ethylene glycol, an antifreeze solution, and dropped through a chute onto the forest floor. Soon after they hit the ground, a delayed chemical reaction causes the balls to ignite.

Temperature and humidity affect the ignition timing of the balls. To get an ignition timing of about thirty seconds, the machine operator adjusts the amount of glycol. To regulate the intensity of the fire, he alters the frequency and number of balls dropped, depending on weather, topography, and the amount of fuel, such as leaves and branches, on the ground.

"The Sandhills are well suited for the use of this system," Terri said. "There's good leaf litter for the balls to ignite. The balls are used not only for prescribed burns," she added, "but also for fire suppression." A wildfire can be suppressed by starting a burn on a forest floor to consume the fuel before the wildfire can reach it.

For an effective burn pattern, the helicopter usually flies from thirty to sixty feet above tree level. "Obviously, the higher you fly, the less effective the drop pattern," said Terri. "Winds or the thickness of the canopy can vary the ball patterns, but it's amazing. The balls drop pretty much in a straight line."

I wondered what happened when a ball became caught in the top of a tree. Couldn't that start a devastating crown fire, with flames leaping from one tree to the next? Scott told me that "the ball will burn and go out because there's not enough dead dry fuel up there. You'll see a small wisp of smoke. The needles will barely get scorched."

The pilot arrived, and the crew prepared to lift off. Scott and I returned to his truck. There was a burst of static on his radio, and a woman's voice gave the cloud ceiling, dew point, and wind direction and speed.

"That's Patricia McCoy, our dispatcher," said Scott. "She checks the weather periodically and notifies the crew before we start a burn. For example, if the humidity drops or the wind direction changes, we have to stop. Every time we schedule a burn, we get permission from the South Carolina Forestry Commission. They issue a permit number and give us the go-ahead."

LATER, BACK AT THE REFUGE OFFICE, I had an opportunity to talk with Patricia McCoy, the CSNWR's accountant, administrative assistant, and dispatcher. Patricia is stationed in the headquarters. Her role in a burn is to monitor weather reports, obtain state approval to burn, coordinate communication between the ground and helicopter crews, and deal with a mountain of paperwork.

"In the morning the ground boss gives me the prescription for the burn, that is, the specific information pertaining to the areas they plan to burn," she said. "Then I phone the South Carolina Forestry Commission [SCFC] to get a permit authorization number. I give them my contact info, the burn location, the nearest road or intersection, and the grid location of the burn area. I also tell them the total acreage of the burn; the tonnage of fuel per acre; the method of burning—aerial or hand; the purpose of the burn, in this case hazard reduction; the time we'll start; the distance in miles the burn is from smoke-sensitive areas such as highways and communities; and the name of the person in charge." If the request is approved, the SCFC issues an authorization number, and Patricia radios the ground boss with the authorization to burn.

Patricia's paperwork includes "the prescription, the day's weather forecast, the resource order [how many people and how much equipment will be on the ground and in the helicopter], the total acreage we plan to burn, and the 'go' checklist," a list of must-haves and must-dos that requires the signature of the refuge's highest ranking officer present. "We can't strike a match without getting that son-of-a-gun signed," Mark told me later.

At the beginning and end of each burn day, Patricia reports the number of acres they intend to burn and the acres actually burned respectively to the South Carolina Interagency Coordination Center, an agency of the Federal Forest Service, which in turn reports to the Southeast Regional Office in Atlanta. When the burn has ended, she notifies the SCFC and faxes the relevant documents and the final number of acres burned.

I scanned the resource order of a previous burn. It listed the date, the name of the burn boss, and the personnel and equipment: a total of twelve firefighters, a helicopter with three crew members, two fire engines and operators, one bulldozer and driver, two ATVs, and one dispatcher.

But there's more than paperwork. "Every hour," Patricia said, "I check the weather, record it, and call it out to the burn crew. Whether it's a helicopter burn or a hand burn, I track what they're doing. The helicopter crew must check in with me every fifteen minutes or I contact them. They tell me, for example, whether they're over Unit 2.4, on route to recon a burn, or heading back to land and refuel. If there's a problem with radio communication, I relay messages from the ground boss to the helicopter."

Patricia must secure a burn permit not just for the day but also for each unit the crew wants to burn. She seeks authorization for another burn only after the first burn has been contained and the burn boss has requested to "fire a new area."

"Sometimes when I call the state with another request to burn, I'm told there's been a complaint about smoke in a certain area. I let the burn boss know of the complaint. If necessary, he'll order the helicopter to see if there is a smoke problem. We get blamed for a lot of smoke from fires that aren't ours," she added.

I asked if things ever got exciting—not a happy question, for who would want drama at a burn?

Not at a burn, she told me. "But one night we had a wildfire." The fire had started on private land within the refuge boundary. The crew, which had been on-site for a prescribed burn, responded. "We were here till three in the morning. One of the firefighters, Jan Tripp, a woman from Savannah, stepped into a stump hole before the sun went down." During a blaze a stump can catch fire and burn down into the ground, leaving a trap of hot embers. "At first her foot and leg hurt, but the pain went away. She had burned and deadened the nerves. She came in here about midnight and pulled her pant leg up. She had skin hanging, third-degree burns. She was taken to the hospital in Hartsville, then flown to the burn center in Augusta, where she had skin grafts."

"She's a tough woman," I said.

"She is tough," Patricia agreed. "That's the only accident we've had on a fire."

AT THE LANDING PAD the pilot started the engine, and the blades of the helicopter began rotating. Scott and I drove off to examine a unit of forest that the crew had burned in March three weeks back. As we rode, I asked if the refuge had many wildfires.

Each year, he said, one or two lightning strikes may start a fire. "One such fire burned about three hundred acres last year. The South Carolina Forestry

Commission has a spotter plane that flies the state searching for fires. But the wildfires we have at the refuge, either we find them or somebody notifies us."

Driving along a narrow dirt road, Scott gestured toward the wide forest on either side, to lupines, clumps of wiregrass, and longleaf pine seedlings that resembled green knee-high fountains.

"Three weeks ago," he told me, "much of this understory was burned to the ground. We got a shot of rain, and everything's starting to green up."

He stopped the truck. I noticed orange needles in the crowns of some pines.

"Heat scorched some of the needles," Scott said. "Those will drop off and be replaced. Longleaf pines are adapted to fire. Fire is part of their life cycle; they have very thick bark. Burning without killing trees is a science and an art," he reflected. "You can kill them by burning too hot."

The voice of Terri Jenkins came over Scott's radio. "Carolina Sandhills office, this is helicopter 8-0 Lima."

Patricia responded, "Go ahead, 8-0 Lima."

"We are on route to Unit 9.3," Terri said. "Three souls on board. Two hours of fuel."

"Copy."

When the radio went silent, Scott continued. "Today is a growing season burn, as opposed to a dormant, winter burn. Research shows that fire often occurs in the growing season. We try to mimic that. It helps curtail the oaks, which are sucking up nutrients from the soil and budding out. If we burn at this time, the fire will kill a lot of them. We haven't pushed the envelope, though, and burned in summer. You can really torch your pines if the conditions—moisture, fuel, and temperature—aren't perfect."

Scott drove on. I recalled what he had said earlier about the threat of an oak midstory to a longleaf forest: in a wildfire flames will jump from oaks into the longleaf canopy and kill the pines.

"Our goal is not to eradicate the oaks," he explained, "but to control them. Oaks are part of this habitat and provide mast, acorns for animals."

The eradication of scrub oaks is as undesirable as it is impossible. Scrub oaks are like a mythological serpent, the many-headed Hydra: the more heads you cut off, the more heads it grows. If fire kills a scrub oak's stem, the stump's response is to grow more stems.

We came to a place where the road divided one kind of forest from another. One side was private land; the other, refuge. The contrast was an object lesson in forestry. The NWR side was pine plantation—an open forest of tall longleaf pines, a scattering of short turkey oaks and dogwoods, and a ground cover of wiregrass, broomsedge, lupines, and a myriad of low, herbaceous plants. The private land, in contrast, was a dense, tangled woods of oaks and taller pines with a thick ground cover of dead leaves and fallen branches. I mentioned that the private land looked like a tinderbox of fuel waiting to ignite.

Scott disagreed. "It would take a tremendously hot fire to get those oaks to burn," he told me. A mat of dead oak leaves had shaded out the grass. "It's hard to get a burn going there. You don't have enough fuel to control the oaks."

I remarked that one would expect to find more animal species on the private land.

Scott replied that most people would think so but that longleaf pine forests are surprisingly preferable for plant and animal diversity. "There are bird species—Bachman's sparrows, for example, a species of concern now—which are adapted to pine savannas. You won't find them on the private land we saw. Quail prefer bluestem, Indian grass, and wiregrass—native, warm-season grasses that grow in clumps. As the clumps grow, there's open space under the grass" where quail and their chicks nest and forage for insects. All of these grasses are part of the longleaf ecosystem. "And all," Scott added, "are fire dependent."

One biologist, tallying the animal diversity of longleaf savannas, placed the number of resident vertebrate species at 212, "including 38 species that are specialists" in this ecosystem. This diversity "is greater than for any other habitat type in the Coastal Plain of the southeastern United States." In terms of diversity, longleaf savannas are among the richest ecosystems "in temperate North America. Such high species richness should be expected, given the antiquity of this type of ecosystem."[3]

Scott and I drove down a maze of dirt roads deeper into the refuge. Ahead smoke was boiling out from the woods. A fire engine sat at a crossroads. The ground crew, highly visible in their yellow fire-retardant Nomex shirts, had started a prescribed burn at Unit 9.3. We parked near a scorched swath of land that paralleled the road bed and stepped out of the truck.

Striding along the firebreak, which in this case was a dirt road, the crew was creating a "black line" about twenty yards wide by pouring fire from drip torches—canisters of slash fuel, a diesel and gas mixture in a 3–1 ratio—onto the ground cover. When tilted, the torches dripped fire from metal spouts tipped with wicks.

Every few yards the crew dripped flames, which flared out in circles, consuming grass and pine needles until they met either the next circle of fire or the firebreak and burned out. The crew also started the fire against the wind, which corralled the flames and pushed them in the intended direction toward the firebreak. After the crew finished the black line, the helicopter would set the whole unit on fire, all 445 acres.

The sky was thick with swirling gray smoke. I heard the growl of an ATV. Mark Parker, the ground burn boss, stopped his four-wheeler beside Scott's truck. Mark was lean and athletic, with close-cropped hair, steady blue eyes, and a goatee. He had a slow country way of talking and an impressive command of the terrain. I found out later that he is an experienced wildfire fighter who had repelled from helicopters to fight blazes out west.

Like the other firefighters, Mark was dressed in fire-retardant clothes and a hard hat. He also wore a black backpack stocked with power bars, a first-aid and CPR kit, and "lots of water." A weather kit capable of giving timely info on temperature, wind speed, humidity, and dew point hung from his belt. With this he could figure critical data such as fuel moisture, ignition rate, and flame height.

"The black line widens out the firebreak created by the road," Mark explained. "Obviously, the fuel we just burned is not going to reburn. You don't want to leave any section along the firebreak unburned," he added. "If we had a wind swap, if the wind shifted 180 degrees, fire would run through the unburned fuel and possibly jump the firebreak," igniting a wildfire on the other side of the road.

The drip-torch crew does not lay down a solid line of flame. "That would push a lot of heat up into the burn unit," Mark said. "Once the fire has backed off fifty to one hundred feet from the road—it's a judgment call—we'll notify the aircraft," which will drop balls from the aerial ignition machine to finish the burn.

As if on cue, a whir of helicopter blades beat the air overhead. The sound repeatedly came and went as the helicopter crew rained down a pattern of fire.

I had been to the refuge often hiking, fishing, hunting, and biking, but I'd never seen it like this. It was a Dantesque scene of an inferno. The ground was smoldering black. Three-foot flames licked the tree trunks. The yellow-shirted, smoke-smudged crew tramped through the firebreak, setting fire to any patch of wiregrass that hadn't yet caught. A yellow fire engine, red lights flashing, stood sentinel on the dirt road.

I looked on from the firebreak with Mark and Scott and watched the thick gray smoke roiling into the sky. I wondered how the devil the helicopter crew could see to drop its pattern of fireballs into the burn zone.

Scott spoke over the noise of the helicopter and pointed to a section of woods across the road. "That area was burned a couple of weeks ago," he said. The pine seedlings and grass had already started to regenerate. "By summer, it'll green up."

An American bird grasshopper, a tawny bug as big as my finger, flew into the burn zone and landed on a trunk that was still smoking. "What about the wildlife?" I asked. "People will look at the fire and say, 'You're burning the squirrels, the toads, the snakes.'"

Mark took a dip of Grizzly smokeless tobacco and put the tin back in his hip pocket. "That's why we don't ring the unit with fire. We light it in strips, not solid lines."

Overhead the helicopter whirred, banked, and turned, dropping another dotted line of balls into the burn zone. The balls fell about five yards apart. Within seconds each fizzed and flared into a spreading circle of flame. Soon the forest floor was aflame with these dotted lines of fire, each line roughly "a chain," or sixty-six feet, from the next. Whenever the fires set by the balls met, the flames died from lack of fuel.

"Not setting the fire in solid lines," Mark continued, "leaves gaps for deer, snakes, rabbits to escape. You'll see turkeys fly out. A lot of animals head into nearby springhead pocosins [upland swamps] and hunker down, because those areas generally don't burn. I've seen deer run through a burn, pop out the other side, and keep right on a-gettin' it. Later this afternoon I'll be surprised if we don't see turkeys foraging in this area while it's still smoking." They'd be looking for toasted grasshoppers, I thought, a backwoods delicacy.

A year later I would see evidence of Mark's assertion about wild turkey behavior after a burn. I was touring Hobcaw Barony, a wildlife refuge near Georgetown, South Carolina, driving past a woods that had been burned the day before. A stump still smoldered in the distance. The ground was black and apparently devoid of anything living. A stone's throw across the road was a green, unburned forest, and yet foraging on the charred earth were three gobblers.

I asked Mark if any animals take a hit during the burns. He paused. "There's always a possibility of killing a few. But on a refuge that's forty-five thousand acres, the benefit of new growth outweighs the small amount of loss."

The argument is that it's better for wildlife to suffer small, periodic burns than a catastrophic wildfire that kills an entire forest community. What's more, rather than leave behind scorched earth, periodic fires encourage new growth and yield "the greatest increases in ground cover species richness and density."[4]

"If snakes have burrows, they can go underground," Scott said. "Sometimes they'll move out onto the road. Because not everything burns completely, turtles may crawl under logs or into pocosins. We're going to lose some animals that can't escape, but the habitat we're preserving is needed by many species."

Just as longleaf pine forests depend on occasional ground fires, many southeastern species depend on longleaf forests. In 1942 J. S. Tanner of the National Audubon Society suspected that the demise of ivory-billed woodpeckers was due in part to the loss of old-growth longleaf pine forests, a loss that resulted from rampant logging and decades of fire suppression. In addition to the endangered red-cockaded woodpecker, seventeen species of amphibians specialize in longleaf habitats. Of these at least three—the flatwoods salamander and the gopher and crawfish frogs—are listed as threatened. The gopher tortoise and eastern box turtle as well as snakes such as the eastern indigo, short-tailed, Florida pine, southern hognose, and eastern diamondback are in decline. That decline goes hand in hand with the loss of more than 97 percent of longleaf pine habitats.

The decimation of native flora and fauna is pervasive. "The northern bobwhite quail, whose 1920s population decline in the Southeast was responsible for stimulating the research that discovered the importance of fire in longleaf savannas . . . has endured a decline of more than 65% over the last 20 years. . . . All three species of mammals that are longleaf specialists," the Florida mouse, the fox squirrel, and Goff's gopher, "have declined." Goff's gopher is believed to be extinct. "The drastic loss of longleaf pine savannas has had an even more severe impact on plants." Depending on which research or government agency you follow, as many as 191 plants endemic to longleaf forests are considered threatened or endangered.[5] Clearly a comparison of the precariousness of longleaf pine ecosystems to that of rain forests is not hyperbolic.

Scott pointed to a pocosin. "A lot of bird and amphibian populations like switch cane. We try to bring cane back into pocosins. If you don't introduce a little fire into the bottoms periodically, switch cane will be overtaken by woody vegetation," he pointed out. Another endangered plant native to the Sandhills, white wicky, also lives in pocosins and needs fire to reduce competition from other plants.

A cluster of red-cockaded woodpecker trees stood in the burn zone. A ring of white paint marked each of these trees. To protect the cavity nests of these endangered birds, the crew had raked a twelve-foot circle of needles and leaves away from each RCW tree. Although the rest of the forest floor was charred and smoldering and the trunks of other trees were blackened, the RCWs' trees appeared untouched by fire.

As the flames died, we watched the ground crew patrol the perimeter of the fire to make sure it did not jump the break. Scott gestured down the road to another unit of forest. "It's been two years since that area burned. If fire jumps there, it'll catch. There's enough fuel to burn."

Scott's and Mark's radios crackled, and Patricia said, "Terri, you might want to fly over to Compartment 17."

Over their radios came the sound of the helicopter. "Copy that," Terri replied. "We're flying to 17."

The radios fell silent. Mark studied the smoke in the sky. "This burn was 445 acres. The one this afternoon at Unit 17.3 will be 470. We have burned up to 2,600 acres a day when the conditions were right and we had a larger crew. But with the smoke we got right now, we might have to cancel," he said matter-of-factly.

After a minute Terri came back over their radios. "The smoke is blowing off the refuge. We have a ceiling that's topping out around two thousand feet."

Mark turned to me. "Smoke will usually rise till it hits the mixing height. Then it'll travel horizontally. The higher the smoke goes, the more it will disperse. The problem is, today's mixing height is lower than what was predicted. The prediction was for an atmospheric ceiling of six thousand feet, but the smoke isn't getting up that high. We may have to call off this afternoon's burn. Terri's flying over to look at Unit 17.3."

Mark unfolded a map on the hood of Scott's truck. This was his fifth burn season at the NWR, and he was familiar not only with the terrain but also with features not shown on the map, for example homes and barns. As the burn boss, Mark would decide whether to continue burning or call it quits. "You can see how Compartment 17 lies. What I'd be most worried about," he said as his finger traced a road along the edge of the NWR, "are residences here and here. With a west-northwest wind, I don't want smoke to set on these houses."

The radios crackled again. "This is 8-0 Lima," said Terri.

"Go ahead, 8-0 Lima. This is Mark."

Terri sounded doubtful. "Mark, if I had to make the decision, I'm not sure I'd burn 17 today."

"Copy that," Mark said, folding up the map. "We still have about forty-five minutes left to wrap up this burn."

Scott said he would drive me back to the headquarters and my Jeep. He offered to let me witness another burn soon.

I shook hands with Mark. I was impressed by his restraint. Ground crew, helicopter, fire engine, bulldozer, ATVs—all dressed up and nowhere else to burn. As much as the crew loved their work, as much as they strained at the leash and hoped to burn a third of the refuge each year, they played by the rules.

On my drive back to town, I noticed that my hands and jeans were smudged. My hair and clothes smelled of wood smoke. It was the smell of orange flames, a blackened landscape, and a crew striding with drip torches as a helicopter beat the air above the pines, their crowns still green in the smoke.

NOTES

1. Alan W. Hodges, "The Naval Stores Industry," in *The Longleaf Pine Ecosystem: Ecology, Silviculture, and Restoration*, ed. Shibu Jose, Eric J. Jokela, and Deborah L. Miller (New York: Springer, 2006), 44.

2. Bill Twomey, address to the annual meeting of the South Carolina Prescribed Fire Council, Columbia, South Carolina, November 18, 2009.

3. Bruce Means, "Vertebrate Faunal Diversity of Longleaf Pine Ecosystems," in *The Longleaf Pine Ecosystem*, ed. Jose, Jokela, and Miller, 200.

4. Joan L. Walker and Andrea M. Silletti, "Restoring the Ground Cover in Longleaf Pine Ecosystems," in *The Longleaf Pine Ecosystem*, ed. Jose, Jokela, and Miller, 307.

5. Means, "Vertebrate Faunal Diversity," 199–200.

Red-cockaded Woodpeckers

"We're the reason they [RCWs] are endangered. Because they are, we are required by law to protect them."

Laura Housh, wildlife biologist

WHEN COLUMBUS DROPPED ANCHOR, an estimated nine hundred thousand red-cockaded woodpeckers (*Picoides borealis*) inhabited ninety million acres of longleaf pines. Many ornithologists who wrote the first books on American birds described RCWs as common. About fourteen thousand RCWs and 2 percent of those forests remain.

The fate of RCWs and longleaf pine forests will always be intertwined. For thousands of years the woodpeckers relied on those trees for habitats in a fire-ridden land. Now, because RCWs are endangered, hundreds of thousands of acres of longleaf pines depend on federal protection.

At first glance RCWs' tree of choice—longleaf pine, which drips more resin than any other pine—would seem a bad place for a cavity nest. Drilling a tunnel through the sapwood into the heartwood of a longleaf pine is a tedious, sticky business; and the tunnel is merely the entrance to the nest, the beginning of the work. Fortunately the heartwood of the tree where the bird excavates its cavity nest produces no resin. A big pileated woodpecker, crow-size and common to the Southeast, may knock out a cavity in a dead sweetgum in weeks. But the longleaf's resinous mess makes drilling through sapwood gooey and operose. RCWs, smaller than cardinals, may take years to dig out their cavities.

"A resin duct in a pine is like an artery which, if cut, will eventually coagulate," said Ralph Costa, red-cockaded woodpecker recovery coordinator for the U.S. Fish and Wildlife Service. Patiently, insistently RCWs drill, wait for the resin ducts to seal "till resinosis sets in," and then drill again. It's slow going.

Endangered red-cockaded woodpeckers, commonly called RCWs, are a keystone species in the longleaf ecosystem. RCWs are the only woodpeckers to excavate cavity nests inside living trees. To deter rat snakes, RCWs flake away bark and drill resin wells to coat the areas surrounding their nests with resin. Photograph courtesy of Dr. William Alexander.

"I've been up to my neck in RCWs since 1985. I've seen some natural cavities completed by RCWs in six months," said Ralph, though excavation can take up to twelve years. Because RCWs live from seven to nine years, excavating a cavity can be a generational project. But a cavity, like a family home, is an investment. A nest of twigs may go up in flames, but a cavity in heartwood may be lived in for over thirty years by six generations. In human life spans it's as though the house you live in had been built by your ancestors before the Revolutionary War.

I was about to ask if it made sense to dig a cavity into a living tree when drilling into a dead one would be so much easier. Then I remembered that southeastern forests endure more lightning-strike fires than any other forests in North America. Dead trees burn. Live ones do too, but thick-barked longleafs are the most fire-resistant of pines.

I recalled watching a sweetgum during one prescribed burn. Fire ate through its bark like acid and boiled its sap. "As a fire licks the bark of a tree, the temperature on the surface can rise to 1,600 degrees Fahrenheit. . . . Fire kills the cambium of sweetgum in less than half the time as longleaf pine."[1] Where better to build your castle than inside the tree most likely to withstand blaze after blaze?

A more frequent and persistent threat to RCWs is the rat snake. Up to six feet long, it slithers up trunks and burglarizes nests for chicks and eggs, even though the nests may be just below the crowns of the trees.

But RCWs are nothing if not resourceful. To deter snakes, Ralph explained, "the bird flakes off bark from around the cavity entrance right down to the cambium, eventually forming a 'faceplate.'" Next the woodpecker drills scores of resin wells around the tunnel and lower down the trunk. To keep the resin flowing, the RCW drills every day. The wells ooze a shield of gluey resin, giving an RCW cavity tree its distinctive waxy, candlelike sheen. The resin becomes armor. It gums up the invading snakes' ventral scales, inhibits movement, and arrests further climbing. What's more, the resin contains chemicals irritating to the serpents. Too much resin can even kill a snake.[2]

"Once at a cluster of RCW cavity trees in Kentucky," Ralph said, "I saw resin wells on a small pine next to a cavity tree. The pine was too small to have a cavity, so I wondered, 'what's going on here?' Then I noticed that further up, limbs from the small pine were touching the cavity tree. RCWs may actually dig resin wells on noncavity trees" to keep enterprising snakes from climbing one tree to invade another. "Which is fascinating. The birds have figured things out."

There may be other reasons why the woodpeckers drill resin wells. Sheens may be territorial warnings to other RCW family groups.[3] Sheens may also be "signposts" to help RCWs locate their cavities, although as one researcher noted, "This view seems to reflect the inadequacies of biologists more than those of birds."[4]

RCWs are picky about choosing cavity trees. They prefer drilling into older longleafs afflicted with red heart fungus, a disease that softens the heartwood and eases excavation. They're also particular about the placement of their cavities in the trees. They often drill their cavities just below the lowest limbs. These sections of trunk are more likely to suffer from red heart. "As the tree grows, it prunes its limbs," Ralph said. "Over fifty, sixty years the lower limbs die, and the fungus can enter through a dead, broken limb. The red heart is usually in that portion of the tree first. This is where you see conks on the trees, exterior manifestations of red heart disease."

Craig Rudolph, another RCW researcher, wanted to see if conks were visual cues to the woodpeckers that trees had red heart disease.[5] "Rudolph and his team strapped conks onto trees. A neat experiment," said Ralph, but the birds weren't fooled. "They didn't select those trees for excavation more than any others."

Curiously RCWs are the only woodpeckers that prefer southwest-facing nests. One reason for this, according to Ralph, may be "that the west-southwest sun increases the flow from resin wells." More resin equals fewer snakes.

Height is yet another consideration in cavity placement. "The further you go up the tree, the smaller the ratio of heartwood to sapwood," said Ralph. The cavities of RCWs are roughly three inches in diameter. The woodpecker needs at least four inches of heartwood so that resin doesn't drip from the ceiling of the nest.

"We're not sure how RCWs know there is red heart disease in a pine," he said, "but historically in old-growth forests they didn't have to know. Probably 90 percent of the trees over 150 years old had the disease," and longleafs can live for centuries. "One day a theory occurred to me when I was lying on my back in the Kisatchie Hills Wilderness of Louisiana looking up at a loblolly pine. The tree was over one hundred feet tall, and an RCW was pecking in the crown. I put my ear against the trunk, covered my other ear, and it was amazing—I could clearly hear the resonance of that pecking. It's possible that when the birds are pecking, they can tell whether the tree has a hard or soft center, as if they had sonar. I don't know if there's any science to that theory or not," he laughed.

I questioned the RCWs' placement of some nests. The cavities I had seen in the Sandhills were often twenty feet up the trunk, sometimes higher but sometimes lower, as low as six feet. The flames of burns often reached that high. Creating a "faceplate" and coating such a cavity tree with highly flammable resin in a fire-prone region didn't seem like a bright idea.

"In today's forests it isn't," Ralph agreed. "But picture the pre-Columbian longleaf pine forest. The trees were often three hundred to four hundred years old—huge, really tall. Because of frequent fires, the understory was essentially grass. De Soto [1540s] and Bartram [1770s] had described those forests as prairies with trees. The bigger and taller the trees, the higher the cavities and the farther the resin from the ground." I was familiar only with young longleaf forests, but in extant old-growth longleaf forests such as the Wade Tract in Georgia, said Ralph, "the cavities are seventy, eighty feet up because they can be." Before the old longleaf pine forests were cut, "it didn't matter that there was resin on trees. The flashy fuel, the low-intensity fires, the shorter flame heights—these probably weren't issues to the red-cockaded."

Because some tracts of longleaf habitat, such as that of the Carolina Sandhills Refuge, are protected now, someday "the trees will be taller and the cavities higher than they are today. But until our pines get bigger, our fuels get lower, and our cavity trees increase in number, the woodpeckers need our help."

Something else puzzled me about RCW behavior. Their roosting habits reminded me of married couples in 1950s sitcoms. No double beds. Each bird slept in his or her own cavity chamber. Each cavity in a cluster, except during child-rearing, was a single-occupancy dwelling. (A cluster is the number of cavity trees belonging to a family of RCWs.) I wondered about this arrangement. It took so much time and effort for an RCW to excavate a cavity, why not share?

"Part of the reason might be size," Ralph said. The cavities that the birds drill often measure a mere three inches in diameter. "There's not room in the bottom of a cavity for more than one adult bird to lie down. If two mature birds were to roost in a cavity, one would be forced to cling to the wall."

RCWs dine alone too. Females forage lower on the trunk, while males forage higher, "probably to reduce competition from their mates and to take advantage of the entire tree," said Ralph. "Jim Hanula did seminal research on insects, trees, and RCWs. He found that the vast majority of insects in their diet come from the ground, although quite a few species of arboreal ants live in dead trees." Hanula, a research entomologist at the University of Georgia, also discovered that "the most common prey fed to nestlings were wood cockroaches, probably selected because they were the most abundant insects on the tree boles." RCWs also prefer to forage on longleaf pines. "During the day, the loose, flaky bark of longleaf pine trees harbored over twice as many arthropods as the bark of loblolly pines of similar size."[6]

"RCWs are flakers and probers," Ralph said. "Pileated woodpeckers, big and powerful birds, drill holes into snags [dead trees] to look for pine sawyer larvae. RCWs, on the other hand, snap the loose bark off of trees and probe to see if insects are underneath. RCWs will forage on snags that still have bark, but primarily they forage on live pines."

By foraging lower on the bole, females may have easier pickings, but there's a cost: the lower trunk is more open to predation. "If you're in the crown, you have more cover," said Ralph. "Fortunately predators are few and far between. For the most part the only day predators would be sharp-shinned and Cooper's hawks. But if RCWs roost outside at night, they are vulnerable to owls."

Hardwood encroachment, for example the growth of a midstory of scrub oaks in the pine habitat, may drive a foraging female higher up the trunk.

"Or it may force her to abandon the territory," Ralph said. "If the neighborhood goes to pieces, if the female can't get groceries, she will leave. She'll look for better territory. A breeding male is a lot more tenacious. He will tolerate pretty atrocious conditions when it comes to oak midstories, but he can afford to. He forages in the crown."

Even if his mate departs, an RCW male is reluctant to abandon his cluster of cavities. "He will usually stay till he dies of old age," Ralph said. "That's when we end up with abandoned clusters."

RCWs are stubbornly territorial. The turf an RCW family defends from other RCWs may range from sixty to six hundred acres, though the average is closer to one hundred. "When one group meets another on the fringe of its territory, it gets excited. The birds do wing displays, the males raise the feathers on their heads, and the little red cockades show up," Ralph told me. It may be that the famous red feathers are as much for defense as for sexual display. "Typically you can't see the red feathers. They are hidden under black ones, but you do see them when the birds are agitated."

In their quest for prime real estate, RCWs have specific requirements. They need, for example, an open stand of pines. To maintain such a habitat, the refuge plants, harvests, and manages timber to keep the basal area of trees at a preferred density.

Imagine that you cut every tree in an acre off at a height of four and a half feet (breast height) and then viewed all of the stumps from above. The basal area would be the total area of the stumps. You might have a sixty-square-foot basal area with five hundred small trees or the same basal area with fifty large trees. For cavity excavation RCWs need larger trees because of the greater heartwood-to-cambium ratio.

According to the USFWS Recovery Plan, RCWs prefer low-density stands with basal areas of forty to sixty square feet per acre. In a May 2005 interview Clay Ware, a forester with the Carolina Sandhills National Wildlife

Refuge, said, "Because there is less competition for resources in open stands, the pines grow larger in diameter, have increased resin flow, and are less susceptible to beetle damage." The expanded ground cover of open stands also provides a greater food source, arthropods, for the birds.

This means more bugs for the babies too, which brings us to RCW families. An RCW family group—breeders, helpers, and fledglings—resembles a wolf pack more than a bird clan. RCWs are "cooperative breeders." There is one breeding pair per group. The pair usually mates for life. Older siblings, or helpers, help defend the territory and feed the young. There are even lone wolves called "floaters."

A new family starts between April and June when the breeder female lays a clutch of two to five eggs, depositing them in the male breeder's cavity. Because the cavities are small, only Dad beds down with the chicks when they hatch. "The breeder male roosts in his cavity," Ralph said, "and broods the young nestlings."

Helper birds put off mating to help their parents raise chicks. Some adult RCW males, like bachelor uncles, stay on to assist the breeding pair in raising young. "In the bird world," Ralph told me, "helping behavior is more advanced." Usually helpers are males, although in some populations "up to 30 percent of helpers can be females." In North America the "red-cockaded woodpecker and the acorn woodpecker (*Melanerpes formicivorus*), which occur in western North America, are the only cooperatively breeding woodpeckers" on the continent.[7]

But helping behavior is not purely altruistic. The effort may pay off. "A male helper may inherit the territory when the male breeder dies," explained Ralph. "Then the helper won't have to spend years excavating new cavities." Some males, it's true, spread their wings to look for new territory, but statistically helper males become breeders sooner than those that disperse. As in human kingdoms, the eldest male usually inherits the land. "Odds are, a helper will get to be a breeder faster" than a floater will.

Still, I wasn't convinced. If I'm a male helper, I wondered, why help? Why not just hang around, lie on the couch, wait for the old man to kick off? Why should I waste energy finding bugs for little sis and bro? Won't I inherit the territory anyway?

"According to Jeff Walters," Ralph said, "helping behavior improves the overall fitness of the group. Helpers aid in raising additional group members."[8] They help dig new cavities and defend the cluster. "Having a healthy group benefits the helper and increases the probability of the male helper becoming a breeder."

Risk is higher for females. Those who survive the first seasons are often the real lone wolves, at least temporarily. In a study of an RCW population by Jeffrey Walters, Phillip Doerr, and J.H. Carter (1998)[9], three North Carolina State University biologists, fewer than one-third of female fledglings survived the first year. Just over half of the males made it. According to Ralph, the reason more female fledglings die is that almost all leave the territory, while only about half of the males disperse. Risk is greater for those that leave. It's safer to stay home.

Of those female fledglings that survive, over 90 percent became floaters, that is, birds without families or territories. "Floaters wander through the forest" or from forest to forest "looking for breeding vacancies or the right place to start a territory," said Ralph. "When females float, they're more likely than males to find breeding vacancies because it's more likely that a male has a territory." In the North Carolina study, over 90 percent of the females that survived found mates and became breeders. "Young females are very adept at locating territory-holding males and reproducing."[10] And very motivated.

Some females even become helpers on a non-natal territory. "In fact, one female," later identified by banding, "actually flew 250 miles from Fort Benning near the Georgia-Alabama border to Fort Gordon near the Savannah River Site," said Ralph. "Talk about floating. That bird became a helper in a group which already had a breeding female. Another female flew from the Carolina Sandhills to Fort Gordon, 200 miles away."

Preoccupied with basic needs, RCWs don't realize how many other species depend on them in their quests for homes. "At least twenty-seven other vertebrate species"—for example bluebirds, titmice, and chickadees; hairy, downy, and red-bellied woodpeckers; snakes and amphibians; flying squirrels; and invertebrates such as bees and wasps—"use abandoned RCW cavities." If pileated woodpeckers enlarge the entrance tunnels so that RCWs are forced to abandon their cavities, "the fox squirrels, screech owls, and wood ducks move in," Ralph informed me. RCWs are a keystone species. When the population of RCWs declines, their neighbors are poorer for it.

"RCWs are also an indicator species. If you have red-cockadeds, it's a good indication that you have a healthy southern pine forest. Some people argue that we're investing all this time and all these resources in single-species management. With RCWs it's easy to shoot holes in that argument. By preserving two-hundred-acre patches of longleaf pine forest for the woodpeckers, we're taking care of everything else that's living out there."

The "everything else" includes "212 resident vertebrate species . . . of which 38 are specialists occurring exclusively or primarily in longleaf pine savannas." A keystone species, red-cockaded woodpeckers promote "species richness by providing shelter for many species. . . . Because the longleaf pine trees are alive when cavities are excavated" and because the trees may live up to four hundred years, the cavities "are used by many other animals over the lifetime[s] of the tree[s]."[11]

LONGLEAF LONGEVITY AND SPECIES DIVERSITY are subject, of course, to saws and storms. In 1989 South Carolina's Francis Marion National Forest was home to the world's second-largest population of red-cockaded woodpeckers, which made their homes in thousands of mature longleaf pines. "In one night," said Craig Watson, then the forest's Wildlife Program manager, "all of that changed."

When Hurricane Hugo rolled over the forest with gusts up to 160 miles per hour, it uprooted cypress and centuries-old live oaks. But longleaf pines, the trees in which RCWs most often dig their nests, were hit the hardest. The morning after Hugo, only 229 of 1,765 RCW cavity trees were still standing. An estimated 63 percent of the Francis Marion RCW population, already listed by U.S. Fish and Wildlife Service as an endangered species, died.

After Hugo the surviving RCWs of the Francis Marion National Forest faced a crisis. Being cavity dwellers, they couldn't toss together new nests from handfuls of twigs. Younger, shorter, twenty-year-old longleafs may have ridden out the storm, but they lacked the sufficient heartwood (a diameter of at least four inches) needed for cavity nests. And even if the surviving RCWs had found pines with adequate heartwood, it would have taken them roughly a year to excavate new cavities. A year without nests would make the woodpeckers easy prey for hawks and owls. A year without nests meant nowhere to hatch and raise the next generation.

Despite the acute loss of habitat, RCWs had one thing going for them. At the Savannah River Site (SRS), where the population of RCWs had dwindled to five birds, biologist David Allen had been at work on a technique to construct and insert artificial RCW cavities into living pines.

The SRS's population of the woodpeckers had dwindled, David said, due to a "lack of fire to control hardwood encroachment. RCWs need the open pine forests that fire provides." The pines of the SRS were young, in the forty- to fifty-year-old range. The only way to get the population to expand was to get these birds to use younger trees.

"When they excavate cavities," David said, "they know what they're looking for—a tree with red heart fungus." He concurred with Ralph Costa: "when RCWs tap on the outside of a tree to forage for insects, they hear the hollow sound that a soft, pulpy interior would make. RCWs don't always excavate cavities in pines with red heart fungus, but they do excavate in relatively old trees. Because the heartwood is dead and produces no sap, an RCW's natural cavity must be entirely within the heartwood. If the bird were to excavate its home in the sapwood of a younger tree, the cavity would fill with sap." A tub of sap would be a lousy place to raise the kids.

David described the construction of artificial cavity inserts. Because sap can force its way in through the seams of a box, the cavities are made from solid blocks of wood. The block, made of southern yellow pine or more commonly western red cedar, measures ten inches high, four wide, and six deep. A three-inch hole is drilled down from the top of the block to within two inches of the bottom. "That's the cavity chamber," said David. "A three-inch diameter is within the range of natural RCW cavities." To seal the cavity, a piece of plywood is then glued and nailed on top of the block. Then from the front, a two-inch-diameter entrance hole is angled slightly upward to intersect the cavity chamber. Sometimes this hole is reinforced with two-inch PVC pipe. A metal plate with a matching entrance hole is screwed onto the front of the block. This "restrictor plate" keeps competitors such as squirrels and pileated woodpeckers from enlarging or "blowing out" the entrance. Finally, to install the artificial cavity, a rectangular hole of the same dimensions is cut into a tree.

Artificial cavity inserts can be used in any pine that's big enough. Although RCWs drill more cavities into longleafs, they also excavate in loblolly, shortleaf, pond, and slash pines.

I wondered if chainsawing a deep hole through the sapwood interfered with the flow of nutrients, with the tree's longevity.

"No doubt cutting a hole in a tree doesn't do it any good," David said, "but we feel confident that the excavation technique doesn't cause major damage. At Francis Marion we've kept track of the trees in which we excavated cavities. Those trees have had no higher rate of mortality than that of neighboring trees.

"We asked the engineering department at Clemson University to analyze how much wood you could take out of a tree of a given size and still maintain its structural integrity. Of course, when you insert the block of wood, you're restrengthening the tree." The engineers concluded that if the diameter of the tree was fifteen inches at the height of excavation, the tree would not be weakened.

Curious about how many years it might take a longleaf to reach that diameter, I contacted Jack Culpepper, a forester at the Carolina Sandhills NWR.

"It's common on 'good' sites to have one-quarter inch annual growth rings with longleaf," Jack e-mailed me. "That would result in an increase of one-half inch diameter per year. Ignoring the grass stage, at that rate you could grow a 15-inch diameter at the stump in 30 years. Sometimes, however, longleaf won't reach this diameter in 100 or even 200 years. Of course, the tree is basically conical, so the higher up the tree, the longer it takes to reach this diameter, although longleaf has limited taper."

For the birds' excavation of natural cavities, wrote Jack, the presence of heart rot is more important than the tree's girth. "If the tree has a 'good case' of heart rot, it doesn't have to be large" to accommodate a natural cavity. "This is what the birds seek out. In some cases, a slow growing tree with an eight-inch diameter will produce a six-inch diameter of heartwood."

"We were just to the point where we felt comfortable with the technique," David said, "when Hurricane Hugo hit. My technician, Sheryl Sanders, and I went to Francis Marion National Forest and taught the folks there how to install artificial cavities." Another biologist, Carole Copeyon, had developed a different technique using a drill to excavate cavities. "All of us were excavating cavities at Francis Marion for several months."

Within a year 537 artificial homes for RCWs had been drilled or installed. Within four years the number rose to 989. Some were artificial cavity inserts; some were drilled cavities; some were "drilled starts," which the birds would finished excavating.

RCWs may move into their new homes within a few days. "Of course, it all depends on demand. After Hugo the birds needed cavities badly, and they took to them fast," said David.

Natural RCW cavities may last generations. I wondered how long artificial cavities might last.

"Sometimes water gets inside an insert and the cavity will rot. Also, as the tree continues to grow, sapwood can wrap around the insert and close off the hole. We've seen this with inserts that are fifteen years old," said David.

To see an artificial cavity insert installed in a longleaf pine, I went on a field trip one April day with wildlife biologist Laura Housh and wildlife science technician Greg Boling, who both work for the Carolina Sandhills NWR. The refuge has the largest population of RCWs on U.S. Fish and Wildlife Service land.

The day was warm and blue-skied. We rode down dirt roads deep into the refuge, where we parked the trucks and hiked a short way carrying an artificial cavity, climbing gear, and a chain saw to an existing cluster of RCW cavity trees.

A "cluster" is the number of cavity trees used by a group of RCWs. I asked Laura how she knew where the clusters were.

"In 1984," she replied, "a survey was done of all 'P-2' stands," that is, of those stands of trees old enough to have RCW cavities. Most clusters neighbor others, but a few are isolated.

I pointed to one cavity, recognizable by the sheen of resin around the woodpecker's entrance hole.

"That's a natural cavity," she said, "but we installed a metal restrictor plate around the entrance to protect it." Earlier the entrance hole had been enlarged, perhaps by a pileated woodpecker foraging for insects. The plate prevented the intruder from "blowing out the hole" and making the home unfit for RCWs. Restrictor plates, she added, are rarely used with natural cavities.

"These woodpeckers are endangered for a reason," said Laura. "We've destroyed much of their mature pine habitat. We've restricted their range. I'd almost guarantee that every endangered species is endangered because of habitat loss."

To reverse this loss, in 1985 the USFWS created the Red-cockaded Woodpecker Recovery Plan. The plan directs the refuge to 1) use prescribed burns to manage the longleaf pine ecosystem, 2) install and monitor artificial nest cavities, 3) reduce competition from other species for cavities, 4) monitor RCW populations and nesting success, and 5) translocate subadult RCWs from the refuge's stable population to other sites throughout the Southeast. The goal is to establish fifteen stable populations of five hundred active clusters each.

"Habitat management is our most important job," Laura continued. "Part of that job is to provide recruitment clusters for RCWs to move into." According to Ralph Costa, "the number of recruitment clusters available in populations should be equal to 10 percent of the current number of active clusters present." For example, "if there are 129 active clusters, there should be 13 recruitment clusters for a total of 142 clusters."

"As long as we have prescribed burns and provide suitable cavities," said Laura, "our population increases." Since 1993 she and her crew have installed about three hundred inserts.

As we talked, Laura and Greg walked the area, surveying the longleaf pines for a good candidate. When searching for a cluster, Laura looks for flattops (older longleaf pines with flat crowns) first. "Flattops are the RCWs' longleaf pines of choice," she said. "Some flattops are one hundred years old, and some with natural RCW cavities are only ten inches DBH [diameter at breast height].” She added that most of the RCW cavities on the refuge are natural. When installing an artificial cavity, however, Laura prefers a younger pine “that’s at least fifteen inches in diameter at cavity height and that’s relatively close to an existing cluster.”

I saw a second natural cavity. “That cavity’s not high on the trunk,” I said. “Six or seven feet.”

“Yes, some of the natural cavities are really low. Artificial cavities need to be a minimum of twenty feet high, though,” to help protect the nests from prescribed burns.

Laura and Greg chose a big, healthy longleaf. The sun was high, so Laura took out a compass to locate the west side of the tree. “Apparently that’s the side RCWs prefer for their cavities,” she explained.

Maybe they’re late sleepers, I thought. Ralph Costa speculates that the west side enjoys greater sunlight. “Solar radiation increases amount of resin flow or perhaps the rate of flow. The more resin, the better the snake deterrent.”

It occurred to me that since RCW cavities are used year after year, generation after generation, the nests might get a little foul.

“The birds keep them clean,” she said. “They carry stuff out—eggs that don’t hatch, chicks that die.”

“Poop too?”

“The adults don’t poop in their cavities.”

“But the chicks?”

“When I’m doing roost surveys at cavity entrances,” Laura said, “I’ve never smelled anything.” According to Ralph Costa, “nestlings’ defecation is enclosed in a fecal sac which the parents routinely remove.”

As Greg readied his tools and assembled the climbing stand, Laura showed me the insert, an artificial cavity made from a block of wood replete with a restrictor plate and a two-inch entrance hole reinforced with PVC, which “keeps other species of woodpeckers and flying squirrels from blowing out the entrance hole.” The population of flying squirrels at the refuge, she added, is “very prolific. They can take over every cavity in a cluster and run the RCWs out. That’s why it’s always good to have several snags in a cluster stand,” that is, dead standing trees to provide other habitats.

This was the last insert that she and Greg would install this year. “Because nesting season has nearly started, we wouldn’t want to come into an active cluster and disturb the woodpeckers.”

Using a climbing stand, Greg scaled the tree. Clinging twenty feet up the trunk, he reminded me of a two-hundred-pound woodpecker. First, he used a draw knife to scrape bark from the trunk. "Scraping mimics the way an RCW clears bark away from the cavity," Laura explained. Removing bark "may attract an RCW to the insert. Depending on how much an RCW needs a cavity tree, the bird may move in that night," although a year might pass before the cavity is occupied.

Holding the insert against the tree, Greg marked off an outline of the box, then revved up the small chain saw. To keep the saw from cutting deeper than six inches, a flange had been welded onto the blade. The saw whined and chips flew as he nosed it into the trunk. First he cut the top, bottom, and sides of the cavity. Next he sliced several horizontal "pages" into the rectangle. Then, after killing the chain saw, he popped out the pages with a small crowbar. After using a hammer and chisel to finish the hole, he painted the insert with nontoxic putty and pushed the insert inside till its face was flush with the outside of the trunk. To wedge the box tight, he hammered in shims of western red cedar. Finally, using the claw of the hammer, he knocked out several resin wells so resin would begin to ooze. "The resin will deter predators and be a visual cue to attract RCWs," Laura told me. As Greg climbed down, she marked the location of the insert on a map. Later she would enter the location into a database.

"Why should humans care about red-cockaded woodpeckers?" I asked. "Why all this trouble and expense?"

"We're the reason they are endangered. Because they are, we are required by law to protect them. It's our responsibility to make sure they can thrive in their natural habitat. It can take them a year to make a natural cavity. If we lose one or two active cavities, it can compromise the family. I mean, why save an endangered species? Because we can."

"I love this time of year," she added as we all walked back to the truck. "I love nesting season. I love bird banding. The most satisfying thing is to install artificial cavities for recruitment clusters, then come back the next year and find RCWs nesting in them. That's the best."

NOTES

1. Lawrence S. Earley, *Looking for Longleaf: The Fall and Rise of an American Forest* (Chapel Hill: University of North Carolina Press, 2004), 22.

2. J. A. Jackson, "Gray Rat Snakes Versus Red-cockaded Woodpeckers: Predator-Prey Adaptations," Auk 91 (Albuquerque: University of New Mexico Press, 1974), 342–47.

3. R. G. Hooper, A. F. Robinson Jr., and J. A. Jackson, "The Red-cockaded Woodpecker: Notes on Life History and Management," USDA Forest Service (1980), General Report SA-GR 9.

4. Robert W. McFarlane, *A Stillness in the Pines: The Ecology of the Red-cockaded Woodpecker* (New York: Norton, 1992), 88.

5. D. C. Rudolph, R. N. Conner, and R. R. Shaefer, "Red-cockaded Woodpecker Detection of Red Heart Infection," in *Red-cockaded Woodpecker: Recovery, Ecology, and Management*, ed. David L. Kulhavy, Robert G. Hooper, and Ralph Costa (Nacogdoches, Tex.: Stephen F. Austin State University, 1995), 338–42.

6. Forest Service, U.S. Department of Agriculture, "SRS Research Highlights from the Red-cockaded Woodpecker Symposium," www.srs.fs.usda.gov/about/news release/nr_2003–02–05-research_highlights.htm (accessed October 12, 2008).

7. U.S. Fish and Wildlife Service, "Red-cockaded Woodpecker *Picoides borealis*," http://209.85.165.104/search?q=cache:xA111j6KmhQJ:www.fws.gov/verobeach/images/pdflibrary/rcwo.pdf+fws+species+birds+rcwo&hl=en&ct=clnk&cd=1&gl=us &client=firefox-a (accessed October 12, 2008).

8. Memuna Z. Kahn and Jeffrey R. Walters, "An Analysis of Reciprocal Exchange of Helping Behavior in the Red-cockaded Woodpecker (*Picoides borealis*)," *Behavioral Ecology and Sociobiology* 47: 376–81.

9. Jeffrey R. Walters, Phillip D. Doerr, and J.H. Carter III, "The Cooperative Breeding System of the Red-cockaded Woodpecker." (1998) *Ethology* 78:4, 275-305.

10. McFarlane, *A Stillness in the Pines*, 138–49.

11. Shibu Jose, Eric J. Jokela, and Deborah L. Miller, "The Longleaf Pine Ecosystem: An Overview," in *The Longleaf Pine Ecosystem: Ecology, Silviculture, and Restoration*, ed. Jose, Jokela, and Miller (New York: Springer, 2006), 5.

Snake Cruising I

"As long as you don't step on one, you're not likely to get bit."

Kevin Messenger, herpetologist

"YOU'LL HAVE TO EXCUSE the housekeeping," Kevin Messenger said, swinging open the door from the carport to the house. "I don't get many visitors." The house, a one-story brick ranch-style in the middle of the Carolina Sandhills National Wildlife Refuge, was a loaner.

Scott Lanier, the refuge manager, told me later that he "let Kevin Messenger stay overnight while he's doing his research. We've done the same for others. His study of snakes at the refuge is important and it's expanding. Before, we had only a species list of herps you might find on the refuge." Now, for example, they know which snakes are more prevalent and when they might be found. "You never know where the information will lead, how it will be valuable. For us, it's about knowing as much as we can about the refuge we manage."

Inside the house Kevin's housekeeping was quintessential male off campus. Way off-campus. In the kitchen, a crinkled dead wolf spider on the linoleum. On the counter, canned ravioli, canned spaghetti, canned chicken. Remarkably there were no dirty dishes in the sink, but maybe Kevin ate out of cans. In the living room, a mattress and blanket on the middle of the floor. No chairs. A computer on a low table. Books and soda bottles scattered across the unvacuumed carpet. On a table more Mountain Dews and four lumpy pillowcases knotted at their necks—"three pygmy rattlers and a black rat snake," Kevin said. He would release these snakes that night. The black rat snake, nemesis of endangered red-cockaded woodpeckers, was what I'd come to see, but I was ready for anything else Kevin had to show.

A rising senior at North Carolina State University in Raleigh, Kevin also worked part-time at a veterinary hospital. In 2000, when he began his research at the CSNWR, he began driving the three-hundred-mile round trip

A pygmy rattlesnake. In the 1970s a snake survey found no pygmy rattlesnakes in the Carolina Sandhills National Wildlife Refuge. Since the introduction of prescribed burns, these tiny rattlesnakes have become the most common snakes in the refuge. Photograph courtesy of Kevin Messenger.

from school to the refuge in a 1989 Ford F-150. In 2003 he bought a 1995 Jeep Wrangler with 124,000 miles on the odometer. It now reads 245,000. In 2005 he spent eighty-nine nights at the refuge. "On average, I cruise about 150 miles per night, hunting snakes back and forth along that 8.4 mile stretch of Wildlife Drive that I love so much." He hunts deep into the night, sometimes past 2:00 A.M.

I asked why, despite the long drive, Kevin had chosen to conduct his study in the Carolina Sandhills NWR.

"Well, the North Carolina Sandhills near Hoffman—that's where a lot of herpetologists go—is more fragmented. More roads break up the terrain." The Carolina Sandhills refuge, he explained, had forty-five thousand acres with just two main roads, Wildlife Drive and Highway 145, to dissect it. "There's a lot more wilderness with fewer people driving around, and since the refuge is closed to the public at night, there are fewer DORs—snakes found dead on the road." Compared to the total number of snakes he captured at the refuge, DORs averaged about 6 percent. If the roads were open to the public at night, he said, "it wouldn't be uncommon to find a ratio of DORs up to 50 percent."

Kevin is a fine nature photographer. We sat on the floor of the living room and perused hundreds of photos of snakes on his computer. I asked about his research.

He took a deep breath. "It's a huge project, a ten-year mark-recapture study. I want to look at the biodiversity of snakes on the refuge, see which populations are going strong, which are dwindling. I hope to finish while I'm in grad school. My goal is to get a Ph.D. in zoology and spend half my time teaching and half in research." His only break from snake hunting at the refuge would be a sabbatical in the summer of 2006 to survey reptile and amphibian species in the Hubei Province of China. In his absence three or four people, including his father, would carry on the research.

"I capture, weigh, measure, sex, and mark snakes, then release them where I caught them. I hope to catch them again, see if they've grown or changed locations, and get an idea of the size of the population here."

Snake populations at the refuge are not static. The first herp study at the refuge, Kevin said, was conducted from 1975 to 1977 by John Garton and Ben Sill of Duke Power Company, about the time of the first prescribed burns at the Carolina Sandhills NWR. That study found no pygmy rattlesnakes. "From 1995 to 1997 Jeff Camper from Francis Marion University did a second study." By then pygmies were the most common species of snake found on the refuge.

"When I began my study, I found two or three pygmies a night. But if you go fifty miles up into North Carolina, they are rare. What makes the Carolina Sandhills refuge so special that pygmies are abundant? That's one of the things I want to figure out. I think that prescribed burning is a huge benefit for pygmies, though I'm not sure why." He speculated that burns benefit fence lizards, a favorite pygmy food. After a burn the lizards are camouflaged on the charred trunks of trees. "They hide more easily from predatory birds."

I wondered how snakes could find lizards if birds could not, then remembered that most snakes' primary sense is smell. More fence lizards, more prey for pygmies. "How do snakes fare during a burn?" I asked.

"Sometimes burns are conducted during the winter or early spring," the months when snakes are dormant. "Occasionally the burn season extends into late spring, which can interfere with snakes. I remember walking up on a burn one time when Mike Housh told me he had seen three snakes leave the burn area." Mike, the refuge fire management officer, jocularly refers to Kevin as "Snake Boy."

"After one burn I also walked up on a corn snake that was trying to go down a hole," Kevin said. "I picked him up, and he had a bunch of burns. I kept him, but he died three days later."

I asked about asphyxiation, whether fire could suck the oxygen out of a snake's hole.

"I don't know, but reptiles have very low metabolism, so they don't require nearly as much oxygen as mammals do."

Not all animals that inhabit longleaf pine forests respond to fire frequency in the same way. In the Florida sandhills, for example, one lizard, the six-line race runner, is more abundant in forests that undergo a yearly regimen of prescribed burns. Another, the five-lined skink, prefers a five- to seven-year burn cycle. Still, despite these varied preferences for fire frequency, ground fires are critical to the survival of these species. "So long as habitat does not succeed into a hardwood forest, both species persist."[1]

Visitors to the Carolina Sandhills NWR, Kevin said, might not enjoy knowing that three of the four most common snakes he finds are venomous: the pygmy rattlesnake, the cottonmouth, and the copperhead. The nonvenomous corn snake completes the quartet. Eastern diamondbacks may have inhabited the area, but they have "definitely been extirpated and are not found on the refuge." Pygmies are nocturnal and therefore are rarely encountered. In fact, Kevin added, "of the thirty-one species of snakes on the refuge, only four are diurnal."

At his computer he clicked on a photo of a white and black anerythristic pygmy. "*Erythr* is the Latin root for 'red,'" he explained; "*an* means 'without.'" Coiled on a bed of sand and gravel, this pygmy, though it nearly filled the photo, was difficult to see.

"Is anerythrism rare?"

"It's about 25 percent of the pygmy population." A true scientist, Kevin has "thirty or forty spin-off studies" in mind. One would be to capture a pregnant anerythristic female and see if her offspring were similarly colored.

We went into the kitchen, where Kevin took a flat-bottomed colander from a cupboard, placed it on the linoleum, and unknotted a pillowcase. Then he gently poured a pygmy rattlesnake into the colander. The snake writhed, coiled, and struck at the air whenever Kevin's hand passed nearby.

"Lively little fellow," I said.

"Oh yeah. This is a large male," he said.

"A *large* male," I repeated, surprised. The snake was hardly the length of two pencils. His rattle buzzed faintly.

"If you walk up on a pygmy in the woods," Kevin said, "you're not going to hear him. It's unlikely a visitor would ever see one. My dad and I have been coming to the Sandhills since I was nine, and we've never seen one during the day, even though pygmy rattlesnakes are the most common species of snake on the refuge. I've caught over three hundred of these little guys. This one is number 118. I caught him once before in June of last year."

"No kidding," I said. The snake coiled and slashed at the air again. "Where did you catch him?"

"Near the same spot."

"Do snakes have distinct home ranges?"

"Most species in the Southeast do. Some, such as coachwhips and black rat snakes—both of which I've captured very few of—have larger home ranges."

I asked if pygmies were dangerously poisonous snakes. Kevin corrected my word choice. Dangerous snakes are venomous, not poisonous. Poison ivy and poison dart frogs are poisonous to touch. Venomous snakes are not poisonous to touch. They inject venom into their prey.

Kevin told me, "I got bit by a pygmy in 2003. The bite was little worse than the sting of a bee." We went back to his computer for a minute, where he showed me photos of his bitten digit: day one, a modest swelling; day two, a slight purple discoloration. By day three, the injury was hardly noticeable.

Back in the kitchen I commented on this pygmy's beautiful color and pattern: an orange-tan body with a weird tint of lavender, an orange stripe along its spine, brown Rorschach markings on its flat little pit-viper head, more dark triangles along its length, and a tiny gray rattler held erect.

"This one isn't so pretty," said Kevin almost apologetically. "But there are so many variations. One pygmy has a background that's almost pure white with a brilliant orange strip on its back. Another's background is lavender. Another's all black and white, no red coloration. Yet they're all pygmies. A newborn pygmy, coiled up, is about the diameter of a quarter," he added. "They're so cute."

Tilting the colander, he slid the pygmy back into the pillowcase and tied it shut.

"Does your mom get upset when her pillowcases keep disappearing?"

"No," he laughed. "Maybe when I was younger. Dad was the one who got me into snakes. He would take pillowcases too. But these were donated by a veterinary clinic."

I asked Kevin what he loved about snakes.

He grew quiet. "I don't know. Dad brought home a python when I was three years old, and I thought it was the coolest thing ever. He'd take me snake hunting. He liked snakes too, and he encouraged me."

Kevin hoisted the four pillowcased snakes, and we exited the house. He placed the three pygmy sacks in a box in the rear of his Jeep Wrangler, which was parked in the carport. He then untied the fourth pillowcase and, without bothering to glance inside, reached in and pulled out the rat snake.

In Kevin's study this was black rat snake number 38. It was a beautiful shiny black, with a head a little bigger than the end of my thumb and creamy white markings on its belly.

"He still has a little of the juvenile pattern," said Kevin. "Baby black rat snakes look far different than adults. Babies are usually white with black blotches—a cryptic coloration so predators can't see them easily. But this one is about four years old and is mostly black. He is four and a half feet long and weighs 453 grams," or one pound. "They'll grow to six or seven feet."

"I've heard that rat snakes are incredible tree climbers," I said, "and I know that they often raid bird nests. But how do they know where a bird nest is going to be? A red-cockaded woodpecker cavity nest, for example, may be seventy feet or more up a tree."

"Unlike birds and many predatory mammals," Kevin explained, "most snakes don't rely on vision. Only two snakes on the East Coast, the racer and the coachwhip, use sight as their primary sense. Those two are both speed-based snakes that see their food and chase it down. For our other snakes, it's all about smell. I don't know much about RCW behavior, so I can only speculate, but if there are bird droppings at the base of a tree, the rat snake smells them and starts climbing." Or perhaps, he added, the hunt is random. A snake climbs a tree and gets lucky. One thing is sure—success doesn't depend on the very audible peeping of the chicks. Snakes are deaf.

I remembered Laura Housh, the refuge wildlife biologist, telling me that RCWs clean their nests by removing dung, feathers, and egg shells. I pictured the birds dropping refuse to the foot of a cavity nest tree.

Consider for a moment the innate intelligence of RCWs—their preference for nesting in longleaf pines, the tree most likely to survive the periodic ground fires to which the Southeast is historically prone; their uncanny ability to identify longleafs afflicted with red heart disease, which softens the heartwood and eases excavation; their skill and perseverance in excavating cavity nests in pines that exude more resin than any others; and their exploitation of that resin to deter rat snakes, to coat the trunk around the nest with a gooey mess. But RCWs had not reckoned on the snake's nose, had not imagined that their ancient foe could track a trail of discarded feathers, shells, and poop. RCWs—betrayed by good housekeeping.

We walked across the grass to a stand of pines. Kevin released the snake onto a large longleaf. Guiltily I realized that the release was for my benefit and asked whether it violated Kevin's policy of releasing snakes where he caught them. He replied that he had caught this snake off the refuge and that sometimes he would release a pygmy, for example, on the opposite side of a lake from where he found it to see if it migrated. And after all, rat snakes are travelers.

The snake stuck like Velcro to the big coarse bark and started creeping up, its ventral scales finding easy purchase in the crevices of the bark, its long black body stretching and contracting. "The snake's ribs flex out and press against the sides of the cracks," Kevin explained.

"It's amazing," I said. The snake was already far out of reach. I asked if there was any limit to how high the snake would climb.

"The top of the tree."

In longleaf pine forests red-cockaded woodpeckers, a keystone species, are vital to diversity. More than two dozen other species depend on RCWs. Therefore, to protect the woodpeckers, wildlife biologists may remove competitors such as flying squirrels and predators such as rat snakes from cavity nests. I had heard that the squirrels and snakes were sometimes killed, and I put forth the argument to Kevin. "RCWs are endangered. Black rat snakes are not. You see where this argument is going. In the tale of the red-cockaded woodpecker, black rat snakes are the villains."

"Yeah," Kevin said slowly, drawing the word out while he considered his position. "If I saw a king snake eating an endangered eastern diamondback rattlesnake, I would let it happen. When it's nature," he concluded, "I find it hard to interfere."

"The prime directive," I said.

By now the sun was setting. We got into his Jeep and wheeled out of the yard and onto the asphalt of Wildlife Drive, the main road through the refuge. It was mid-July, and a late afternoon downpour had cooled things off. Kevin hoped that the rain would not ruin the hunt.

He mentioned that he had recently equipped the Jeep with a "snorkel," a vertical intake that, if the Jeep ran through deep water, would feed air to the engine. "Once I was in water up to here," he said, placing his hand halfway up the driver's door. "I was afraid the air intake would suck in water and the engine would lock up."

Nervous, I confessed that I had never been snake hunting, adding that I hoped we wouldn't be driving through any lakes.

We turned down a dirt road that was more of a wide path and proceeded to "the bone yard," a small area where the refuge temporarily dumps building materials and where Kevin had found scarlet king snakes, coachwhips, black racers, and southeastern crowned snakes—a weak-venomed reptile that injects its venom not through front fangs but rear ones. Full grown, black-capped crowned snakes may be about ten inches long—not much bigger than a common earthworm—but Kevin said he was impressed by "a tiny snake that will take down huge centipedes."

Helping him flip over sheets of rotting plywood and discarded metal siding, I steeled myself so that if a crown snake was uncovered, I would not jump back too quickly, then felt embarrassed at being scared of the thought of a snake the size of a gummy worm.

"Trash and tin sheets are gold mines to a snake hunter," Kevin remarked.

Cautiously picking up one corner of a piece of plywood, I asked about copperheads.

Copperheads are sometimes referred to as "highland moccasins and are, in fact, of the genus *Agkistrodon*, which includes water moccasins. I prefer not to call cottonmouths water moccasins," he added, since so many snake-fearing people believe that any water snake is a moccasin. "I find a tremendous amount of copperheads in April," he added. "In the summer I might find one or two, but in August the number increases again. I also find a lower number of pygmies throughout the summer. In August and September, though, the numbers jump up. On August 20, 2004, I caught eleven pygmies in one night."

We left the bone yard snakeless, however, and drove up an embankment and back onto Wildlife Drive. Kevin cruised at a sensible 25 miles per hour. Dark forest bordered both sides of the road. Caught in the headlights, a frog leaped across the road to escape our vehicle. We saw hundreds of toads and frogs warming themselves on the road; they looked like little Jabba the Hutts. Kevin swerved to avoid another leaping amphibian. "Fowler's toad," he said.

Kevin's eyes were keen and well trained. I almost thought he was kidding when he said he could see the eyes of wolf spiders reflected like tiny purple diamonds in the headlights. "There's one," he said, breaking and pulling up beside it. I opened the door and looked down at the road. It took me a few seconds to see the arachnid, which seemed to blend in with the gray of the pavement. Kevin later remarked that success in hunting doesn't hinge on having good vision, "but having a good search engine," that is, by knowing when to look for what, and where.

Overall Kevin's hunt methodology was to cruise back and forth along Wildlife Drive, scanning for snakes to capture. He began half an hour before dusk and drove about an hour and a half after he found his last snake.

"Is there any night when you're tired and just say, 'I've had enough'?"

"Nope. I've been out there till 5:00 A.M." After he found his last snake, he always made two passes on the road before he called it quits.

As we cruised, he asked me to hand him the infrared thermometer from his knapsack in the back of the Jeep. The device looked like a gray plastic Star Wars gun with a little digital screen. Driving, Kevin pointed it at the road and pulled the trigger. The gun gave an instant read-out of the temperature of the asphalt—85 degrees Fahrenheit. Later he entered this datum into a college comp book that he kept in the glove compartment.

"What does the road temperature tell us?" I asked.

"It's not very warm for this time of the year. It's usually in the 90s," he replied, adding, "Pygmies prefer mid-80s."

I commented that the afternoon rain had cooled things off and then asked where he hoped to find snakes this evening.

"The higher, drier elevations," he said. "That's where the pygmies usually come."

"Why higher elevations?"

"I don't know yet. It's real strange. In southern South Carolina—Jasper County, for instance—pygmies often prefer swampy areas; but here on the refuge, the drier it is, the more pygmies I find. That's one of the questions I have, one of the reasons I'm doing this study. When a snake crosses a road, is it a once-in-a-lifetime event? Or are they aware of the road? Do they come to it each night to warm up? If a snake's had a meal or is pregnant, it will often seek out warm places to bask and soak up the heat, which aids digestion and helps embryos develop." Kevin was speculating that pit vipers, given their higher recapture ratio, seem attracted to the warmth of the road, when he slammed the brakes, shouted "banded water snake!," and jumped from the Jeep.

"I didn't even see it," I said, climbing out, flashlight in hand, but Kevin had already snatched up the snake by its tail before it could escape into the roadside grass. The serpent was charcoal gray with a pale yellow belly, smiling jaws, and, true to its name, brown bands across its back. Hanging from Kevin's fingertips, it writhed and lashed, describing curlicues and question marks in the air and biting him twice.

"You've got some blood on your fingers."

"Yep. Nonvenomous snake bites are overrated." He gripped the snake by the base of its skull. "The bite looks worse than it is. There are anticoagulants in the snake's saliva, so the tiniest prick will bleed. A lot."

Snake saliva often contains anticoagulants. "Especially water snakes and garter snakes," he said. "Evolutionarily, venomous snakes are more evolved. Some water snakes are on the verge of becoming venomous. Their saliva is slightly toxic. Water snakes eat fish, and when they bite, they want the fish to succumb as fast as possible. The more toxic the saliva, the faster the fish dies."

He dropped the snake into a pillowcase; retrieved his pen, comp book, and infrared thermometer from the Jeep; and recorded the time, place, snake, road temperature (82.5 degrees Fahrenheit), and air temperature (74.5 degrees Fahrenheit). "Later tonight I'll measure his snout-to-vent length and record his total length and weight. If I haven't captured and marked him before, I'll mark him and sex him. Tomorrow I'll bring him back here and release him and hope to find him again. Recaptures give you an idea of how healthy a population is and what the recruitment is—in other words, if there are new snakes in the population. If you find nothing but recaptures, it indicates that no new snakes are being born. If you find few or no recaptures, that indicates that the population is very, very big."

He placed the bagged snake in the rear of the Jeep, and we drove on until we reached the drop-off point for one of the pygmy rattlesnakes. Following Kevin several yards into the woods, I watched in the glare of the headlights while he unceremoniously released the snake into the wiregrass—a ritual that he had already performed about thirteen hundred times, once for every snake he had captured in the past five years. He released two more snakes that night.

Walking back to the Jeep, I noticed a small pendant glinting on a leather cord around Kevin's neck. It was an Australian gold coin from 2001, the year he had traveled "down under" after graduating from high school. "The year of the snake," he added.

Well after dark he said it was a good time to head to "the sluice," his favorite hunting ground for cottonmouths, a site where within 125 feet of the road he had already captured forty-six cottonmouths that year. It was the only place he regularly hunted off-road. "My dad and a friend grew up hunting snakes together," Kevin reminisced. "Today when I catch a big cottonmouth, Dad will say, 'Oh, that's nothing. When I was young, every one was a six-footer.'" Kevin added wistfully that "the days of six-foot cottonmouths are gone."

"What if you were bitten by a cottonmouth or rattlesnake?" I asked. "You're out here in the middle of the night alone."

"A cottonmouth would be bad. A canebrake rattlesnake would be worse. They have potent, deadly venom. If I'm bitten, I'll remove anything constricting. When I was bitten by the pygmy, I took off my ring and watch. I have a snakebite kit with a suction and syringe, and if I can apply it within a few seconds of the bite, it'll help. Otherwise it won't. You should keep the bitten area below the heart. Don't wait, don't call the police or an ambulance or suck out the venom. Drive to the hospital as fast as you can."

We parked by the sluice. It was the Sandhills' answer to a tropical forest. A culvert from the other side of Wildlife Drive fed the stream. Because of the afternoon downpour, the flow was rushing through the sluice and down a small creek. "This strong a current is bad for a cottonmouth hunt," said Kevin, surveying a pile of brush on the opposite shore. "The cottonmouths will probably have moved downstream."

I had mixed feelings on receiving this intelligence.

Carrying his snake stick, a long-shafted handling hook, Kevin strode down the trail. I followed. Closely. The terrain was dark and tangled, a grassy bank leading to a precipitous path so narrow and overgrown that I had to place each foot directly in front of the other. Large orange spiders, orb weavers, hung in lacy webs from branches. I had brought a flashlight, an inconsequential thing with two AA batteries that was about as useful as a birthday candle in a haunted castle. Kevin's flashlight was as big as a car headlight and lit up the area like a 400-watt metal halide lamp.

Waist-high cane brushed us on either side of the path. I was clad in heavy jeans and high lace-up leather boots, wishing I were armored in the snake-proof plastic shin guards I had bought for deer hunting around swamps. Kevin wore cargo shorts and tennis shoes. "Kevin," I said, "it's pretty jungly through here. You're traipsing around through tall weeds, stepping through mud puddles and over rotten logs, and you're dressed for a day at the beach."

He laughed. "I've never seen a cottonmouth on the trail. I used to wear jeans and boots, but when you have to run through the water"—chasing a cottonmouth, I presumed, or maybe running from one—"you're wet for a long time." The beam of his flashlight fell on a six-inch alligator gar treading water in an eddy.

I said I had heard that cottonmouths are aggressive.

"They are to other cottonmouths. But they are not as aggressive as people think. As long as you don't step on one, you're not likely to get bit."

"Where do you find them?"

His beam played across a brush pile and several low-hanging limbs. "They are usually half in the water, half out."

"What about the stories one hears of cottonmouths dropping from high limbs into canoes and johnboats?"

"Those are probably brown water snakes. A cottonmouth might lie on a branch like that one," he said, pointing to a limb two feet above the creek as he tightroped along a log that paralleled the stream. I started to follow, unsteady. "You don't have to come out here," he said.

"OK," I said and stepped back down.

He searched the opposite bank with his light. "In 2002," a year of drought in South Carolina, "I would sometimes find six cottonmouths per night. Then in 2003 there was a lot of rain, and I found nowhere near as many." The faster, heavier current had pushed the prey downstream, he reasoned, and the snakes had followed.

Gently probing some matted leaves with the toe of his sneaker, he mentioned that this was also good habitat for mud snakes. When grown, mud snakes are forty to fifty inches long, black with pale red markings along their sides. "They are active in late April and early May. They're inactive in summer and become active again in late August."

He cocked his ear to a distant *pu-tunk pu-tunk* from across the pond. "That's a carpenter frog. And lookee here," he said, shining his light on a tiny orange frog clinging to a waist-high green leaf. "A spring peeper."

For me, this was the real find. Every year in February I listen for spring peepers. The sweetest chorus in the world, they sing the end of winter. But I had never seen a peeper before. I thought of how great it would be to cruise the refuge on summer nights and catalog the different species of frogs and toads.

We found no cottonmouths and left the sluice with empty pillowcases to ride the road twice more, dodging the toads and frogs that were dodging us.

Over the growl of the Jeep, I asked, "How seasonal is your research?"

"I start in March, but I usually don't find much. I may find some snakes under trash, but the heart of my study is road cruising at night. It's not until mid- to late April that I start finding snakes. I usually finish around mid-October. Last year, though, I actually found some snakes crossing a road the night of November 1st."

I asked if there were any surprises in his study.

"The moon. My moon-phase theory came to me one night in 2003. I was cruising along, and the road temperature, air temperature, everything was great, but I wasn't finding any snakes. Usually six snakes is a normal find. I couldn't figure it out. Then I happened to look up and see a full moon. Later I went back to the house and started pulling data together and made some graphs, which showed that there were very significant differences in snake activity levels during a full moon, a half moon, and a new moon. There are a whole bunch of ways to dissect the data, and I may turn that theory into my master's thesis."

We rode without talking for a few minutes, then over the sound of the engine Kevin said, "I wish I could hunt for tiger salamanders. I wish I could find gopher frogs—they've never been recorded here. Both are threatened species. Finding them would be significant. I wish I could put radio transmitters in cottonmouths," and he went on reciting half a dozen more wishes, driving through the forest, eyes focused on the road ahead.

BACK IN HIS KITCHEN with the banded water snake in hand, Kevin demonstrated how he marked snakes by counting and cauterizing their scales. "The anal scale differentiates the snake's tail from its body," he said, turning the lively, corkscrewing snake belly-up. "This is the anal scale here, right above the cloaca. I count the anal scale as zero. Every scale above it, I count in ones—one, two . . ." He burned the second scale with a medical cauterizer, a delicate tool generally used for cauterizing blood vessels. There was a wisp of white smoke. The snake writhed a little more than usual. "Once I—," Kevin began, when the snake, which had already bitten him a few times on the road, whipped up and nailed his finger. "He's really trying to latch onto me," Kevin observed. "Once I get to the tenth scale, I count by tens—10, 20, 30, 40, 50. . . ." Another wisp of smoke. The snake struck again. Kevin's hand and fingers dripped blood onto the linoleum. "The cauterizing tool makes a permanent scar. After the snake sheds his skin a couple of times, the cauterized scales turn white." Kevin had experimented with implanting microchips in the reptiles for identification, but "microchips are really expensive," especially if the microchipped snakes were lost to cars or predators.

"This is banded water snake number 52. Say next year I catch him again, I can see how much he's grown, see if he's been injured, if he's changed location . . ."

"How many times has this snake bitten you?"

"Probably eight."

"Ever think about wearing gloves?"

"I could, but I'd lose dexterity." The snake lashed up through the air again. This time its jaws locked onto the side of Kevin's hand. It did not release. "Ever been bitten by a kitten or a puppy?" Kevin asked. "That hurts more. The way I feel, if I'm taking the snake out of its habitat, I deserve to get bitten."

"You're too obliging."

"Bites from these nonvenomous snakes are clean. They heal quickly. Tomorrow morning there'll barely be a scab," he said, although he told me later that this snake was the first to leave a scar, albeit a tiny one. Gently unlocking the snake's jaws from his hand, Kevin returned the reptile to its pillowcase and washed his hands at the sink.

Since we had captured only one snake that night and no cottonmouths, Kevin invited me to cruise with him again. I jumped at the chance, made a mental note to bring a bigger flashlight, bade goodbye, and left him at the sink staunching his wounds with a kitchen towel.

NOTE

1. D. Bruce Means, "Vertebrate Faunal Diversity of Longleaf Pine Ecosystems," in *The Longleaf Pine Ecosystem: Ecology, Silviculture, and Restoration*, ed. Shibu Jose, Eric J. Jokela, and Deborah L. Miller (New York: Springer, 2006), 194.

Staging a Burn

"You can burn only what Mother Nature and the government let you."

Mark Parker, burn boss

ON A MORNING IN LATE APRIL at 7:00 A.M. I received calls from Scott Lanier, manager of the Carolina Sandhills National Wildlife Refuge, and Mike Housh, fire management officer. "We'll try a prescribed burn if we can round up a few extra bodies." They invited me along to watch.

I made a cup of coffee and switched on the TV to the Weather Channel. Low of 46 degrees. High of 80. Unlimited visibility. Humidity 93. Dew point. . . . Sleepy, I wondered what a dew point was.

The extra bodies Mike rounded up were Terri Jenkins, fire management officer at the Savannah Coastal Refuges Complex, and her crew of fire technicians, who had left Savannah at 6:30 A.M. for the long drive to the Sandhills.

At 8:00 A.M. I was in the office of Mark Parker, the refuge's burn boss. "I got two fire techs and two ADs," he told me, ADs being "administratively determined" part-timers. "Terri's bringing four, but they got delayed. We should burn by 11:00 A.M. Mike Housh tells me it'll be a short day. We'll burn only about eight hundred acres."

I sensed his frustration. He'd hoped for an earlier start. With the approaching summer heat, the safe season for prescribed burns was closing quickly.

A map of the refuge was thumbtacked onto Mark's wall. The map was divvied up into compartments, the compartments into units. The units were shaded orange, pink, white, and green.

"This year we'll try to burn the pink areas," Mark told me. "The green ones are where we're experimenting with seasonality—winter burns, fall burns, in different rotations. Those areas are small enough to burn by hand, so we don't need a helicopter." A helicopter is often used to drop incendiary "Ping-Pong" balls to ignite controlled burns within a unit.

A helicopter crew assists with a prescribed burn. Using a Premo Aerial Ignition Machine, the crew drops incendiary plastic spheres into a forest unit to be burned. Photograph courtesy of Andy Smith, Vanguard AIS.

"If on a given day we don't have a pink block to burn because of wind, we'll burn an orange block. The next year we'll substitute that orange for a pink. The white spaces are what we burned last year. We were hit hard in 2001 because we burned only seven thousand acres."

The fire crew tries to burn one-third of the NWR's forty-five thousand acres each year. "That year we didn't have a helicopter stationed here. It took two and a half hours to fly it here. The crew was guaranteed three hours of on-the-job flight time. If the burn was canceled, the helicopter would cost forty-two hundred dollars to get here and back, plus per diem and mileage, so you've spent about forty-five hundred dollars—even though you accomplished nothing." This year, fortunately, a helicopter was stationed at the refuge.

Swiveling in his chair, Mark showed me a map of the acreage he hoped to burn that day—Unit 2. The area was a Florida-shaped swath of forest bordered by Black Creek, a dirt road, and a bulldozed firebreak.

"Normally you'll have crew on both sides of the unit." Using drip torches, the fire techs lay down a "black line against the wind," which pushes the fire in the intended direction. "If there is a firebreak or road, you'll have to pull a black line along it. The helicopter can't drop fire along the road." There was no need to lay a black line along Black Creek. "The fire will burn up to it and quit."

Mark pointed to numbered dots on the map. "See these trees? Red-cockaded woodpecker clusters. There's a nest in this one, so today while the aircraft is lighting this area, a crew member on an ATV will rake fuel away from these trees to give them a buffer. It's nesting season. We definitely don't want to mess up any RCW cavities."

Mike Housh entered from the hallway. It was the first time we had met. Strongly built, with a goatee, a day's growth of beard, a dip in his lip, and the can in his back pocket, he wore a black T-shirt, green fire-retardant pants, and a ball cap lettered "Carolina Sandhills NWR Fire Region 4 District 2." In earlier years Mike had played rugby in Washington State, Texas, and Columbia, South Carolina. I found out later that the helicopter pilot was a former semipro rugby player. I wondered if there was a Pavlovian connection between the brutal contact sport and firefighting or just some shared, unconditioned need for the rough-and-tumble.

Immediately Mike and Mark fell into the shorthand dialogue of those who had worked together a long time and knew the terrain. "Which way's the wind?" Mike asked.

"Southeast," replied Mark. "According to the forecast, it's supposed to stay steady."

Mike asked about mixing height, the height where smoke stops rising and travels with the transport wind.

"Right now, mixing height's low," Mark said. "Just over two thousand feet. But it's predicted to be fifty-five hundred feet this afternoon. Transport wind south at 12 miles per hour." He leaned back in his chair and stretched. "It's a high Category 4 day, almost a 5." Category 5 described the optimal conditions for a burn. "I think we can get the smoke up there, but I'm not gonna push my luck. I also hoped to do Unit 16.3 today."

"You might be able to burn this one," said Mike, pointing to a pink unit on the map.

"It'll push smoke right on what's-his-name's house."

"Is he there, though?"

"I came through the other day and his gate was open. His truck was sitting there. He may be gone today."

"We could swing in and ask if he'd mind leaving for a couple of hours," said Mike. "You know he'd like to get that stuff burned."

"Unit 16.3 has a good firebreak on the south end down to the river, and there's no black line to set. That unit is about 500 acres," Mark said, turning to his computer monitor and checking a spreadsheet. "No, 655 acres."

"And it's mostly upland," said Mike.

"It shouldn't take long to burn. What's gonna be slow is getting there," said Mark, referring to the logistics of moving the crew, trucks, ATVs, fire engines, and bulldozer.

"Right."

"Terri and Ray will be in the helicopter. There'll be two fire engines and me and Greg on ATVs, since we know where the RCW trees are. We need to use the helicopter because it'll be off contract Wednesday," Mark added.

"I'd stick with 2.2 first," said Mike. "That way you'll have a point to cut off if things aren't going the way you want. I wouldn't commit to burning 2.4."

"That unit is mostly grass," Mark said. "If we burn there, we're gonna have some heat in it. That might be rolling the dice a little more than I should. My feeling is, get started, get the fire up. With the ceiling predicted to get higher and higher, if we start at 11:00, we'll be done by 4:00."

"Remember the last time you had a Category 4 day, but the ceiling squatted right on top of you." Mike pointed to the map. "You'll know once you get to this little ridge here. You'll know."

"I'll work up 16.3."

"I'd use it as a backup. I'd stage the dozer right by 16.4. That way it could go either right or left. Because with the southeast wind, if the fire's gonna do anything, it'll just jump onto us."

"And if we burn all of this and we still got time—" said Mark.

"—just roll everybody over. Load up with fuel and Ping-Pong balls and get on it," said Mike. "You just need a couple of ATVs on that disk line."

Mark rose to go. "I got the ATVs loaded already."

I LEFT THE HEADQUARTERS of the refuge with Mike and headed to the maintenance area, where Mark would meet the crew for a preburn briefing.

On the drive over, Mike told me that the previous day Mark had worked a prescribed burn at the Congaree National Forest near Columbia, South Carolina. This spring Mike, Mark, and their crew had worked burns at Pinckney Island, the ACE Basin (the basin of the Ashley, Cooper, and Edisto Rivers), Cape Romaine, and the Francis Marion National Forest. "That's what we're paid to do."

Mike and Mark had also battled wildfires out west. They would later train my son Aaron as a wildlands firefighter, an experience that would inspire him to get a master's in forestry at Clemson University. As Mike drove, he gave me his take on fighting wildfires in grizzly bear country: "Make a lot of noise. Clank your tools as you walk. Give the bears time to run off so you don't surprise them."

Mike loves his work. "When we're not starting burns, we're putting out wildfires." He parked his white Dodge Ram 4WD truck on the gravel lot of the maintenance area. The Savannah crew was still en route. Mark was leaning against a truck, perusing the day's National Weather Service forecast. To kill time Greg Boling, a biologist and fire tech, was sweeping the garage floor.

Several of the fire techs were young, tough-looking men in their early twenties. They invited me to the next "Weenie Wednesday"—a weekly party where they roasted hot dogs and quaffed immoderate quantities of refreshing beverages. At a recent Weenie Wednesday, an impromptu wrestling match had ended in a broken collar bone. Mark informed me that there'd be no more Weenie Wednesdays this year.

Mike noticed that I'd worn white jeans to the burn. Whether to keep my pants clean, protect me from stray sparks, or maybe as a joke, he handed me canary yellow Nomex coveralls to wear. Size 44 long. I'm a 38. I looked like a kid in his dad's pajamas.

I followed Mike into the briefing room. Hayden Bergin, the helicopter pilot, was sitting on a table. Mike introduced us. Tall, tan, with rock-star hair and wearing a green jumpsuit and dark tortoise-shell sunglasses, the pilot had an accent I couldn't place. English? Australian? "Nee-ew Zayland," he said.

This year Hayden and the helicopter were stationed at the Carolina Sandhills NWR throughout the burn season, from February to May. At the refuge Hayden had two responsibilities: one, fly patterns above the burn zone so the helicopter crew could drop lines of incendiary balls to start fires; two, get the crew back safely.

At an earlier prescribed burn, I had stood in a firebreak and watched Hayden's helicopter hover, bank, and shuttle back and forth along the edge of smoke, fifty feet above the trees, while a crew member, leaning from the open door and manning the aerial ignition machine, dropped balls to seed the flames. I wondered how Hayden could see the forest through the smoke.

"You don't often get into the smoke," he said, "because the fire is backing into the wind. So you're staying in front of the smoke. Basically we fly backward and forward, perpendicular to the wind direction."

When dropping the fire balls, Mike said, the helicopter crew has to concentrate on two distances: the distance between the lines of balls; and the spacing between the balls within each line. "The distance between lines depends on the fire behavior," said Mike. "You adjust your between-line distance depending on how the fire acts. Your in-line spaces are determined by the craft's forward air speed and the frequency at which the aerial ignition machine drops the balls. You want the balls to burn together between lines before they burn together within lines. That way you get a little backing fire, a little flanking fire, and a little head fire. You don't want a solid line of fire going through the forest. And if the fire gets too hot, you 'bump' or decrease the distance between your lines."

"The rate at which you drop the balls is weird," explained Hayden, "because it's the opposite of what you'd think. If the fire starts to get too hot, you put more fire in it. If the fire's not burning hot enough, you put fewer balls in the line to build up some heat."

"On this burn, the between-line distance will be about a chain—sixty-six feet—or a chain and a half," said Mike. The helicopter's burn boss usually determines the frequency of dropped balls and the distance between the lines.

"I'm glad somebody figured all of this out," I said.

"It's definitely an art," Hayden told me.

"Some days, because of temperature and humidity, the balls don't ignite fast enough," added Mike. "And because the ignition of the balls is delayed, the helicopter crew won't have a visual on their last one or two lines. They might lose the pattern and drop more balls than they should. Then the pilot will radio, 'I'm sorry. I crossed my line.' I'll say, 'Don't worry about it. We're just painting the landscape with fire.'"

Mike tossed out that phrase in an offhand way, but I thought how apt it was: like some nineteenth-century landscape painters, the foresters and fire crews were attempting to re-create a landscape that had been nearly lost, a landscape that relatively few in the world had ever seen.

I didn't bother to ask for a ride in the helicopter. There was nothing I wanted more, but I knew the fire management officer and burn boss would nix it. I also knew the helicopter crew didn't need me looking over their shoulders and asking questions while they worked. As close as I would get to flying was my conversation with the pilot. Hayden, age thirty-three, was from a small town near Wellington, New Zealand, where he learned to fly helicopters. He initially came to the United States to play rugby, the sport that he shared with Mike Housh.

I mentioned how rough rugby looks when I watch it on TV. Hayden said that rugby's "not as bad as American football. There are a lot of rules in the game to protect the players. You can't tackle someone around the head, you can't tackle someone who doesn't have the ball, you can't block. Most of the injuries in football occur when players get blindsided when they don't have the ball."

To Hayden, rules and safety are a matter of life and death. "This job at the Sandhills—you really have to know how to fly. A pilot who isn't comfortable won't be able to do it. Firefighters don't want to fly with pilots who are 'cowboys' who try to show off. You can't show government firefighters something they haven't seen before. It's not like you need to impress them. They're more impressed with getting the job done safely and efficiently and getting home at night."

Hayden and the Bell LongRanger helicopter were on contract from Skylane, Inc., of Decatur, Texas. "Skylane has really good maintenance," Hayden said. "We have an in-house mechanic, and the helicopter has timed inspections." Skylane contracts with both the U.S. Forest and U.S. Fish and Wildlife Services.

"I've flown on U.S. Forest Service contracts. Often their objective is to use controlled burns to protect the timber because it's going to be logged. If those trees catch fire, someone's out millions of dollars. The objectives of the U.S. Forest and U.S. Fish and Wildlife Services are different—one manages timber; the other also manages wildlife. For the Forest Service, I usually burn huge, square, three-thousand-acre blocks of land. It's easier. You start flying at one end and work your way down. But for Fish and Wildlife, the burns are a lot more technical. A refuge is not a big block of land. At the Sandhills my main focus is prescribed burning. Firebreaks and black lines are all over the place. You have to watch for a firebreak here, make sure you don't drop balls there."

I asked about his training.

"Learning to fly a helicopter is not overly hard. When a pilot learns to fly, he has lessons in safety and emergency landings. For example, he follows flight profiles that protect him if his engine fails. On a prescribed burn, though, I may fly thirty feet above the pines. If something goes wrong, we're going into the trees. It's a calculated risk. You do everything you can, but the risk is there. Everyone on the helicopter knows that.

"A lot of your trainers are the people you work with. The people I work with—Mark, Mike, and Terri—are awesome. This is my third year, and these guys are by far the best I've seen. Mark and Mike have a lot of fire experience. Mark rappeled out of a helicopter for years—one hundred, two hundred feet up. Those guys are pretty highly regarded."

I mentioned that, in the event of a mishap, the helicopter could be going down in a forest that's on fire.

"That's the least of my worries," he said. "Sometimes the trees are 150 feet tall. If you hit the canopy, you've still got 150 feet to fall."

I asked if he had experienced any close calls.

"You get in situations where you say, 'I can't believe I just did that, and if I keep doing that, I'm not gonna get away with it.' Sometimes the others in the helicopter don't realize it. When you're firefighting in mountains, for example, there's a whole different set of aerodynamic factors. You can't let your performance fade. You've got to *be* even farther out in front of the helicopter. You've got to think ahead. You can get into a spot where the helicopter is 'settling,' or descending, and you can't stop it. You may get into a spot and think, hey, if the helicopter does start to settle, I've got a big gap in the trees where I can use my air speed to carry on out. But if you're in a spot where there's no gap in the trees and you start settling, you're gonna hit the ground, whether you land or crash."

I wondered if the intense heat and smoke of a fire affected aerodynamics.

"My rule of thumb is that if smoke is white, I can fly through it. I don't make a habit of it, but it won't affect the helicopter as far as turbulence. But if the smoke is black, it's hot. It'll bump the helicopter and it's not good on the engine, which is a turbine. If I fly through hot black smoke, it'll make the engine hot as well."

Hayden knew that the burn season at the Sandhills was coming to an end. Rains were forecast for the next several days, and his contract ended soon. The next summer he would be on fire detail out west, where he would drop one-hundred-gallon buckets of water from his helicopter onto fledgling wildfires so we wouldn't hear about them on the evening news.

"In June I'll be in Moab, Utah, on an initial attack crew. The crew will be three other fire personnel and me. We just stand by, and if a fire is reported, we launch, dispatch to the fire, size it up, see what can be done. If we can land, the firefighters will try to cut firebreaks and put it out. If there's water available, we'll hook the helicopter's bucket up. It's usually a hundred gallons. Huge fires—even five-hundred-thousand-acre fires—start less than the size of a room. If you can put one out before it gets big, you don't need thousands of gallons of water."

Or hundreds of firefighters and millions of tax dollars. And we don't lose hundreds of homes, thousands of acres of forest, and lives, both human and wild.

AFTER THE BRIEFING we walked to the trucks. Because of adverse weather conditions that year, Mike said, they were falling far short of their goal of burning one-third of the forty-five-thousand-acre refuge.

"It was late spring, and we had burned only about seven thousand acres," Mark later told me. "We were way off our target, and we were getting into summer," the end of their burn season.

With the day's late start, the helicopter going off contract, and the favorable forecast of a Category 4 or 5 day, I asked Mark if he felt pressured to make up lost ground.

"No," he said, "we're already far behind. No reason to push it. We aren't gonna knock out seven thousand more acres." Still, the hope that day was to get another nine hundred acres under their belts.

Mike dropped me off at the burn zone, out of harm's way on the corner of a dirt road and a bulldozed firebreak, then drove off. Parked along the road were ATVs, white 4WD refuge trucks, and yellow 4WD fire engines. The helicopter hadn't flown in yet.

The plan was to burn Unit 2.2 (230 acres) in the morning and Unit 16.3 (655 acres) in the afternoon. But odds were against it. The crews were getting a late start, the forecast had changed, and the weather was threatening.

To complicate matters, the helicopter, essential for big burns but already on an extended contract, was off the job in two days. A dozen shifting variables, all out of burn boss Mark Parker's control, determined if the burn could go forward. If the cloud ceiling remained too low for smoke dispersal or if the temperature hit 75 degrees, Mark would be forced to scrub the afternoon burn.

Compared to the last prescribed burn I had witnessed, Unit 2.2 was trashed with undergrowth—abundant pine needles and leaves, fallen branches, and an encroaching midstory of hardwoods, mostly turkey, red, white, and water oaks. The excess fuel on the ground made me nervous.

I waited with Don Cockman, assistant refuge manager, by his truck. I hoped to get a photo of Mark or his drip-torch crew stitching lines of flames along the firebreak or the edge of the road, but they strode too fast for me to focus my camera.

Don said that the lines of fire they were laying down would be visual cues for Terri Jenkins, the helicopter's burn boss. If not for these, the helicopter's crew "would have a hard time seeing the road" and might accidentally start a fire on the wrong side.

We stood on the road and watched the flames grow while music from a Christian radio station played quietly from the FM in Don's truck. A moment later over his handheld radio I heard Terri say something about a dozen blue herons.

"There's a beaver pond in this unit," Don explained, "and a heron rookery in a big old pond pine snag."

The rookery, Mark later said, was "down in Black Creek bottom in a beaver pond. It's too wet there; it won't burn. The herons ate a little smoke, but that's about it."

Soon the helicopter was shuttling overhead and things heated up. As the aircraft banked fifty feet above the trees, I could see a crew member in its open door manning the aerial ignition machine. The white plastic balls fell in lines, fizzed, and burst into small circles of fire seconds after impact. Soon orange flames jumped through the woods and gray-white smoke wrapped the crowns of the pines.

Terri's voice came over the radio again. "This is 8-0 Lima. We'll start filling in the interior." She paused, then remarked, "I'm still not too sure about the smoke today."

"Copy that," I heard Mark say.

"There's a lack of smoke dispersal," Don said. "Too much smoke hanging down low, getting on the roadway." The smoke was thick. Fire snapped and popped. Flames whipped chest high up the trunks of hardwoods. "Mike, Mark, and Terri are trying to make sure the smoke goes where they want and keeps off the highway."

I was watching a wolf spider clamber down the road bank to escape the heat when a deer bolted out of the smoke. Seeing us, it ran back into the forest. I recalled what Mark had said. The crew did not set the fire in solid lines but left gaps for deer, snakes, and rabbits to escape.

Across the road behind us was more pine forest. Though the tree trunks were charred from an earlier burn, the ground was covered with bright green bracken ferns.

"How long ago was this area burned?" I asked.

"About a month, six weeks ago back in March. That burn had a flame height of about eight feet," he said, looking at the charred trunks. "Flame height depends on fuel. There was pretty heavy fuel in there. Pine litter, pine straw. Not many hardwoods, though."

We crossed the road and climbed the bank. He bent to show me a knee-high longleaf pine. "This one's in the grass stage. After the burn it would have looked dead for sure, but now you can see the regeneration. The needles were scorched orange, but the terminal bud is still alive. If this were a loblolly pine," he added to underscore the longleaf pines' adaptation to fire, "it'd be dead."

I commented that it didn't take long for wiregrass to green up after a burn.

"No, it doesn't." He stood up and walked to a small turkey oak. "You can tell that fire has burned the midstory oaks. This one is still alive, but it's been weakened." He pointed to a tall hickory. "When a hardwood gets that big, it's pretty hard to burn it without killing your pines. If that tree was a problem, we'd cut it down with a chain saw. You don't want any midstory hardwood in a red-cockaded woodpecker cluster." A midstory of hardwoods is a ladder: a ladder for rat snakes to climb into RCW cavity nests and a ladder for flames to climb into the forest canopy.

Sooner than I would have guessed, Terri was on the radio again. "Mark, we've completed firing down the interior of the unit."

"Copy that," Mark responded. "What's the smoke doing?"

"It's not getting up a whole lot. It's still in that hardwood area. If we get away from the creek, we might be OK. Stand by. We'll get you a better smoke report." She paused and then, concerned about smoke descending on nearby private land, asked, "How are your neighbors?"

"They're fine," said Mark. "The fire will burn a lot better once we get out of that hardwood bottom down by Black Creek."

"Mark," Terri said, "it looks like the smoke's hitting the ceiling, mixing about eleven hundred feet or so. If we can get into a higher unit of pine, we'll be OK."

Mark later explained that "if the Weather Service predicts Category 4 conditions and a fifty-five-hundred-foot ceiling, we expect good transport winds. But if the smoke hangs at fifteen hundred feet, we think about shutting down the burn. Otherwise we might smoke our neighbors out." Hardwood smoke, he said, usually has less "lift" because its leaf litter holds more moisture. But pine straw held off the ground by wiregrass produces more heat when it burns, sending the smoke up to the wind's transport height.

Mike's voice came over the radio. "Terri, we probably ought to see what the smoke does on that pine ridge before we take another bite." If, due to the low ceiling, the smoke still failed to disperse, the burn would be canceled.

"8-0 copies that," said Terri, "and yeah, Mike, we want to watch the fire for a few minutes. It's building up some heat now."

"A little more to worry about now than just smoke," Mike added. There was a pause. Then Mike's voice again: "We're making a determination whether we're gonna burn another unit."

There was another burst of radio static, then Terri said, "Flames six to eight feet high on the converging lines only. The rest of the fire looks to be around four feet."

"Copy that," Mark told her matter-of-factly. "Seventy-four degrees is knocking on the door of our top end."

"Understand," replied Terri. "Top end is 75 degrees."

Later I asked Mark about the role of the weather. "Today the determining factor was temperature. Some days it could be wind speed or humidity. Seventy-five degrees was written into our prescription. We were bound by it. If we went outside the prescription and killed trees or somebody got hurt, we'd be held accountable."

Terri came back over the radio: "Mark, this is 8-0. We're here to do whatever you'd like."

"Everything's got to line up just right," Mark replied.

"Understand," said Terri.

There was another pause. Then Mark said with a tone of resignation, "You guys head back to the barn."

"Copy that," said Terri. "8-0 will be returning to the base."

As the burn ended, Don and I watched a snag. Fifteen feet up its trunk, fire was eating through. The trunk flared and smoked, and the dead tree teetered in the breeze. I thought the snag might fall any second.

"It might stand till nighttime," Don said.

Minutes later Terri spoke over the radio: "Landing secured."

On an ATV, Mark roared up toward us on the dirt road. I was going to take his photo but put my camera away. It wasn't a good time.

"Mark," I said, "you look pissed."

"Not pissed," he said. "Distraught. The crew likes to keep burning, but we have to call it quits. No use to push it. You can burn only what Mother Nature and the government let you."

I was as much impressed by the crew's restraint as I was by their toil and sweat. The next day the crew burned Unit 2.4. That was the end of the burn season that year at the Carolina Sandhills National Wildlife Refuge. They had burned 7,720 acres, about half of their goal. The shortfall would mean harder work next year, if the weather cooperated. If not, the risk of a wildfire would rise with the number of unburned acres.

After a Burn—Longleaf Pine Strategy

"If you are thriftily inclined, you will find pines congenial company."

Aldo Leopold, conservationist

I WENT IN MAY with forester Clay Ware to the Carolina Sandhills National Wildlife Refuge to study how longleaf pines survive fire. Earlier that month and well into the growing season, the refuge crew had staged one of the last burns of the year to preserve their portion of this threatened ecosystem.

To determine if an area has recently burned, Clay said, look for wiregrass (*Aristida stricta*) with long stalks of seed. "Wiregrass won't produce a big seed crop unless it's been burned." In some parts of the Sandhills there's typically more broomsedge, "but the Carolina Sandhills NWR has a lot more wiregrass." Native bunchgrasses such as wiregrass, Indian grass, bluestem, and broomsedge are essential to the longleaf ecosystem and beneficial to wildlife, such as quail.

Wiregrass encourages fire. Each clump of bunchgrass catches falling pine straw; prevents it from settling into a thick, hard-to-burn mat; and leaves plenty of air space to stoke the flames. "Wiregrass carries the fire through the ecosystem," said Clay. Combined with highly flammable longleaf pine straw, which is more resinous than that of other pines, wiregrass creates "the ideal condition for fire to run hot and fast."

In the burn zone we visited, dead leaves dangled from the blackened branches of five- to eight-foot scrub oaks. Last fall, Clay said, these oaks had stored nutrients in their roots for this growing season. "This spring those nutrients were allocated to leaf production. By the time of the burn, the oaks—which we're trying to control—had already leafed out. When you burn this time of year and kill the scrub oaks' leaves, you really put the hurt on them. They have limited nutrients stored in their root systems to produce new leaves."

A longleaf pine in the grass stage. Longleaf seedlings, which may exist in this stage ten or more years, develop deep taproots and have a survival strategy tested under fire. Photograph by the author.

As we walked through the woods, he pointed to the base of one seven-foot oak. "See, this tree has not resprouted at all. It may actually die."

Some young oaks were sprouting new leaves about a foot above the ground, but the ability of the hardwoods to recover had been visibly set back. I asked if they would live. "Those will make it," he said, "but they won't grow as vigorously, and we'll burn them again."

The goal of the burns is not to eliminate the oaks but to prevent them from maturing into a hardwood midstory beneath the taller longleaf pines. Although individual longleaf pines can stay healthy surrounded by a midstory of hardwoods, Clay said, "a longleaf forest won't regenerate sufficiently if there's a heavy oak understory. The longleaf forest will eventually die from old age, insect outbreak," or wildfire. During a fire a midstory allows fire to jump up above the pines' corky fire-resistant bark and into their treetops, igniting a wildfire that destroys the entire forest community. Such a midstory also degrades the habitat of red-cockaded woodpeckers, an endangered and keystone species.

The ground we stood on was still black and charred. At first glance the only color I noticed was a sprinkling of orange longleaf needles. "Needle cast," explained Clay. I was surprised by the length of the longleaf needles, which were up to eighteen inches. Heat-singed needles also hung from the lower branches of more mature pines, which were often fifty feet tall and twelve inches or more in diameter at breast height.

"The flame length probably stayed below five feet," Clay said. "A few pines may die, but longleaf is well suited to fire." He pointed to the branches of the pine beneath which we stood. Needles were sprouting on its lower boughs. "See how rapidly the new leaves are growing around the lateral buds?" On higher branches the needles were still green.

For an overview of the evolutionary importance of fire to longleaf pines, it's worth quoting D. Bruce Means of Florida's Coastal Plains Institute and Land Conservancy:

> Fire is responsible worldwide, if not for the origin, then for the perpetuation of pine associations known as savannas. . . . Pines may have evolved their special relationship with fire early in the evolutionary history of the group going back to the Jurassic [150 million years ago]. . . . Longleaf pine, as a species, probably does not go nearly that far back in time, but it may have evolved from ancestors that were part of grassland/fire habitats throughout the later half of the Cretaceous [105 million years ago] and all of the Cenozoic [65 million years ago to present]. Longleaf pine savannas are pyrogenic communities that require periodic fires in order to exist through time. . . . In the absence of fire, longleaf pine savannas succeed to southern mixed hardwood forest . . ., a completely different ecosystem, but fires associated with summer lightning probably have been characteristic of the climate of the Coastal Plain of the southeastern United States at least since the Miocene [25 million years ago]. Longleaf pine savanna plants are so completely adapted to the periodic effects of fire, and fire has been so continuously present in the Coastal Plain, that the longleaf pine savanna is considered a climax vegetative type.[1]

"Compared to other pines species," Clay said, "longleaf pine is not a prolific seed producer." It takes at least three years for their seeds to develop, and seed crops may occur only once every six to eight years. What's more, the large, heavy seeds don't carry far on the wind, and this lack of wide dispersal keeps longleaf pines from "colonizing and establishing in areas" far from their source. Another obstacle to reproduction is that longleaf "requires an exposed mineral soil seedbed that is free of surface litter." The suppression of fire, therefore, "results in accumulation of forest litter that hinders proper germination of longleaf pine seeds."[2] Fire isn't a midwife to this pine species alone. The seed cones of the pocosin-loving pond pine, *Pinus serotina*, often germinate after a fire.

After germination longleaf pines have three basic life stages: grass stage, sapling, and mature tree. For longleaf pines in the grass stage, fire is usually no problem whatsoever. "Look at this little longleaf," Clay said, squatting by a grass-stage pine that was hardly bigger than an Easter egg. Though bristling with charred needles, it was already rebounding from the fire that had swept over it. Baby green needles grew from its white center.

I surveyed the black forest floor again and for the first time noticed hundreds of little grass-stage pines. Although each of these was blackened, nearly all boasted a spray of green needles. I was impressed and asked if most grass-stage longleaf pines can survive fire.

"Oh yeah," said Clay. At this stage their terminal buds are small, hard, and fire-resistant. Even if a fire kills the bud, at the root collar is a latent bud that may step up, enabling the seedling to survive. Longleaf pines bide their time in this pint-size stage "from three to five, even ten years or longer." The number of years a longleaf spends in the grass stage, in fact, "varies depending on site resources and competition. This stage may last as long as 10–25 years."[3]

"All that time they are developing a long taproot, storing nutrients," said Clay.

We were not the first to appreciate the frugality of pines. "If you are thriftily inclined," writes Aldo Leopold, "you will find pines congenial company, for, unlike the hand-to-mouth hardwoods, they never pay current bills out of current earnings."[4]

When longleaf pines finally accelerate out of the grass stage and into saplings, said Clay, "they'll be about five feet tall within two growing seasons. Then they are usually out of harm's way, as far as fire goes. I have seen young longleafs up to twenty feet tall without a single lateral branch. It's so unbelievable—straight up without a single limb."

In the sapling stage, the terminal bud is "enlarged and almost fleshy. If the bud is burned at this time, another bud will not form and the tree will die." To Leopold, the pine's terminal bud resembles a candle: "the new shoot is waxy, upright, brittle. But he who lives with pines knows that candle has a deeper meaning, for at its tip burns the eternal flame that lights a path into the future."[5]

"Grass-stage longleafs tend to become saplings after a fire," Clay said. Maybe this growth spurt results from the boon of nutrients that fire bequeaths to the soil. Or maybe the transformation "is a physiological or genetic response to fire."

Clay knelt by a small longleaf in the sapling stage. Dead orange needles hung from its slender trunk. "This sapling is at the worst size for fire susceptibility," he told me. Fire might have killed the tree's terminal bud, the embryonic tissue at the tip. Although the very existence of longleaf forests depends on fire, prescribed burns "must be prudently timed because longleaf seedlings remain highly vulnerable to fire-caused mortality until they reach a ground-line diameter of 7.5 mm and a height of 1 m."[6] Fortunately the terminal bud of the sapling Clay showed me was green-white and unscathed. Tiny green needles emanated from the bud. "All new growth," he announced.

Clay demonstrated the sapling's strategy for surviving fire. He wrapped his hand around the long, dead needles and pulled them up and gathered them into a thick sheath around the bud. "When fire comes, these needles close around and protect the bud. As they burn, they emit moisture," hopefully enough to cool the bud and push the flames away. This strategy, however, is hit and miss. Two feet away a second sapling of the same size was scorched, its terminal bud, well, terminated. "But out of the fifty or so saplings I see," Clay said, "it's the only one that hasn't developed new growth."

I asked about other threats to longleaf, such as fungus or southern pine beetles. The beetles, Clay said, were present, but because longleaf pines produce lots of resin, they are fairly resistant. His theory is that "when a beetle bores into the tree, the bug is often 'pitched out' by the resin."

Brown-spot fungus, however, is a real menace and the pine's "most serious pathogen." Again it's fire to the rescue. "Timely application of prescribed fire, which consumes the infected needles, is the most effective remedy for this needle blight."[7]

Interestingly, it is the longleaf's ability to wage chemical warfare against bugs and fungi that helped Britannia and later the United States rule the seas. Naval stores production, that is, the "use of the pine products for building and maintaining wooden ships during the seventeenth through nineteenth centuries . . . is based upon exploiting the terpene chemical defense system of the pine tree, which protects against wood-decaying fungi and insect pests such as bark beetles."[8]

It's difficult to guess the age of a mature longleaf at the refuge by eyeing its girth. Some are over one hundred years old. Still, owing to the fairly xeric, or dry, soil of the Sandhills, they may not be large. A tree with a mere fifteen-inch diameter may be fifty years old.

In the 1940s, under authority of the Resettlement Act, the federal government had planted this longleaf pine forest "to restore this badly damaged, barren land to a healthy, rich habitat for the plants and animals that once lived here."[9] At about the same time Aldo Leopold was engaged in a similar act of restoration, planting white pines and bringing back to life an equally desecrated tract of farmland in Sand County, Wisconsin. It was good to see scientists, bureaucrats, and environmentalists thinking the same thoughts, doing the same work.

NOTES

1. D. Bruce Means, "Vertebrate Faunal Diversity of Longleaf Pine Ecosystems," in *The Longleaf Pine Ecosystem: Ecology, Silviculture, and Restoration*, ed. Shibu Jose, Eric J. Jokela, and Deborah L. Miller (New York: Springer, 2006), 194.

2. Shibu Jose, Eric J. Jokela, and Deborah L. Miller, "The Longleaf Pine Ecosystem: An Overview," in *The Longleaf Pine Ecosystem*, ed. Jose, Jokela, and Miller, 4.

3. Ibid., 5.

4. Aldo Leopold, *A Sand County Almanac* (New York: Oxford University Press, 1989), 82–83.

5. Ibid., 82.

6. John Kush cited by Dale G. Brockway, Kenneth W. Outcalt, and William D. Boyer, "Longleaf Pine Regeneration Ecology and Methods," in *The Longleaf Pine Ecosystem*, ed. Jose, Jokela, and Miller, 110.

7. Brockway, Outcalt, and Boyer, "Longleaf Pine Regeneration Ecology and Methods," 109.

8. Alan W. Hodges, "The Naval Stores Industry," in *The Longleaf Pine Ecosystem*, ed. Jose, Jokela, and Miller, 43.

9. U.S. Fish and Wildlife Service, "Carolina Sandhills National Wildlife Refuge" [brochure].

Groundwork

"Imagine that three hundred million years ago Himalayan-like Appalachians loomed on our horizon."

Fred Edinger, geologist

"TO SEE A WORLD IN A GRAIN OF SAND," writes Blake, "And a heaven in a wild flower / Hold infinity in the palm of your hand / And eternity in an hour."[1] Geologists, like poets, have visions, and if they may not grasp infinity, they may still spy a hundred million years of Earth's history in a handful of sand, see oceans come and go and mountains brought low.

Most folks in the Carolinas, if they think about the Sandhills at all, believe them to be dunes deposited by the advance and retreat of an ancient sea. Skim some books and Web sites on Carolina's natural history or ask some locals and they'll probably tell you the same.

After all, when we think of sand, we usually think of oceans. And if we know anything about geology, we probably know that continents drift and sea levels, like tides, are cyclical. Oceans have transgressed and regressed numerous times in the past sixty-five million years. "Like the teeth of an abused saw-blade, each supercycle rises rapidly, slows to a standstill, then drops precipitously."[2]

Each regression leaves sand in its wake. Because the Sandhills are full of the stuff and the region, roughly midway between the Blue Ridge Mountains and the ocean, is relatively flat, it's not hard to imagine that primeval seas washed over the land. According to Dr. Fred Edinger, a geologist at Coker College, "the shoreline of an ancient sea did run somewhere between the Sandhills and Pamplico," a town about fifty miles southeast of the Carolina Sandhills National Wildlife Refuge. "If you go to Pamplico, you'll find fossils of oyster shells and crocodile teeth," signs of a marine environment, "in the sand."

The evidence needed to nail down the theory that Sandhills sand is oceanic, however, is conspicuously absent. "I've been in the region for thirty years," said Fred, "and I've never seen any Sandhills fossil that looked marine—with one possible exception."

The exception was southwest of Patrick, a town five miles to the east of the Carolina Sandhills National Wildlife Refuge. In a low-lying field, a student believed she had found fossils of seashells. "I went to that field, searched and searched, and found a couple of fragments which might have been shell material," said Fred. The question was, were those fragments original or had a farmer limed the field "with crushed limestone which had been mined in a coastal region? That type of rock often contains shell fossils."

To get a truer picture of the origin of the Sandhills, several of us, including Carolina Sandhills National Wildlife Manager Lyne Askins, her eight-year-old son Josh, my wife Allison, and nonagenarian John McLeod, met Fred for a field trip on a cold, wet, windy morning outside the refuge headquarters. Lyne had taken the reins of the refuge when manager Scott Lanier moved to the Alligator River and Pea Island NWRs in North Carolina in 2006.

"Imagine," said Fred, gazing to the northwest, "that three hundred million years ago Himalayan-like Appalachians loomed on our horizon." Those peaks, thrust up by the collision of tectonic plates, might have towered four times as high as today's Smoky Mountains. "Our region would have been in the foothills of those ancient mountains, which would have extended upward in a massive range. They were a great mountain belt, and as they slowly eroded over an immense amount of time, their granite weathered."

Granite is an igneous rock, formed by magma and composed primarily of quartz, feldspar, mica, and pyroxene. As granite weathers, the feldspar turns to clay; the quartz, to sand.

About 270 million years ago when the supercontinent of Pangea formed and the drifting, colliding continents pushed up the Appalachians, "our part of North America was probably south of the equator," Fred informed me. I tried to visualize the Smokies, where I had spent much of my youth, ice-capped and twenty-five thousand feet high; and I wondered if the Appalachians would have had icy summits in a jungly primordial past when our region was covered by humid tropical forests.

"It's reasonable to speculate that if the Appalachians were really high, they might have been ice-capped," said Fred. After all, Mount Kilimanjaro, which is three degrees south of the equator, has ice on it, although according to National Geographic that mountain has lost 82 percent of its ice since 1912 and may be ice-capless by 2020. "Of course," Fred added, "any evidence of

Appalachian glaciers would not have survived. It would have been worn down." As the peaks eroded and the mountain granite weathered, the glacial melt would have spawned rivers and floods to wash clay and quartz sand down to create the Sandhills, coastal plains, and the continental shelf.

BEFORE WE HEADED INTO THE FIELD, Fred opened the back of his van to show us some Sandhill fossils. "Plant fossils. Petrified wood. All terrestrial fossils," he said, handing Lyne a rust-colored chunk. "Hold it. Feel how heavy it is. It's obviously not wood anymore. It's a mineral called hematite. As the mountains wore down and floods occurred, trees were buried in the sand. Later iron-bearing water trickled through the sand and petrified the wood." Lyne passed the fossil around. "You can see the bark on that one," Fred pointed out. "Petrified wood is common evidence of ancient life in the Sandhills. Of course, petrified wood is a land fossil," he added, "not a marine fossil."

Next he exhibited a small chunk of Sandhills clay that he had coated with polyurethane to keep it from crumbling. In the clay were fossilized imprints of leaves—the midvein of one leaf, its outer edge, and some smaller leaves. "I'm not a botanist, but these look like willow leaves. This fossil is Cretaceous, the age of the dinosaurs, about eighty million years ago. Leaves would drift into the waters of river deltas and coastal plains and be buried in mud. Something as delicate as a leaf would be preserved. This fossil is typical of what you find in the Sandhills. You can find fossils of pine needles, leaves, twigs, and berries in the clay where a railroad cut a line through the state forest. I'd like to find a dinosaur bone," he mused, storing the fossils away. "In Kingstree they've found dinosaur fossils."

I reported that someone had found the fossil of a theropod tooth near Quinby, South Carolina.

"That's Cretaceous. Here in the Sandhills we have a lot of Cretaceous rock that's land material. But down by Pamplico, their Cretaceous rock is marine. Marine fossils are a sure indication that it's marine rock. I'm sure dinosaur fossils are here," he added. "That would be more evidence that the Sandhills was a land environment."

Piling into our vehicles, we headed east along Highway 1, then south down a dirt road to a clay deposit. As we rode, John McLeod reminisced about growing up in the Sandhills in the early twentieth century. "We heated our houses with open fireplaces. For kindling, we'd go out into the woods with two-horse wagons and load up fat lightwood. To get a load wouldn't take any time, it was so plentiful. People didn't use it just for kindling, though. They put it in pits, covered it over with pine boughs, and burned it to get rosin out. Rosin would run out of a trench below the fire and down a hill, where they'd bottle it up."

This tar was known as "common tar," writes Lawrence Earley, author of *Looking for Longleaf: The Fall and Rise of an American Forest.* "North Carolina tar burners made tar by collecting lightwood from the forest floor and burning it in their homemade kilns."[3] Fat lightwood "was the wood that had become especially saturated with resin. When people first settled in the region, lightwood from branches and dead tress littered the forest floor. According to one nineteenth-century writer, 'With these dry bones the surface is very much covered—not entirely covered, but so thick as to fill the body of a horse-cart, in many places, in a square of ten yards. . . .' Because they were saturated with flammable resins, lightwood pieces burned easily; the settlers used them as torches and burned them in tar kilns to make tar and pitch."

Quoting Aubrey Shaw, a retired North Carolina biology teacher, Earley adds, "'In the forests of today, you don't find lightwood because the trees are normally cut before they grow old enough to form it.' After the old trees died and fell, the sapwood rotted away, leaving the dense heartwood."[4]

To transport longleaf logs, recalled John, "railroad companies laid spur tracks that ran out of the main tracks. There are several places on the wildlife refuge where you can find spikes and see old cross ties." Because of logging and clear-cutting around the turn of the twentieth century, "there weren't so many pine trees. More scrub oak. Farmers burned the woods around the cotton fields to kill boll weevils. That was their theory," although they later concluded that burns "didn't have much effect" on the beetles. "At night sometimes I could see the sky lit up with fires. They would keep burning all night till they died out. Back then there wasn't a fire department to put them out."

WE PARKED AT THE CLAY DEPOSIT and stepped out of our vehicles into a cold wind and onto slippery, sticky mud. Across the road, grading and erosion had carved out a bank that was crowned with pines and oaks. At its crest the half-bowl of the bank was about twelve feet high. The top three or four feet of soil were brown, dark with decaying organic matter.

"The next layer is whitish clay," said Fred, arming himself with a rock hammer and a shovel from the back of the van. "Underneath, the earth is mostly typical Sandhill deltaic sand. It's made of quartz from weathered mountain rock and not of marine organisms. When granite weathers—the granite that made the Appalachians, for example—its feldspars and micas change chemically to clay. Its quartz grains, however, do not change chemically. They break down into sand."

Clay, like sand, is important to the ecology of the Sandhills. A layer of clay can form an underground pan to hold rainwater. "Sometimes," said Fred, "you can guess where these underlying clay areas are by looking for blackjack oaks. In fact," he added, pointing to a tree growing atop the bluff, "there's one right above us. Blackjack oaks need more water. A clay layer keeps water from draining so fast."

In addition to the blackjack on the crest of the bank, Lyne noted high-bush blueberry, bay bush, bracken fern, longleaf pines, and bluejack, laurel, and turkey oaks. "Up the road I saw an Atlantic white cedar," she said. "That might also indicate moist soil."

The swirling layers of clay and sand in the cutaway bank looked like a Georgia O'Keefe landscape—creams and magentas the colors of vanilla and boysenberry ice cream. In front was a big mud puddle.

"The pinkish-purple we see is manganese oxide," Fred said. "The reds are iron oxide. The yellow ochre is limonite." His boots squished and slid on the steepening bank. My own boots, thick with wet clay, weighed several pounds now.

With the edge of the shovel, Fred scraped at the bank of clay and sand to get a clean face. The thin layers of soil resembled a fabric woven with yellow, pink, and purple threads. "See the cross-bedding? See this thin orange layer that rises and cuts across horizontally? It was caused by shifting deltaic environments," by water and wind. Just as tree rings gauge years of rain and drought, these layers of sand have recorded the floods that washed sand and clay from the mountains to deposit them here, where the land flattens out. Unlike tree rings, however, each flood might alter the record of previous floods.

"The layers are a combination of erosion and deposition. Each flood deposits a layer. The next flood erodes some layers, deposits more. Sand was deposited in times of flood, but clay was deposited when rivers were still and calm and the clay settled out. You won't, for example, find clay deposited on mountain slopes." Fred gestured broadly with the shovel. "This region was probably a delta where a river slowed down as the terrain leveled out. You get a lot of deposition near an ocean."

CURIOUS TO SEE THE DIFFERENCE between terrestrial and marine sand, I later joined Fred in his geology lab at Coker College. On the lab table were several discrete piles of sand on index cards. I had brought along bags of sand from the Carolina Sandhills NWR, courtesy of refuge manager Lyne Askins, and some oceanic sand from Pawley's Island on South Carolina's coast.

First, Fred gave me a geologist's definition of sand: "a sedimentary particle between 1/16th and 1/256th of an inch in diameter." Then he sprinkled some of the Sandhills particles on a clean card and positioned it under a dissecting microscope. The Sandhills sample was dark and loamy. "Pretty dirty," he commented. "There's probably some organic matter in there."

I looked first, dialing the image into focus. He asked what I saw. "Looks like little grains of glass with detritus mixed in," I replied. I asked if this sand was "granitic," the residue of weathered granite from the old Appalachians.

"Quartz sand is a more accurate term than granitic," he explained. "Granite is an igneous rock. Sand isn't rock anymore; it's sediment made of one or more minerals." This quartz might have come from granite, but it might also have come from gneiss, another igneous rock; or from sandstone, a sedimentary rock; or from schist, a metamorphic rock. "So if you say 'quartz sand,' you're naming the mineral."

To prove the point, Fred showed me a coconut-size chunk of schist. "A metamorphic rock typical of the Appalachians," it also contained quartz, feldspar, and mica. "Our Sandhills quartz sand might have weathered out of schist." He handed me a magnifying glass and an egg-size chunk of granite from Pageland, a town about twenty miles northwest of the refuge. With the glass I could see gray crystals of quartz as well as feldspar and flakes of mica embedded in the rock.

Fred returned to the sand specimen under the microscope. "The little clear grains with jagged, sharp edges are quartz," he explained. "The mucky stuff is probably organic matter or clay."

Next, for comparison, Fred placed under the microscope a card of quartz sand from a desert in Utah. "This sand is very old. It's from the Permian period 250 million years ago." He focused the microscope and asked what I saw.

"No sharp edges," I responded, peering through the eyepiece. Each small grain of glassy sand was rounded like a little river stone.

"It's been blown around in the wind. More work is done in wind than in water. The grains bump against each other in the wind." More bumping and grinding means smoother grains. Although the sands from the Sandhills and Utah were both of quartz, Fred said, "they have a different history."

Under the microscope we examined a second small piece of granite from Pageland. This sample looked stuccoed. "As the crystals grew together," he explained, "quartz was the last mineral to crystallize, filling in the cracks and crevices."

He slid a card of mystery sand under the microscope. "See if you can guess what this is."

I recognized glassy grains of quartz, although these had rougher edges. "Not weathered by wind," I said. But I also saw little chunks and cylinders of unfamiliar white stuff mixed in. I couldn't figure out what they were.

"Fossils of shell fragments," Fred said, including possible micro-fossil remnants of shipworms, gastropods, or echinoderm spines. This sand, about five million years old, was from a layer of bedrock in Timmonsville. That area, about thirty miles south-southeast of the refuge, would have been within reach of the ancient sea.

"This example is typical of our beach sand. It's quartz sand mixed with bits and pieces of shell. A lot of the sand you find on our present-day shoreline is quartz because quartz is very abundant in our rivers," which carry sediment down from higher elevations. Our beaches are a mix of terrestrial and marine sand.

Last, Fred showed me another card of sand from Chesterfield County, which lies within the Sandhills. Looking through the microscope, he said, "This seems to be deltaic sand from rivers that flowed down out of the Piedmont and dumped their materials. Most of the Sandhills share that origin. There may be a cross-bedding of delta sands with shoreline dunes, but it's unlikely you'll see any shell fragments in this."

Admittedly our samples were not exhaustive, but Fred's assertion that Sandhills sand is terrestrial, not marine, was supported by two observations: The sand from Timmonsville, a town within the range of a primordial sea, contained fossilized shell fragments; but the samples of sand from the refuge were devoid of marine fossils.

MY FIRST ENCOUNTERS with longleaf pines had been in the Carolina Sandhills; and just as many Carolinians wrongly assume that Sandhills sand is oceanic, I had assumed that longleaf pines prefer sandier, drier soil. In the 1700s Philip Miller, the Scottish botanist who gave longleaf pine its Latin name, by chance encountered the trees in a flooded plain and dubbed them *Pinus palustis*, that is, "swamp" or "marsh pine"—hardly a pine for xeric soil. In his *Gardner's Dictionary* of 1768, Miller conjectures that "in dry ground they [longleaf pines] will not thrive." First impressions, as we know, can mislead. A more accurate name, *Pinus australis*, that is, southern pine, was recommended by the French botanist François André Michaux, but Miller's moniker stuck. (Commonly longleaf has many nicknames, among them Georgia pine, pitch pine, fat pine, yellow pine, and southern yellow pine.)

A key reason why we often associate longleaf with drier, sandier soil is, in a word, us. When Euro-Americans logged out the vast original forests of longleaf, those clear-cuts were converted to agriculture, often to cotton and later to loblolly pine plantations. Longleaf inherited the leavings, the dry, sandy regions less suitable for profitable farming.

Historically, of course, longleaf pines were not restricted to sandy sites. In fact, their growth is stunted by the slim nutritional pickings of these regions. In the Sandhills, for example, it's difficult to guess the age of a flattop by eyeing its girth. A longleaf with a relatively slim bole may be a century old. Truth be told, a longleaf would be happy to sink its teeth into richer earth.

Yet these pines may thrive in more xeric soils. The secret of a longleaf's success in deeper, drier sites such as the Sandhills or Apalachicola's pine-palmetto flatwoods is due in part to its taproot, which bores deep underground to find water and nutrition that most other plants are incapable of exploiting. Loose, sandy soils also make the work of digging a taproot easier.

Another reason that a longleaf may flourish in sandy, drier soils is that it doesn't like competition. "Longleaf pine is a very intolerant pioneer species . . . and does not compete well for site resources with other more aggressive species."[5] Before a longleaf flexes its muscle above ground, therefore, it bulks up for years below. Then, in a growth spurt from grass stage to sapling, it may grow four to five feet in two growing seasons, thrusting its terminal bud skyward to compete for space and light. A turkey oak sprout, said USFWS forester Dave Robinson, may grow nearly as fast as a longleaf's after a burn, but only for the first couple of years.

Scrub oaks, of course, are not the longleaf's most fearsome competitor for terrain. Oaks and longleaf pines have begrudgingly coexisted on the same turf for millennia. Soon I hoped to tour the Francis Marion National Forest, a longleaf community increasingly threatened by East Coast urban development.

NOTES

1. William Blake, "Auguries of Innocence," in *The Poetry and Prose of William Blake*, ed. David V. Erdman (Garden City, N.Y.: Doubleday, 1970), 484.

2. Tjeerd H. Van Andel, *New Views on an Old Planet*, 2nd ed. (New York: Cambridge University Press, 1994), 188.

3. Lawrence S. Earley, *Looking for Longleaf: The Fall and Rise of an American Forest* (Chapel Hill: University of North Carolina Press, 2004), 91.

4. Ibid., 93.

5. Shibu Jose, Eric J. Jokela, and Deborah L. Miller, "The Longleaf Pine Ecosystem: An Overview," in *The Longleaf Pine Ecosystem: Ecology, Silviculture, and Restoration*, ed. Jose, Jokela, and Miller (New York: Springer, 2006), 4.

Sandhills Botany

"I always thought that U.S. Fish and Wildlife doesn't owe me anything. I owe them for letting me enjoy my work. Thirty years, I got to walk this whole refuge. Beautiful, isn't it?"

Dave Robinson, forester

PINES, GRASS, SCRUB OAKS—before I started this book, when I drove through a Sandhills forest that's all I saw. It wasn't until I escaped the office and town and began digging into the role of fire in longleaf forests that I discovered, outside of my door, one of the world's great ecosystems.

I was never immune to the seduction of pines. Years ago, attending the Bread Loaf School of English in Vermont, I made several pilgrimages to a cabin where Robert Frost had lived and written poetry. The cabin was rustic.

Inside was a simple straight-backed chair with wooden arms, across which Frost would lay a board as a writing desk. "One could do worse," he might have said. In front of the cabin was a meadow. Behind, a woods of stately pines. Even the mosquitoes and black flies kept their distance. The pines had a quiet, eternal feeling. Maybe they seemed so old because, evolutionarily, they predate flowering trees.

Thoreau also celebrates pines, writing that they are as immortal as he is, "and perchance will go to as high a heaven, there to tower above me still."[1] James Lowell, editor of the *Atlantic Monthly*, disapproved of Thoreau's pantheism and, without permission, cut this sentence from an article by him, thereby ticking off the transcendentalist righteously and ensuring that the words are even more famous than they might have been. I've hiked in old-growth forests in the Great Smokey Mountains and in the redwoods of California, and I'd be hard-pressed to imagine a better heaven than a virgin forest.

Despite a longleaf forest's air of timelessness, however, it's a busy place, one of the more botanically diverse ecosystems on Earth. Longleaf pine forests

Trumpet pitcher plants and purple blazing stars grow near Oxpen Lake in the Carolina Sandhills National Wildlife Refuge. Pitcher plants need fire to reduce competition from woody shrubs. Photograph courtesy of USFWS.

"have one of the richest species diversities outside the tropics. Although the overstory is dominated by one species [*Pinus palustris*], the understory is host to a plethora of plant species."[2] These tropical and temperate habitats share another, more dismal fact: like rain forests, longleaf forests are among the most imperiled ecosystems on the planet.

On a hot July morning, my wife Allison and I met Lyne Askins, manager of the Carolina Sandhills National Wildlife Refuge, and Dave Robinson, a retired forester, for a botanical tour of the refuge. I wanted a tour of the plant community in a longleaf forest, and Dave, who had worked this refuge for thirty-two years, knew the plants as well as anyone, probably better. Before coming to the Sandhills, Dave worked for the U.S. Fish and Wildlife Service in Kentucky, Georgia, and Mississippi and fought wildfires in northern California. "Best time I ever had. I saw fire all over California. Got to see beautiful country—Tahoe, Pumice, Eunice, and Cinch River. Oh, it's beautiful country."

As longleaf forests go, those of Carolina Sandhills NWR are not as botanically diverse as those grown in richer soil. Old-timers referred to the forests of the Sandhills as longleaf–scrub oak. Even so, despite the refuge's fairly xeric environment, it boasts nearly eight hundred plants.

Fire is one determinant of plant diversity. By knocking back duff, the layer of leaves and needles, and reducing a hardwood midstory, fire stimulates the growth of wildlife foods, such as legumes and herbaceous plants. Soil is another determinant. Typically the soil of the Sandhills is dry, sandy, and acidic.

"Overall," said Lyne, "there are two kinds of soil in the refuge: not-so-dry sand and really dry sand. Plant diversity at the Sandhills is more related to topography and other larger scale features. On a stand scale, the Sandhills' longleaf ecosystem is rather homogeneous. On a landscape scale, inclusive of topographic features such as hills, streams, and seeps, plant species are more heterogeneous. In a ten-by-ten-square-foot area of the Sandhills, I would expect to find an average of twenty to thirty plant species, with maybe fifty to sixty species on rich sites. Our diversity is across the forty-five thousand acres of the refuge."

The day's weather forecast was clear but with a heat index of 107. That didn't bother Dave. "Sweating is good for you. I never did turn on the air-conditioner in my government truck unless I was traveling on the highway," he said. "I'd roll the window down. I have air-conditioning at home, and I'd take a shower after work. But air-conditioning during the day? Uh-uh. In my truck at work? Uh-uh." Mercifully we were riding in Lyne's USFWS truck. A breeze and her truck's AC kept us cool enough.

Life in the forest had been good to Dave. Dressed in boots, blue jeans, a khaki shirt, and ball cap, he looked healthy and fit. Usually on the quiet side, this morning he was animated and happy to get back into the woods, and we were happy to be with him. Standing on the porch of the headquarters while the flag snapped in the wind and its rope clanged against the metal pole, I asked Dave what changes he had witnessed at the NWR.

"In 1969," before he arrived, "there was an ice storm." Perhaps a third of the trees on the forty-five-thousand-acre refuge were down. Much of that timber was salvaged, but "because of the heavy fuel load, there were no burns for a number of years. When I got here in 1974, you couldn't see a hundred feet off the road on either side because of scrub oak. Then we resumed burning. Back then we didn't have big fire crews. No helicopters, just two or three men with drip torches. There was a lot of heavy duff [accumulated leaves and branches on the ground], and we started slow-moving backfires." Smoke guidelines were much less stringent then. "We'd set a fire in the afternoon, let it burn all night long." The low-intensity fires burned small units of forest, sixty to eighty acres. Penned in by firebreaks, "the fires burned cool, knocked back the duff. We'd check on a fire throughout the night. Driving these Sandhills, you'd see a red horizon. It was like the sky was on fire, and boy, it was beautiful.

"We burned like that for several years, then got into strip-head fires [lines of fire that burn with the wind and toward a firebreak] and then helicopter burns," he remembered.

The unchecked advance of hardwoods into the longleaf savanna had begun more than a century before. As early as 1883 one writer documented the "resultant vegetation changes in South Carolina." Before the suppression of fire, "a deer might then have been seen, in the vistas made by their smooth stems [of yellow pine], a distance of half a mile, where now, since the discontinuance of the spring and autumn fires, it could not be seen fifteen paces, for the thick growth of oak and hickory that has taken up the land."[3]

"If you read descriptions of this region in the 1880s, it was longleaf-scrub oak," said Lyne as we climbed into her crew-cab truck. "You'll never kill them all off. Oaks are part of this ecosystem."

Dave chronicled the introduction of prescribed burns to the refuge. "In the 1970s I had just a small crew. We were on a five-year burn cycle. U.S. Fish and Wildlife recommended that we go to a three-year cycle. I said, 'OK, you give me fire money and a burn crew, we'll go to three years.' That's when we started getting fire money. In 1996 I hired a fire management officer, Mike Housh, and we started burning in February," when sap flowed in the scrub oaks. "We were amazed at the top-kill we'd get for hardwoods. If we kept burning, we eventually killed their roots. Then, when we started helicopter burns in January, February, March, we got a lot of hardwood kill."

Lyne drove us along a gravel road bordered with chest-high lespedeza, a member of the pea family *Fabaceae*, which had been planted to prevent erosion and feed quail. "I heard a quail whistle this morning," said Dave.

"Our quail population is one of the best in the state," said Lyne. "Every year when we do our quail survey, we're right on top as far as the number of quail." During the state's quail season, from late November through February, the refuge allows quail hunts on Wednesdays and Fridays.

We turned left onto Wildlife Drive, traveling no more than a couple of hundred yards before Dave directed, "Stop here" and, turning to me, asked, "Are you familiar with scrub oaks?"

I said I was, then realized that I had enrolled in Sandhills Botany 101. There would be frequent quizzes. I have a good memory for some things—telephone numbers and lines of Shakespeare I read years ago—but in the woods I'm sometimes a remedial student. We exited the truck and climbed up a sandy bank. Lupine and scores of grass-stage longleaf pines, which were little more than finger-high tufts of needles, sprouted along the crest of the bank.

Dave was in his element and excited. "We got all of them near here," he said, gesturing expansively to scrub oaks as we stood on the ridge. The little hardwoods were only waist high.

I identified a turkey oak easily by the turkey-foot shape of its leaf and the blackjack by its fist-size, club-shaped leaf. By process of elimination, I got lucky with the bluejack, though its thin, delicate leaves reminded me more of a willow oak and didn't look particularly blue at all.

This not-so-dry, less xeric soil often had underpans of clay, which retained rainwater that otherwise would have drained through the sand like water through a sieve. Dave explained how subtle soil gradients helped to determine the niche of each of these oaks. "The poorer the soil is, you'll find turkey oaks. Down the hill, a little better site yields blackjack oaks. On the best sites are bluejacks."

Standing next to the bluejack was a persimmon, a clay-loving species more associated with the Piedmont, or foothills. "And here's your southern red oak," Dave said.

"It's known by its bell-shaped leaf," added Lyne.

"In longleaf sites," explained Dave, "you mainly find the three scrub oaks, but in sites with better soil, near Black Creek or Lynches River, you get typical bottomland and coastal plain hardwoods," such as southern red oak, water oak, willow oak, maple, and blackgum.

We climbed back into the truck. The heat was stifling. As Lyne accelerated, we rolled down the windows for a cooling breeze and rolled them up again when the air-conditioner kicked in, but not before several horseflies had hitched a ride. I swatted at two on the ceiling. Dave rolled down his window. One flew out. I glanced out of my window. A posse of horseflies was escorting our truck down the road. Lyne said that the flies might swarm us as we stepped out, but they'd stay at the vehicle when we walked into the woods. "They're attracted to the white truck," she remarked. "A unique phenomenon."

"Let's drive slow," said Dave. "We might see some false indigo." Pointing to the ditch, he added, "There's poison oak. I bet Allison knows it." My wife, a biologist, is highly allergic to poison ivy and poison oak. Both plants seemed to have scattered themselves strategically throughout the woods.

We passed a wiregrass restoration site that had once been a barrow pit of pink clay. Most of the sand and topsoil were gone. All of the layers of soil were disturbed. "Years ago," said Lyne, "the refuge took clay out of here for roads. Then in the mid-1990s the refuge planted wiregrass seed in the pit," which was now full of the native bunchgrass. "Little bluestem and broomsedge," she added, were other native bunchgrasses common to the Sandhills.

I asked if the refuge had problems with invasive species, such as cogon grass (*Imperata cylindrical*). Also known as Japanese bloodgrass, cogon is an aggressive "exotic rhizomatous grass" that "can displace native grasses" and may even affect species diversity "because it burns more intensively than the native bunch grasses" and may change the fire regimen.[4] Although cogon plagues the Francis Marion National Forest, the Carolina Sandhills NWR is currently free of it. "But we have Chinese love grass," Lyne said with some dismay. "The refuge planted it in the 1940s and '50s along Wildlife Drive as a soil stabilizer." Love grass was also touted as being good quail habitat. Not surprisingly refuge officials discovered that over time the love grass spread, not aggressively like kudzu but through "equipment transfer" when its seeds hitched rides to new locations on the bumpers and frames of trucks. "We're concerned that love grass is getting into the woodlands. We're starting a five- to ten-year love-grass eradication program."

Like cogon, love grass burns extremely hot and is therefore "very dangerous to firefighters," said Dave. "If fire hits love grass, I guarantee that sparks will jump across the firebreak, so you better be ready."

"Love grass flares up quickly and puts out a lot of heat," agreed Lyne. "You may think that all fires have the same temperature, but there are different degrees of fire. Love grass burns so much hotter than wiregrass" that it can catch a firefighter off guard. "At the briefing for each burn, we always say, 'Beware the love grass,' because if you're standing in it when the fire hits . . ." She shook her head, leaving the sentence unfinished.

We taxied past a woods crowded with young longleaf pines. "Twelve years ago this area had a lot of scrub oak," said Dave. "That's when we first used the herbicide Velpar ULW. Look at it now." The area was thick with saplings. It was not the open, spacious woods we associate with longleaf. Dave said that the pines would be mechanically thinned, and he then pointed out of the window to some sparkleberry and switch cane.

The growth and dispersal of switch cane, Lyne said, had been tracked over ten years by a Ph.D. student in Louisiana, who confirmed what foresters already believed: "Cane follows fire" because fire reduces competition. "If shrubs creep into an upland from the bank of a stream," she said, "then you're not using enough fire. That shrub layer should be restricted to the ecotone between the wet and upland areas." A canebrake, she added, is "excellent habitat for Swainson's warbler, a species of concern."

We got out at a roadside bank near the natural bowl of a pocosin and walked down a gradual but steepening slope past sourwood and through inkberry, featherbush, and bracken fern, which grew thicker as the soil grew wetter.

Of the forty-five thousand acres in Carolina Sandhills NWR, about thirty-eight thousand acres, or 84 percent, are pine forest. About four thousand acres, or over 11 percent of the refuge, form pocosins. "The refuge has thirty ponds," said Lyne, "and each was put in at a pocosin drain."

Dave showed me a red bay with the customary "warts on its leaves." Lyne pointed out the leathery green leaves of a sweet bay, also known as swamp magnolia. The vegetation was dense. "This site has not been burned for six years," she said. "Now there's only an occasional cane. It's time for a fire. When we run fire through here, the first plant to respond will be cane."

"It needs a hot fire in here," Dave agreed. "Knock this stuff back, open it up. This pocosin is fed by a small spring that drains into a lake. In the winter, when the acorns are gone, or if you have a dry spring and a crop failure, pocosins are what support the deer."

"We also hear a lot of quail at the edges between pocosins and upland pines," said Lyne.

"If a quail hunter comes by here," Dave said, "the covey will fly into the pocosin for cover every time." He pointed to a patch of blueberries, a favorite quail feast.

Wiregrass surrounded the pocosin. Around its top edge was a hardwood area of blackjack, bluejack, hickory, southern red oak, red maple, and bracken ferns, which, Lyne said, "are indicative of dormant season burns." The longleaf pines gave way to yellow poplar, loblolly, and pond pines deeper inside the pocosin. I asked how the pond pines would fare in a prescribed burn.

"They need it," Lyne told me. "All pine species are shade-intolerant. Their terminal buds need all the sunlight they can get. Fire reduces competition from other species."

Both longleaf and pond pines need fire to survive, but pond pines, Dave explained, are serotinous, as their Latin name, *Pinus seritona*, implies. "Their cones," which are small and compact, "need the heat from fire to pop open and release their seeds." By comparison, longleaf cones, which are often the size of small footballs, "don't need fire to release their seeds. They need fire to germinate, to clear off the forest floor down to mineral soil."

"When you look at the composition of vegetation in a pocosin," said Lyne, "you know that fire has been part of that ecosystem because pond pines are in the canopy." The fire regime for pocosins at the refuge varies from three to seven years. "You know it's time to burn when the shrub layer dominates and you begin losing other species, such as switch cane."

"For wildlife, we need diversity," said Dave. "That's why we need pocosins."

We walked back and crossed the road. The woods on the other side had been burned recently. We bent down to examine a longleaf seedling. Its needles were black and orange, but the terminal bud was a cheery greenish white. A few feet away a sweetgum had been top-killed by the fire.

It occurred to me that I didn't often see sweetgums, the bane of foresters, in the NWR. "Foresters and landowners regard sweetgum as a prolific pain," I said. "Why don't we find more sweetgum on the refuge?"

The reason, Dave explained, was the soil. Sweetgums prefer less sandy, wetter terrain.

We got back into the truck. As we rode, Lyne spoke of the Brosnan Forest, a privately held, seventeen-thousand-acre longleaf forest on South Carolina's coastal plain. "They have a horrible problem with sweetgum, but they've found that frequent fires, at least every three years, go a long way to controlling them."

The seasonal timing of burns affects not only the population of sweetgum but also that of the endangered red-cockaded woodpecker. Joan Walker, of the U.S. Forest Service, and Ralph Costa, of USFWS, conducted a research study of dormant and growing-season burns at the Brosnan Forest. "One site was burned in January, another in April. They found that the April burns didn't just top-kill the sweetgums. There was an incredible herbaceous response. Both sites also had red-cockaded woodpecker colonies. The sites that had April burns every three years had higher nest production, higher numbers of chicks that fledged, than the sites with January burns." Costa and Walker hypothesized that the increase in RCW population, Lyne said, "was related to the increase in insects and biomass produced by the grassy, forb understory" typical of a healthy longleaf forest.

Along the roadside grew rye, panic grass, bluestem, Indian grass, partridge pea, and sericea, a lespedeza similar to clover but taller and nonnative. Sericea is another soil stabilizer often used for erosion control along interstates. Farther down the road were false indigo, lupine, turkey oaks, longleaf seedlings, big pinecones, and spurge nettle, also known as stinging nettle. "It'll make you itch," said Lyne.

Nearby was a dead pine that had been struck by lightning. "We have thousands of lightning strikes on the refuge every year," said Dave, "but because our fuels have been so reduced by burns, the strikes usually don't result in wildfires." When lightning recently sparked a blaze on the west side of the refuge, "the wildfire was a tenth of an acre. Last year we had a two-acre wildfire. It's amazing how prescribed fire does what researchers predict. This is what we're telling people across the nation. If you put fire back in the system, you won't have huge, catastrophic wildfires."

Dave casually mentioned that the upper edges of pocosins were also "good places for rattlesnakes," and the conversation inevitably turned toward snakes. I thought of the huge canebrake rattlesnake that Allison and I had seen on the trail to Forty Acre Rock in Lancaster County and recalled the bushwhacking I'd done through chest-high switch cane and shrubs. I questioned the wisdom of wading through the dense foliage of a pocosin.

Years before, Lyne had been bitten. "I was busting out a beaver dam on a farm in Darlington County. I stuck my left hand into the dam to shake a log and was bitten underwater. It felt like an ice pick in my knuckle. What really hurt was the swelling caused by the venom. I never saw the snake but knew it wouldn't have been a rattlesnake or a copperhead." As the swelling advanced from her hand up her arm, she drove to a shed where workers were having lunch. The foreman put her hand in a five-gallon bucket of ice and helped her to remain calm and control her breathing while they waited for an ambulance. "At the hospital they gave me eleven shots of antivenom. I was in the hospital six days. Initially I pretty much lost the use of my hand, but after seven weeks of therapy, I regained full mobility. I'm still not scared of snakes." She added that she recently had been kneeling by a plant on a seepage slope and had seen "a great big cottonmouth coiled a yard away."

AS WE CRUISED IN LYNE'S TRUCK, Dave discussed the restoration of pine plantations on the refuge. "Back in the early 1960s during a scrub-oak eradication program, the state allowed timber to be cut off financially unproductive areas." The disruption of soil and herbaceous layers was an unforeseen result of the clear-cutting. "When I first came here, we called these areas 'biological deserts' because that's what they looked like. Over a ten-year period, we planted ten or eleven thousand acres, mostly in longleaf, some in slash."

We drove past an area of longleaf that had been planted about forty years before. "We thinned it mechanically, opened it up, burned it every three to five years," Dave said. "It took all this time, but native species such as wiregrass are starting to come back. Look at all this reproduction."

Thousands of hand-high longleaf seedlings grew in close quarters. I tried to picture the thickness of the forest if they all lived to maturity. "Obviously they all can't survive. What will reduce their population?"

"Fire will thin some," Dave answered.

"A lot of research about the management of longleaf forests comes out of the red hills of Georgia," said Lyne, "which is a completely different site. We can't apply their yield and growth tables to the Sandhills. Our long-term goal is to open up, for example, two-acre pockets in areas of mature longleaf. We'll let these longleaf seedlings grow so that we have an uneven-aged pine plantation," that is, a landscape with areas of mature longleafs as well as those with longleaf pines in the grass and sapling stages. "Although we've used even-aged regeneration, over the refuge we have an uneven-aged forest. Every age is represented."

"That's right," agreed Dave. "For years I've been beating my head on the wall telling people, 'We don't have to manage for an uneven-aged forest. Mother Nature is doing it for us.' In my thirty years at the refuge, I've seen tornadoes, I've seen Hurricane Hugo, and what happens? Nature knocks holes in the forest. Young trees fill the gap. A single-tree event might be a lightning strike. Other events, such as storms or tornadoes, impact larger areas." If a tornado downs twenty acres of trees, the next generation of trees that grow there will be even-aged, and the greater forest will be uneven-aged.

"There's no other way to grow a pine forest," said Lyne.

In *1491: New Revelations of the Americas before Columbus*, Charles Mann similarly argues why forests, if untouched by humans, do not end up as "climax stage vegetation: a world of great trees, dark and silent. . . . A few years or decades of tranquility may see grasses replaced by shrubs and trees which are in turned flattened by a violent thunderstorm," permitting early successional species "to thrive again." Another frequent disturbance, of course, is fire. "For more than 10,000 years, most North American ecosystems have been dominated by fire."[5]

I remembered a stand of pines outside my town, roughly seventy miles as the crow flies from the coast. Hugo snapped trees halfway up their boles. At the 275,000-acre Francis Marion National Forest, ground zero for that hurricane, the storm smacked down nearly three-quarters of the mature trees. An uneven-aged forest is desirable for the Carolina Sandhills NWR. The long-term survival of the ecosystem depends on it.

"We're not gonna live forever," Dave said. "It's important to have grandchildren growing up."

We parked at an open area where a tornado had knocked down some mature trees. In their place were Dave's grandkids—hundreds, even thousands of longleaf seedlings and saplings and other slender pines. "Once this gets pulpwood size," roughly four to nine inches in diameter, "we can thin it out. Of course, longleaf saw timber brings the best price," but saw timber trees must be ten or more inches in diameter. "When I first came to the refuge, a lot of the saw timber sales were for light poles."

Lyne added that timber sales, like fire, are important tools for the management of the refuge, but "we only do forestry for habitat improvement."

Wary of the stinging nettle and poison oak, we tramped through native bunchgrasses, goat's rue, and pinecones. "Look at the wiregrass," said Lyne. "It just blows me away. The response we've had to burning is phenomenal. We have all three age stages of longleaf here: grass stage, sapling, and mature tree. This is what you read about in the literature."

In the site were two longleafs with red-cockaded woodpecker cavity nests under construction: one about fifteen feet up; the other, about twenty. "Both are natural starts that a woodpecker has been excavating," said Lyne. "Those excavations may take from one to eight years." RCWs live an average of eight years. "In addition to lots of fire," she added, "the area surrounding this RCW cluster probably had mechanical and chemical treatments. But here the scrub oaks are greatly reduced as compared to the area outside of this cluster."

We walked past dwarf huckleberry, *Gaylussacia dumosa*, an herb with gilt-edge leaves and fat little bell-shaped flowers with green pistils; and blue-petaled Sandhills gentian, *Gentian autumnalis*. A second species of huckleberry, *G. frondosa* or blue huckleberry, Lyne said, also grew on the refuge.

Another nearby site had been recently burned. The charred trunks of longleaf saplings rose straight and branchless up to their green crowns, which were about twenty feet overhead and well out of the reach of most ground fires. I wrapped my fingers around one trunk. My hands were black from the charcoal.

"I wish the folks who read and write these grand ideas about restoration would come and work here for a year," said Dave. "Their mind-set would change. You cannot micromanage a forest or program it like a computer. Some people might think they can, but they can't."

An effort to restore longleaf savanna habitat at the Savannah River Site in South Carolina exposed several obstacles. Experience at the SRS "demonstrated that prescribed burning alone is rarely sufficient to redevelop the native species composition or structure." Competition from woody plants and the scarcity or absence of native flora and fauna such as the threatened gopher tortoise inhibited restoration of the ecosystem. Strategies for restoration at the SRS included prescribed burning, tree thinning, the chemical and mechanical removal of midstory shrubs and hardwoods, and the reintroduction of native species.[6]

I said that I had read articles and texts on restoration. To some "green activists," the restoration of a "long-ago, putatively natural state is a task that society is morally bound to undertake."[7] I asked Lyne and Dave if they agreed, if it was possible to restore, let alone envision, a landscape unshaped by Man the Tool Wielder. And what should be the paradigm for restoration? What long-lost model, which previous epoch, should we attempt to re-create?

Lyne and Dave shook their heads. With some exasperation, Dave responded, "You can't set the clock back to a certain time."

"We're managing for a mature longleaf forest with areas of regeneration necessary for species survival," explained Lyne. "In an uneven-aged forest, a third might be mature, a third might be middle-aged, and a third might be in regeneration. We don't want forty-five thousand acres of mature longleaf. We want diversity."

"This right here," Dave pointed out with a sweeping gesture, "is a pine plantation. But forty years from now, you won't be able to tell it was planted. By then there will be openings, it will have been thinned, and ground species, such as this dwarf huckleberry, which is typical of a longleaf stand, will have recovered."

I marveled at Dave and Lyne's vision. Living as most of us do, week to week, paycheck to paycheck, job to job, I admired foresters and geologists for their ability to take the long view. Lyne and I plucked and ate some of the sweet, seedy blue huckleberries.

The talk turned to a recent wildfire at the Okefenokee National Wildlife Refuge. The lightning-strike wildfire, the largest in the southeastern United States in the last century, had raced thirteen miles in one night and ultimately torched more than half a million acres in and around the NWR. Surrounding the refuge, commercial forests that had not undergone prescribed burning had "suffered nearly 100 percent mortality." Long-term investments were reduced to ashes. But the longleaf forests that had been under a burn regimen exhibited "beautiful fire behavior" with negligible tree mortality, said Lyne, who had attended a postburn briefing at Okefenokee. "Now people are beginning to think, 'Maybe we should use prescribed burns.'"

We walked down a hill past common sweetleaf, *Symplocos tintoria*, which bears furry-looking white flowers beloved by butterflies; winged sumac, *Rhus copallinum;* blackjack oaks; and smilax, also known as greenbrier or catbrier. "Deer like its shoots," said Dave. Near the bottom of the hill was goat's rue, pea flower, and staggerbush, *Lyonia mariana.* For a moment a blessedly cool breeze dispelled the heat and humidity. Our feet crunched and swished through wiregrass, dead needles, leaves, twigs.

"Glad to feel that breeze," I said.

"Supposed to be a breeze all day," replied Dave, leading the way down a moderately steep slope of another pocosin. The vegetation grew higher and thicker: hickory trees, sweetleaf, inkberry, smilax briers, persimmon, more persimmon, an indigo bunting, and johnsongrass—"not native," Lyne commented.

Another large staggerbush stood at the edge of the depression. "It grows around the edges of pocosins," said Dave. A red bay with insect galls on its leaves, sourwood, mushrooms, and more staggerbush were there.

"Years ago when we first started burning," recalled Dave, "we put firebreaks around these pocosin heads. Back then we had small crews and would just burn the upland sites because if we started a fire in a pocosin, it would burn for days. Now we use helicopters for aerial burns, but if we drop fire in a pocosin, it'll go out or just smolder. We have to burn hot, let the fire roar, run down the slope, and penetrate the pocosin head."

Lyne drove us next to the seepage slope at Oxpen Lake, another Sandhills habitat. We parked and traversed a meadow of grass and tall, yellow-flowered plants. "Mullein," remarked Lyne, "an herb that people made tea from."

"Seepage slope" is not a pretty term, but walking down the slope was like descending into a flower basket. "I wish people would come out here every month," she said. "Something new is always going on. In April this slope is a sea of purple with dwarf locust, *Robinia nana.* Gorgeous." At the present time, in July, another purple flower, meadow beauty, *Rhexia virginica*, was blooming.

"Here's elderberry," Dave pointed out. "White blooms. Old-timers used to make elderberry wine. My dad used to."

"Come back here in a couple of weeks," said Lyne, "and you'll see *Liatris*, also called blazing star." Blazing star is a butterfly bush, yet another purple flower. "It will take your breath away."

As we descended the wet slope, there were bogs of pitcher plants and tiny red sundews, another carnivorous plant; daisy fleabane, with white flowers, a treat for butterflies; hat pins, also called bog buttons; cinnamon ferns; orange milkwort; and white fringed orchids, also known as snowy orchids. "The others may be yellow fringeless orchids," Lyne said, "but I can't tell because the blossoms haven't opened up yet. The refuge has four or five species of orchids."

The sundews put me in mind of Venus flytrap, another carnivorous plant that makes its home in the nitrogen-poor bogs of the Carolinas and needs fire to reduce competition—"a mean fire frequency of at least three years to survive." Evolutionarily this plant's thirst for fire "may be millions of years old."[8]

I wished I'd worn waterproof hiking boots. Even on the slope there were mud puddles that would swallow your feet. I walked to a big crowd of yellow pitcher and sweet pitcher plants. I bent over to look at one. Inside its pitcher it held rainwater like white wine in a glass. A small bee flew inside and fell into the liquid, destined to be slowly turned into plant food by digestive enzymes.

Rising above the slope were thin dead black stems and branches, "remnants of shrubs," Lyne said, "mostly sumac and sweet bay."

"The slope was burned?" I asked.

"Oh yeah," said Dave. "We burn this every year, every March." Turning to Lyne, Dave said, "You make sure they burn this every year."

"I will," said Lyne. "Every March."

OUR LAST QUEST THAT DAY was for pyxie moss, *Pyxidanthera brevifolia*, the *brev* probably for the diminutiveness of the subshrub, which is less than four inches tall, but also perhaps for the limit of its range, a handful of counties in the Carolina Sandhills. Lyne drove us to a remote part of the refuge, one of her favorite retreats. We parked and hiked up an atypically steep hill of longleaf pine, wiregrass, smilax, *Baptisia*, fallen branches, rocks, rust-colored boulders, and trailing arbutus, *Epigaea repens*, which Dave called "an indication of pyxie moss" habitat—a propitious sign.

"Trailing arbutus, along with blueberries," said Lyne, "is in the *Ericaceae* acidic soil family."

Dave found the pyxie moss easily. It was well past its bloom. Its little leaves were succulent and evergreen. There was a blissful breeze. The day's work of driving, hiking, pointing, naming, and talking ceased. We all took deep breaths. "There's a site similar to this in Compartment 11," she said. "This is Compartment 19."

I let out a deep sigh. Where we stood was steep. We felt we were on top of a little mountain. I thought of Emerson's transcendental tenet of correspondence, that nature mirrors our souls. I fear what happens to our souls when that mirror is broken. Endangered plants, endangered animals, endangered souls. I envied Dave for his life in the woods, his love and respect for nature, and the thousands of times, alone, that he's felt this oneness. Let me put a little camper here on this hill, I thought. I'll live right here.

"This is pretty," said Dave.

"This is . . . this is . . . a neat spot," said Lyne, at a loss for words. I thought of Poe, that although "there are combinations of very simple natural objects which have the power of thus affecting us, still the analysis of this power lies among considerations beyond our depth,"[9] and of how impossible it is to speak that depth. This totality of hill, trees, rocks, plants, sky, sun, and wind was greater than the sum of its parts, and the greater sum was deposited in our spirits.

Lyne expressed her frustration with people "who see just a bunch of pine trees and don't get it. Our vision statement speaks about 'stirring the soul.' That's what this does for me. It's just right here. Listen to the wind. The refuge awakens the senses. It stirs the soul."

"It's peaceful," I said.

"I like that peace and quiet," Dave told us. "When the wind whispers through the treetops, it's the good Lord speaking to you."

"I think the reason I have this connection," said Lyne, "is because I did my graduate research in habitat like this. That was a great time in my life. I always knew—well, no, I didn't know what I wanted to be, but I knew what made me happy. This is what I want to do for the rest of my life."

"I always thought that U.S. Fish and Wildlife doesn't owe me anything," said Dave. "I owe them for letting me enjoy my work. Thirty years, I got to walk this whole refuge. Beautiful, isn't it?"

NOTES

1. Henry David Thoreau, *The Maine Woods* (New York: Thomas Y. Crowell, 1966), 160.

2. Shibu Jose, Eric J. Jokela, and Deborah L. Miller, "The Longleaf Pine Ecosystem: An Overview," in *The Longleaf Pine Ecosystem: Ecology, Silviculture, and Restoration*, ed. Jose, Jokela, and Miller (New York: Springer, 2006), 4.

3. Cecil Frost quoting the South Carolina State Board of Agriculture, 1883, in "History and Future of the Longleaf Pine Ecosystem," in *The Longleaf Pine Ecosystem*, ed. Jose, Jokela, and Miller, 34.

4. Joan L. Walker and Andrea M. Silletti, "Restoring the Ground Layer of Longleaf Pine Ecosystems," in *The Longleaf Pine Ecosystem*, ed. Jose, Jokela, and Miller, 310.

5. Charles C. Mann, *1491: New Revelations of the Americas before Columbus* (New York: Knopf, 2005), 249–50.

6. Walker and Silletti, "Restoring the Ground Layer of Longleaf Pine Ecosystems," 331–32.

7. Mann, *1491*, 5.

8. Frost, "History and Future of the Longleaf Pine Ecosystem," 15.

9. Edgar Allan Poe, "The Fall of the House of Usher," http://www.enotes.com/fall-house-usher-text/the-fall-house-usher (accessed September 7, 2010).

Banding Red-cockaded Woodpeckers

"Yeah, the chicks get a little nervous. They are probably thinking, 'Gosh, my parents told me about snakes, but they never warned me about the noose.'"

Laura Housh, wildlife biologist

JUNE 2. ANOTHER BLUE SKY, cool breeze, and warm sunny day. My hands were spotted with pine tar from helping wildlife biologist Laura Housh load gear and a Swedish climbing ladder from her truck onto a four-wheeler. Laura was banding red-cockaded woodpecker chicks and had invited me along to watch. It had been a good nesting season, she said. She had banded fifty.

Because the Carolina Sandhills National Wildlife Refuge has a stable population of the endangered birds, it donates RCWs to other refuges. A big reason for banding, therefore, is translocation—supplying RCWs to other refuges to help save the species. The bands on each RCW indicate the year it was banded and the refuge and cluster, that is, family community, from which it hailed. Only subadults, four- to five-month-old birds, are translocated in the fall. Subadults adjust better to translocation; adults usually have already established territories.

I followed Laura into the forest to a cluster of red-cockaded woodpecker trees. "We installed four artificial cavities in these trees last February," she said. "I was pleasantly surprised to see RCWs already nesting in them this year."

The longleaf pine that Laura was after stood straight and tall, about twenty-two inches diameter at breast height. She guessed the tree might be seventy-five years old. It was a beautiful tree, a nice place for a home.

Two adult RCWs flitted high in the branches overhead. One had something in its beak—probably an insect for a chick, Laura said. The adults did not come closer.

To determine if a given cavity contained chicks, Laura used a specially designed "peeper scope." The device had a telescoping pole with a cigar-shaped video camera at the top and a viewing screen at the bottom.

The cavity was about twenty feet up. Standing on the ground, Laura extended the pole and inserted the camera into the entrance tunnel of the cavity. Although the chicks had not yet opened their eyes, they could sense light and dark and probably assumed the camera was an adult delivering a breakfast bug. They began a high-pitched trilling that we could easily hear from the ground.

Laura showed me the video screen. I could see the interior of the cavity and see the chicks breathing. "There are three in there," I reported, viewing their heads, backs and wings.

"No, only two," she said. "They're all tangled."

"Good lookin' guys."

"They're probably eight days old," she said.

"How can you tell?"

"The skin is a little lighter, and the quills aren't as developed. What a difference a day can make," she added, assembling the climbing ladder.

The ladder rattled and clanged as she connected the ten-foot sections and leaned it up against the pine. After chaining it to the trunk, she secured herself to the tree with a stiff, resin-glazed climbing belt, slung over her shoulder a canvas pouch containing a ziplock bag of cornstarch and a small rubber noose, and started climbing.

Laura would dust her hands with cornstarch if they became sticky with sap or apply it to a chick as a kind of topical Band-Aid if it got nicked in the banding process. "But that's rare," she told me. The noose—a scary name for what pulls cute, defenseless chicks from their nests—was a simple homemade device consisting of a pencil-size rubber tube and a length of thin coated wire. A chick-size loop of wire is fed through one end of the tube and dangled into the cavity to fish for a baby. The loose wires are then pulled through the other end of the tube to snag one. I asked if she could use the peeper scope to help see and lasso them.

"No," she said, "I have to go in blind with the noose. There's always a risk. I don't know whether I'll get the chick by the neck, leg, or wings. But they're very resilient, sturdy little birds. I've never injured one."

Atop the ladder and at the cavity, Laura placed her hand over the entrance hole to block the light. The chicks, expecting food, began peeping and raising their heads. "That makes it easier for me to catch them with the

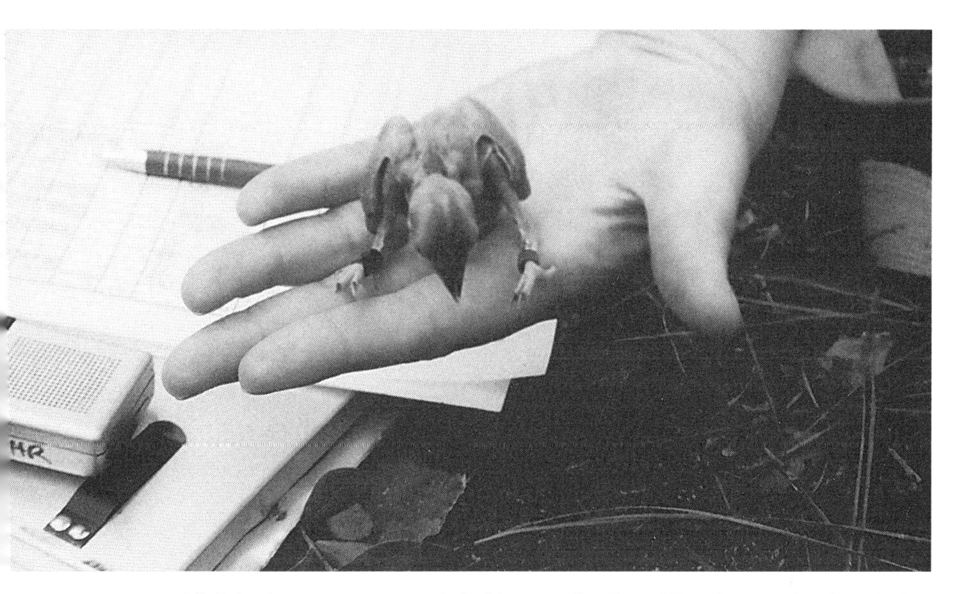

Wildlife biologist Laura Housh holds an eight-day-old endangered red-cockaded woodpecker. For identification, the chick is banded with one aluminum and four colored bands. As a subadult, this bird may be translocated to a group in another refuge to aid in the species's recovery. Photograph by the author.

noose. But they get wise to the trick. If I don't get them on the first couple of pulls, they lie flat, which makes things a lot harder."

I had always heard, I told her, that if you handle a baby bird and put it back into its nest, the parents would reject it.

"That's a myth," she said. "Most birds don't have much of a sense of smell." A fledgling you might find on the ground, unless it's taking its first solo flight, has probably been rejected by its parents, pushed from the nest for being too frail or, as Laura said, "a runt. Once we've put the baby back in the cavity," she assured me, "the adults will return to feed it. I've never found a baby RCW on the ground," she added.

The trunk around the cavity's entrance glistened with tear-shaped drips of sap, which splotched Laura's USFWS shirt and pants. "I have to wash my clothes with Gojo to get the sap out," she said. "Once I got stuck to a tree." The resin flowed from wells that the RCWs had drilled to discourage snakes; but because this tree had hundreds of wells near the base as well, Laura speculated that the woodpeckers had also been foraging for bugs.

Fortunately for the chicks, Laura's noose fishing was undramatic. On the first try, she looped them both around the wings, then pouched them and descended the ladder.

When she was on the ground, I peered inside the canvas pouch. The chicks emitted a plaintive trilling. Curled up next to the bag of cornstarch, they were gray and mottled pink. "They look like tiny dinosaurs," I said. "Good strong beaks. Their legs are folded up. I see the stubs of feathers on their tails and the edges of their wings. They're shaking."

"Yeah, the chicks get a little nervous. They are probably thinking, 'Gosh, my parents told me about snakes, but they never warned me about the noose.'"

Kneeling on the needle-strewn ground, Laura took the chicks from the pouch, placed them on a cloth, and opened a small compartmentalized box, the kind a fly fisherman might use. There were ten compartments of different colored plastic bands, not counting the aluminum ones.

"All of our banded birds—RCWs, wood ducks, and doves—have an aluminum U.S. Fish and Wildlife Service band." On each USFWS band is a number that Laura forwards to a center in Maryland, where it's entered into a nationwide database. If the band is ever recovered and returned to the lab in Maryland, it will indicate the origins of the bird.

With deft fingers and special pliers, Laura fastened three colored plastic bands on one leg and one aluminum and one colored band on the other. She repeated the process with the second bird. Then she recorded each chick's colors and number on a spreadsheet. Every banded bird on the refuge has its own color combination.

"We have to identify each subadult that we translocate," she said. She held up a chick. "For example, if this bird is the cluster's only helper male," referring to the RCWs' remarkable family structure, "I wouldn't translocate him. I'd keep him here on the refuge."

I asked how she decided what birds were helpers.

"Roost surveys." With a spotting scope, Laura and her crew will observe the RCWs coming in to roost, determine the birds' sexes, and note the color combinations of their bands. Then Laura would decide which birds to translocate.

She handed me the chick. It was warm, with well-developed talons and skin so transparent you could see the internal organs.

"RCW chicks can be banded at five to ten days old, but between six and eight days is preferable," she said. "At nine days their eyes open." She checked the chick's toes to make sure that none was caught in the bands.

"When will it fly?"
"At twenty-six days."
I asked about the life span.
"Seven to nine years is average in the wild. In captivity one lived fourteen years, I think."
The chick peeped nonstop, flopped in my palm, and struggled to raise its head. "It's getting feisty."
Laura took it, picked up the other, stood, and dropped the siblings unceremoniously into her pouch. "Goin' back up," she said. As she climbed the ladder to return the babes to their bed, I tried to imagine what kind of life they would have—whether they'd be helpers or breeders; whether they'd stay at the refuge or be translocated to Virginia, Arkansas, or elsewhere; and whether folks like Laura could keep them from going the way of ivorybills and Carolina parakeets.

Under a Red Flag

"This is my work. As a wildlife biologist, I'm making
a difference. . . . It makes me feel good."

Pat Ferral

IN THE 1920S THE U.S. GOVERNMENT, along with the states of Florida, Georgia, Mississippi, and South Carolina, were hot to stamp out the "estimated 200,000 woods fires [that] burned annually in the South." Believing fire to be "the greatest deterrent to renewed timber stands and to permanent forest management," state governments dispatched fleets of trucks equipped with generators, movie projectors, and screens to show films such as *Trees of Righteousness*, which caricatured some southerners as Burnin' Bills who "practiced the old southern custom of burning woods." Playing at schools and fairs, the films were a successful if misguided attempt to "enlighten" rural folks about the evils of all forest fires.[1]

Bad science weighed in with those who distrusted fire. In the late nineteenth century most foresters "regarded fire as the unrelenting enemy of forest regeneration," even going so far as to insist that in North Carolina, "the burnings of the present and future, if not soon discontinued, will mean the final extinction of the longleaf pine in this state."[2]

Fire, however, had shaped the New World long before man—Native American or European—arrived. "Before the immigration of Indians into the Southeast near the end of the Wisconsin glaciation some 12,000 to 13,000 years ago, essentially all fires would have been caused by lighting. . . . The emerging picture suggests that terrestrial vegetation has evolved with fire from its very beginning in the early Devonian Era, some 400 million years ago."[3]

Whether the early southerners mimicked nature's processes or copied the Native Americans' use of burns is up for grabs, but apparently the custom of setting fire to the woods was not imported to America by settlers from

A prescribed burn. Converging lines of fire are set with drip torches or the aid of a helicopter and an aerial ignition machine. The intensity of the prescribed burn may be controlled by altering the distance between lines of fire. Photograph by the author.

England. "A British traveler in South Carolina in 1829 was astonished to discover a recently burned stand of longleaf pine: 'There was no underwood properly so-called, while the shrubs had all been destroyed a week or two before by a great fire. The pine trees, the bark of which was scorched to a height of about 20 feet, stood on ground as dark as if it had rained Matchless Blacking for the last month. Our companions assured us that although these fires were frequent in the forest, the large trees did not suffer. This may be true, but they certainly did look very wretched, though their tops were green as if nothing had happened.'"[4]

Before Europeans arrived in the New World, the humans already here had managed much of America's forests and grasslands with fire, and not just in the Southeast. In the Northeast in the mid-1600s Adriaen van der Donck, a Dutch settler in the Hudson River Valley, wrote that the Haudenosaunee burned "'the woods, plains, and meadows' to 'thin out and clear the woods of all dead substances and grass.'"[5] In the Southeast, "Accounts from the

Colonial Period describing Indian burning practices indicate that use of wildfire . . . peaked in fall and winter when fires were set to drive game."[6]

Most hunters and hikers will find the image of precolonial America as a wildlife preserve ecologically advanced and a lot of fun. In *1491: New Revelations of the Americas Before Columbus*, Charles C. Mann expands on the idea of Native American as caretaker:

> Rather than domesticate animals for meat, Indians retooled ecosystems to encourage elk, deer, and bear. Constant burning of undergrowth increased the numbers of herbivores, the predators that feed on them, and the people who ate them. . . . Incredible to imagine today, bison roamed from New York to Georgia. A creature of the prairie, *Bison bison* was imported to the East by Native Americans along a path of indigenous fire, as they changed enough forest into fallows for it to survive far outside its original range. When the Haudenosaunee hunted these animals, the historian William Cronon observed, they "were harvesting a foodstuff which they had consciously been instrumental in creating. Few English observers could have realized this. People accustomed to keeping domesticated animals lacked the conceptual tools to recognize that the Indians were practicing a more distant kind of husbandry."[7]

Twentieth-century foresters, however, were slow to pick up the torch. In the 1920s a conservationist as progressive as Aldo Leopold derided the use of fire by Native Americans as "Piute Forestry" and its proponents as "propagandists": "It is, of course, absurd to assume that the Indians fired the forests with any idea of forest conservation in mind." Leopold did grasp one core concept of prescribed burns: "Light-burning means the deliberate firing of Forests at frequent intervals in order to burn up and prevent the accumulation of litter and thus prevent the occurrence of serious conflagrations." Early in his career, however, he failed to grasp other key concepts and argued, "Light-burning gradually reduces the vitality and productiveness of the forage."[8] Leopold, writes Curt Meine, "had been conditioned to a simple response: fire was evil." By 1923, however, Leopold showed sparks of recognition regarding the regenerative role of fire in forestry. He "still regarded fire as 'the scourge of all living things,' but admitted that forest fires sometimes caused an increase in vegetation beneficial to game."[9]

For nearly a century the government's wholesale suppression of fire was a death knell to many natural ecosystems. Despite the executions of this misguided policy, however, there were still intelligent, observant voices crying out in the wilderness. As early as 1913 Roland Harper, a forward-thinking botanist for the Geological Survey of Alabama, argued that "it can be safely asserted that there is not and never has been a longleaf pine forest in the United States . . . which did not show evidence of fire, such as charred bark near the bases of the trees; and furthermore, if it were possible to prevent forest fires absolutely, the long-leaf pine—our most useful tree—would soon become extinct."[10]

In the last decades of the twentieth century, the winds shifted. Recognizing the role of fire in maintaining southern pine forests, the powers that be made a U-turn. The new road, however, is thorny and contentious, complicated by the encroachment of smoke into the suburbs and suburbs into the wildlands. Not surprisingly liability costs and lawsuits have increased.

Forester Pat Ferral of Ferral Environmental Services troops through these hot issues holding a drip torch in one hand and a briefcase stuffed with college degrees, petitions, legislation, insurance policies, high-tech gadgets, data, weather reports, and fire prescriptions in the other. He works to enlighten the public and restore the tradition of setting fire to the woods.

IT WAS A MORNING IN MID-MARCH, and there had been no rain in recent memory. The forecast was for a cold front to move in the next day and drop the temperature into the unseasonably low 50s. But this day would be blue-skyed, dry, and in the 70s. A Category 5 day. A perfect day to set fire to the woods.

"I'm aware we've been under a red flag," Pat Ferral had said over the phone the evening before, "but that's not a burning ban, and we're burning a safe area," a tract of loblolly pines. "If the weather doesn't change, expect a call from me dark-thirty tomorrow morning to confirm."

Issued by the state Forestry Commission, a red flag fire alert is "a wildfire danger warning" that "asks people to postpone burning" but "does not prohibit outdoor burning as long as all other state and local regulations are followed."[11] A burning ban, in contrast, is a legal prohibition.

I had witnessed big, all-day burns of hundreds of acres at the Carolina Sandhills NWR; but because Ferral Environmental was burning a small tract, I expected an uneventful burn. Instead I got a hands-on lesson in what could go right and what could go wrong.

Pat met me at a Citgo station off I-20. I left my Jeep there and rode with him in a red F-150 to an expansive horse ranch, a thousand acres of rolling pastures, white fences, and pine stands in the upper coastal plain. The landowners were the CEO of an international firm and his wife, who raised thoroughbreds. They lived in Pennsylvania and jetted down to South Carolina on weekends "to hunt and relax," Pat said. He had worked for these clients about six years.

Pam, Pat's wife, waited for us at the ranch's equipment shed. The two ran their environmental service out of Camden, South Carolina. Both were dressed in Nomex pants and green Nature Conservancy T-shirts.

Pat has degrees in natural science, biology, and forestry resources from Winthrop and Clemson Universities. "Worked at the Savannah Ecology Lab for a while," he said. "Took a job with the state as a botanical technician. Did my master's on red-cockaded woodpeckers." Pam has a master's in wildlife management from North Carolina State.

I asked about the T-shirts.

"I went to the Nature Conservancy fire schools," he said. "For six years I monitored red-cockaded woodpeckers for them on Sandy Island." (Located in the Waccamaw National Wildlife Refuge, Sandy Island is the largest undeveloped freshwater island in the eastern United States.) Pam had worked for the Nature Conservancy as a project director in Winyah Bay, South Carolina, and later as director of science and stewardship.

After lowering the tailgate of the truck, the two began filling pillow-size yellow bladders with water from a garden hose. Each rubber bladder held eight gallons (about sixty-seven pounds) of water and was fitted with shoulder straps and a hose. Pat called the bladders "backpack pumps." In the event of a spotover—that is, if flames leaped across a firebreak—a crew member could shoulder the bladder and "attack the fire with backpack pumps and hand tools, squirt it with water, throw dirt on it with a shovel. But we're not expecting any spotovers," he added.

Pat also represented the Association of Consulting Foresters to the South Carolina Fire Council. The previous fall I had attended a meeting of the S.C. Fire Council in Columbia. The chief topic had been liability. I asked Pat about it.

"Liability's our biggest problem. We're trying to make changes at the state level to address it. We want to change 'negligence' to 'gross negligence.'" The Florida legislature, he said, had already instituted the change.

I later asked Mike Baxley, judge of the Fourth Circuit in South Carolina, about the legal definitions of negligence and gross negligence. Simple negligence, he said, is the failure to use due caution or reasonable care. Gross negligence is when one acts with a reckless, willful, and conscious disregard for the rights and safety of others. Under South Carolina law, negligence can give rise to actual damages, whereas gross negligence can give rise to not only actual damages but also exemplary and punitive damages. Judge Baxley added that it was not unusual for an industry or profession to petition the General Assembly for protection from litigation.

"The threat of liability is one reason why there hasn't been enough fire on the ground," said Darryl Jones, forest protection chief for the South Carolina Forestry Commission and chairman of the S.C. Prescribed Fire Council, in a September 2012 interview.

For years the S.C. Prescribed Fire Council, supported by the Wildlife Federation, the Nature Conservancy, and other conservation groups, petitioned South Carolina's legislature "to improve the legal climate for burning," Darryl said. In the spring of 2012 they succeeded. The amended law states that if a certified prescribed fire manager is on-site supervising the burn, writes and follows a prescribed fire plan, and properly notifies the Forestry Commission, he gains legal protection. Liability relating to fire—for example, if a prescribed fire escapes and burns a neighbor's house—still falls under simple negligence. But liability related to smoke—for example, if smoke from a smoldering fire obscures a road and causes an accident—now falls under gross negligence. "Once smoke is up in the air, it's harder to control," explained Darryl.

"This is a significant improvement to the law," he stated. "It makes it easier for us to encourage burning. If weather cooperates, in years to come we expect to see an increase in the number of acres burned." He added that "the state has never restricted the right of a landowner to conduct burns. You don't have to be a certified prescribed fire manager to burn, but only certified burners are eligible for added legal protection under the Prescribed Fire Act." The Forestry Commission offers training and certification for prescribed fire managers. In 2012 there were about fifteen hundred certified prescribed fire managers in South Carolina. "Already, the number of applicants for certification has gone way up."

Done filling the water bladders, Pat and Pam began pouring slash fuel from a ten-gallon plastic can into drip torches. We continued talking about liability. "State and federal agencies want to increase the number of burns, but it's increasingly difficult to afford insurance. My insurance has jumped eight hundred dollars this year because I do a lot of burning. By the end of the month, I gotta come up with four thousand dollars. I have to pass the cost along to my clients, but how much will they be willing to pay? It's enough to make you want to hang up your torch," he added, capping a drip torch, "but I believe in what I'm doing."

Pat and Pam aren't the only foresters who question the future of prescribed burning. "One of my first tasks on the Fire Council," he said, "was to come up with a list of contractors who do prescribed burning in the state. I canvassed all the members of the Association of Consulting Foresters. Everybody said, 'We don't recommend that our clients burn anymore because of the liability and the risk.'"

The dilemma of whether to burn or not is a matter of life and death to longleaf pine forests. Over two-thirds of South Carolina—over twelve million acres—is forested. Although the state and national governments manage 10 percent of these forests, nearly 75 percent is in the hands of private landowners, and roughly half of these privately held forests, well over four million acres, is fire dependent. The health of the state's pine forests and the wildlife therein is therefore largely a private affair.[12]

The U.S. Forest Service agrees that the "significance of land ownership in the South for the provision of species habitat cannot be overstated. Each major landowner has an important role to play in the conservation of species and their habitats."[13] Reality, however, can be a wet blanket. An increasing number of private landowners are reluctant to conduct burns. This bodes ill for the health and survival of many species. Because of liability, development, and a forest-as-product mind-set, "it's getting tougher and tougher to get people to burn," Pat said.

As he worked, he mused about changes in the landscape. "A lot of woods are going to developers for residential developments. Forests are just one part of the portfolio" of timber owners and investment associates. "Their main focus in timber management is growing trees for fiber production. They don't want fire in their stands because it inhibits growth."

"Smoke management has become our biggest challenge. I'm a certified fire manager. On all my burns, there's a written prescription and a certified fire manager present, the whole nine yards. I've asked my insurance agent, 'With all the training I've had, why can't I get a lower rate?' He tells me, 'The only reason we insure you at all is because of that training.'" Pat and his associates recently "pitched an idea to Lloyds of London," an international insurance firm, asking that the provider of specialist insurance services offer liability insurance "to private landowners for a certain window of time—a week, a month, even a six-month period, pretty much the length of the burn season—to burn a piece of property as opposed to taking out an annual burn policy."

"Can any landowner go out and burn?" I asked. "What if I had forty acres of woods? Even though I have no training, even if I were clueless, could I burn?"

"Yes, unless there's a state ban," he said, unfolding some paperwork to show me a routine prescription for a prescribed burn on private land. Because Pat is a fire manager, he can approve his own burns. "This is a generic prescribed fire plan. Today's plan lists where I'm at, the coordinates, the address, who to contact, objectives. . . ." Next he showed me a GPS map of the area they would burn and the weather forecast. "Partly cloudy, west wind in the morning, northwest transport wind at 18 miles per hour this afternoon. Ceiling's 5,500 feet. Multiply those two for your ventilation rate, that's 99,000."

According to the S.C. Forestry Commission's "Smoke Management Guidelines," ventilation rate indicates "the capability of the lower atmosphere to diffuse and disperse smoke."[14] A high ventilation rate, Pat said, "allows the smoke column to lift better," keeping smoke off a neighbor's property and, more important, off roads, where smoke inversion could cause—and has caused—accidents, injury, and death. "If the ventilation rate is below 25,000, I won't burn. Today I know we can keep smoke off the county road. You gotta watch out for your smoke-sensitive areas. Here we have to wait for a north wind to keep smoke off the hardtop road. But we got a Category 5 day," he said, folding up the prescription. "It'll burn good. I've already called the Forestry Commission and got my notification number. The last thing I had to do was call county dispatch, the 911 people, and let them know where I'm burning."

"So if somebody calls 911 that there's a fire here, a fire truck doesn't show up," Pam explained.

Pat expressed his frustration, however, at the occasional lack of communication between the state Forestry Commission, dispatch, and local fire departments. On one burn in Kershaw County, despite securing approval for a prescription and notifying the local dispatch, Pat, patrolling the perimeter on an ATV, turned a corner to find eleven fire engines from two counties and a brush truck hosing down his fire. Pat was hotter than the fire that day and ended the burn.

Because today's was a private burn, I wondered if all the paperwork and contacts were required.

"For my insurance, yes. The state has a prescribed fire act that says if you follow all prudent measures, get your firebreaks in, check for snags, write a burn plan, have a notification number, it's tougher to be sued for negligence."

With all the expense and risk, I was curious how much Ferral Environmental charged for a burn.

"Eighteen, sometimes twenty dollars an acre."

I said that the price sounded amazingly inexpensive.

"It does until you're burning a 30-acre block and 150 acres a day." This day, said Pat, they were burning "a pretty darn small parcel of 16 acres," or about $320 worth of woods. Clearly this was no way to get rich.

"I don't just burn, though. I also scout and sell timber for clients." Pat's focus is managing wildlife habitat, mainly for quail. "Most of my clients burn for wildlife enhancement, not so much for hazard reduction or the prevention of wildfires. For example, I wrote a prescription for a burn on this property detailing what we need to do to promote grasses and legumes for quail habitat. Quail is a keystone species," much like red-cockaded woodpeckers, he explained. "If you manage the habitat for quail, you're taking care of other species—wild turkey and songbirds such as Bachman's sparrow."

Pat hopes to be conducting burns twenty years from now if he's "still alive and can afford the insurance." But like others, he is uncertain about the future of burning. "I'm on the Fire Council to help bring more awareness to the public as to the benefits of fire. People who have no idea about the need for fire are moving to the South from other parts of the country, particularly to our coast. Because of smoke, there are complaints and lawsuits. It's like every bubble boy in the Southeast has moved next to the Francis Marion National Forest. Talk about a wildland-urban interface," he said.

The S.C. Forestry Commission concurs that "urban sprawl is rampant" and that "wildfires in these areas are tough to control. As development increases, lives and property will be threatened as never before."[15]

"You know," said Pat, "we don't burn just any area. Woods next to a major highway, chances are they'll never get burned," which ultimately increases the risk of wildfire. He cataloged the current wildfires in California, Texas, and Oklahoma. "Build a house surrounded by sage chaparral, eventually it's gonna burn. Those areas are supposed to burn. What's happening out West is a prime example of why fire needs to be on the ground. Fire has been excluded for so long—eventually it's gonna explode. That's why the South Carolina Forestry Commission came up with Firewise, a program to help protect the homes of people who live near woods."

A white Ford Expedition drove up, followed by a Honda ATV. We were joined by Scott Poole, the ranch manager, and Mike Adamson, who would watch for spotovers. A little boy looked out over the dashboard of the truck. I shook hands with Scott and Mike.

As Pat and Pam continued readying gear, I thought about the inherent risks of fire and asked Scott about the options of using chemicals or machinery instead to reduce not only the fuel load but also the risk of liability.

"We've used all three on this land," Scott said, "herbicides, machinery, and fire. Chemicals won't do it alone, and their costs are prohibitive." The choice, he continued, "depends on your objective, whether you're harvesting trees or developing wildlife habitat." As for machinery, the use of bulldozers and Bush Hogs to clear undergrowth is expensive, as well as labor intensive. What's more, machines often disturb the soil. They may inadvertently transport and disperse invasive, nonnative seeds that hitchhike on frames and bumpers, and they destroy habitat. Prescribed burns, in contrast, return nutrients to the ground and encourage plant and animal life. Despite the rising costs of insurance, burns are still the most cost-effective strategy.

"There's a new machine called a Gyro-Trac," Pat commented, "basically a drum with teeth that pulverizes everything into mulch. But you're talking $350 per acre. With chemical treatment, you're still looking at about $100 per acre. If you've got the money, a combination of herbicides, machinery, and fire will get you what you want a lot quicker."

"It's nice to be able to work for a landowner with these resources," said Pam. "A lot of landowners don't have them, and we have to bring everything in, for example Bush Hogs and ATVs, and do all the necessary prep work, such as cutting firebreaks."

I did some math. A hundred acres times twenty dollars per acre per burn is two thousand dollars. If I bought a hundred acres of pine forest, I'd have trouble enough making the payments, let alone hiring someone to run a burn.

"Land management is not cheap," Pam said. "Cost is another factor that limits prescribed burning."

And burning alone may not always do the job. A recurring problem on this land was the control of sweetgums (*Liquidambar styraciflua*). "Sweetgums can really be a problem. They're prolific seeders. Once they get established, you can burn and burn, but they just keep comin' back with more sprouts. Sweetgums drop hardwood leaves that lay flat on the ground and retain moisture. They just don't burn that well. Even with a growing season burn, you're just top-killing the sweetgums. I'll burn as late as June, but sometimes it gets so dry you can't burn. For the past three years we've used herbicide to control unwanted hardwoods and followed up with a burn. Last year we sprayed the area we're going to burn today with glyphosate. Glyphosate is a foliage spray. You have to spray the leaves to kill the plant. Another chemical we use is Imazapyr—it goes by the name Chopper. Imazapyr is a defoliant, and it's active in the soil. In Florida," he added, "there are oak domes or groves out in the middle of fire-maintained pine systems. Fire will burn right up to them but won't burn the hardwood leaves."

I knew that mechanical treatments often disturb the soil, and like many, I distrust chemicals. I wondered what choice was best for the forest.

In Pat's opinion, "Tordon and Garlon blitzkrieg the soil. Those are real nasty chemicals. Some chemicals, however, have become more earth friendly, breaking down in the soil faster. Fire is usually the friendliest treatment, but things"—urban development, liability, and litigation over smoke management—"have gotten so out of control that you almost have to use different treatments."

Pat and Pam finished loading up their truck, and I rode with them down dirt roads and through more woods to the burn site. Scott and Mike followed in their vehicles. "Good quail habitat," said Pat, driving past a meadow of splitbeard bluestem, a species of bunchgrass in the *Andropogon* family. "Here we have areas of mature loblolly and slash pine. The trees are about eighty feet tall. About six hundred acres are uplands. The rest is creek drainage. We've also got about fifty acres of longleaf. It's my biggest project on this tract. Once we reduce fuels with winter burns, we get into rotation with growing season burns.

"With a winter burn, you're just going to get top-kill. Winter burns are more for hazard reduction. Now I'm experimenting with herbicides and winter-season burns as opposed to just growing-season burns. One of those won't totally kill your hardwoods. Once you scarify the canopy oak or the sweetgum, it may take four or five years for disease to set in and kill them. To really control hardwoods, you've got to have successive growing-season burns.

"Growing-season burns really improve the wire-grass component. Wiregrass needs growing-season burns to flower. Quail and wild turkeys like wiregrass. The owner hunts quail and has a healthy deer herd."

"A healthy deer herd," I repeated. "A lot of hunters will say you won't have many deer in a pine forest, that they need hardwoods for mast."

"Where we have a cluster of mast trees, we protect them by encircling them with permanent firebreaks. Before a burn, run a disk over the breaks. We also plant a lot of food plots."

A gray squirrel scurried up a pine, and my mind wandered to eastern fox squirrels (*Sciurus niger*), the titan of North American squirrels and an indicator species of habitat health. I had read that fox squirrels shied away from hardwood forests, preferring an open habitat of longleaf, wiregrass, and herbaceous ground cover; and that their southeastern populations had declined, not surprisingly, due to loss of habitat. The great precolonial forests of longleaf pine, estimated to have encompassed ninety million acres, have fallen by about 98 percent. I asked Pat if he encountered many fox squirrels.

"To my observation, they like a pine–scrub oak habitat. Six years ago I'd see one fox squirrel. As we increased the burn program, I've seen as many as a dozen out here."

WE PULLED UP AT THE CORNER of the burn site, which was bordered on the west by a dirt road and on the south by a wide firebreak with loose, freshly disked earth. South of the firebreak the woods sloped gradually to a bog.

"I recommend that all of my clients establish permanent firebreaks," Pat said. "It makes things easier. When you want to burn again, just disk the break with a tractor and you're done."

"Scott disked these breaks this morning," Pam added. Firebreaks not only help corral the flames, they also make it easier for someone on an ATV, in this case Mike, to patrol the perimeter and search for spotovers. All in all, Scott and Mike had about two hours of prep time before the burn.

There was a lot of fuel on the ground in the tract to be burned. It was more fuel than I was accustomed to seeing—fallen branches, dense patches of briers, tall grass, and occasional deadfalls. "How tall will the fire get today?" I asked.

"Ten-, fifteen-foot flame lengths."

Recalling that the flames I had seen during burns at the Carolina Sandhills NWR rarely got over six feet, I commented that fifteen feet was pretty high.

"It's an adrenaline rush," he laughed.

"Yeah," smiled Pam, "when we burn he gets excited and starts talking louder and louder."

On the west side of the road was a tract that had been burned two weeks earlier—an area of blackened ground, charred blackberry briers that looked as tough as twisted rebar, and tall slash pines with green crowns.

Pat donned a hard hat and yellow Nomex shirt, lifted a drip torch from the truck bed, lit the wick, then poured some fire onto the grass at the corner. Eager little flames danced up.

"Pat's checking wind direction," said Pam. "Based on what we know about today's weather, we want to see if we're in the right place to start the fire."

"We always start with a test fire," said Pat. "See how the wind is gonna cooperate. Today, because we're burning near a paved road, we need a north-northwest wind."

Depending on how the fire acted in the unit, Pam told me, "we can slow it down or intensify it as we need to."

Scott parked in the burned-out zone across from the corner and, without stopping to talk, walked down the firebreak toward the other side of the tract carrying his drip torch. With their torches he and Pat would create a black line along the firebreak and back the fire into the wind.

Talking louder now, Pat judged that the test "looked good." He took a Motorola two-way radio from his belt and traded "Check" with Scott, Mike, and Pam to test communication.

I asked what was essential to conduct a burn.

"Radios. Communication is key for the progress of a burn and especially for safety. Water. And matches," he laughed as he stepped aside to use his cell phone.

There was the chugging of an approaching ATV, and I turned to see Mike drive up with the little boy perched on the back. I asked Mike the name of the boy, who was cradling a plastic rifle.

"Little Ross, Scott's boy." Today was St. Patrick's Day, and Little Ross had a green four-leaf clover painted on his face. Four years old, blonde-haired, and blue-eyed, he was a knockoff of his father.

"What kind of gun you totin'?" I asked.

"Rifle," said Little Ross. He aimed the rifle into the woods and squeezed the trigger. The gun made a twangy, ricocheting sound. "Takes three bullets." Working the bolt, he ejected three silver plastic cartridges, which fell onto the ground. I helped him pick them up. "I have a BB gun too. My sister has a .22. She's older."

Pocketing his cell phone, Pat announced, "Just notified 911 dispatch. We're ready to roll!" He strode off with his drip torch along the firebreak, dripping fire to start the black line as he went. Little Ross jumped down from the ATV to join Pam and me, and Mike turned and rode off to police the firebreak.

Pam said, "The black line should be at least five feet wide. It depends what's on the other side of the firebreak. Pat's burned these stands so many times, he pretty much knows what's going on. It's difficult to get the hardwood litter to burn on the other side of the break, even in low humidity."

Pat's voice came over the radio. "Pam, get that Kestrel out of the glove box and take some measurements."

Pam entered the truck cab and after a moment emerged with a pocket-size weather meter hanging from a lanyard around her neck. She pointed the device into the wind. "The Kestrel has a little fan to check the wind speed and direction," she said as she took readings. "It also gives relative humidity, ambient temperature, and dew point."

Soon Pat was striding back toward us through a head-high brier patch, one hand dripping flames from the torch and laying down a line of fire, the other pushing brambles away from his face.

"Briers are pretty bad," he remarked as he stepped out of the woods.

I contemplated how hot and hard a struggle it must be to hike through brush and briers in full gear and hard hat, all the while making the woods even hotter. Nomex fabric, though flame retardant, is no protection against thorns. If wildfire fighters were to wear heavy canvas pants in this intense heat, they'd sweat to death.

There was a loud pop and hiss of fire. "How's it going so far?" I asked.

"Good, no spotovers."

"You seem to be putting down a continuous line of fire," I said.

"I was spotting some areas. It's so thick in there. Scott Bush Hogged some trails for me, but . . ." His face was already smoke-smudged and sweat-streaked. He was breathing hard—half from exertion, I thought, and half from exhilaration. He set down the drip torch, wiped his brow on his sleeve, and tossed his hard hat into the bed of the truck. "I usually wear a hard hat, but it's not too bad in there."

The wind was easy. Though the flames at times were over ten feet, hardly any smoke had drifted into the firebreak, and the fire appeared to be well contained. "We'll see how the fire behaves before we really attack it. We'll probably be done with the burn in an hour," he added, stepping aside to call Scott over the radio.

As I looked at the smoldering black line, I wondered if that time frame was possible. At that point the fire seemed to be going nowhere fast. I asked Pam about the process of conducting a burn by hand without the aid of a helicopter and aerial ignition machine. "Do Pat and Scott just zigzag back and forth with their torches?"

"It depends on how the fire's behaving. If they want to intensify the fire and get the flame lengths up, they'll start stripping it, putting down continuous lines of flame for a really intense fire. And if they want to decrease the intensity, they'll change the ignition pattern and drop a line of spot fires."

Over the radio Scott said, "There's a pretty good wind shift on this side. I think I oughta be working down this front line."

"The wind is getting a little shifty," Pat agreed, "but it's working to our favor on this side."

"OK," replied Scott. "I'll go around."

Pat hung the radio back on his belt and hooked his thumb toward the previously burned zone west of the dirt road. "The stand behind us was sprayed six years ago with Chopper. After that we went through a wet spell and couldn't burn, then through a spell so dry we couldn't burn. We've finally reached a time when we can burn a lot."

In his ATV Mike rode up to the corner, U-turned, and headed back down the firebreak to watch the perimeter again.

"We thinned this stand five years ago and got more light onto the forest floor," Pat said, turning back to the woods. "Then, because of the drought, we couldn't burn for a while and sweetgum came up. The next year we came in with backpack sprayers and sprayed the sweetgum—nothing else—with glyphosate. This year we're burning up dead sweetgums."

Scott's voice came over the radio. "I have a black line pretty much along the firebreak. I'm doing good here so far, though I've run into some thick briers. I'm gonna rip my line on down."

Pat hoisted his drip torch again. "As we get further into the unit, we'll let the fire burn bigger chunks. Right here we're still concerned with spotovers," he said and strode off into the woods, lighting a pile of brush and fallen timber, presumably sweetgum. He laid down more fire and disappeared into a stand of tall loblollies. In seconds the brush blazed up into scorching twelve-foot flames.

"When the fire's hot, I feel like a roasted marshmallow," said Little Ross.

"I feel like a hot dog on a grill," I said. Surprised by the blast of heat and fire, I asked Pam what was going on.

"We're in an area that's open to the north wind, which is traveling down the road, so we have some eddy effect." I thought of wind flowing like a river down the road until the fire sucked it spinning into the burn.

"At this point," Pam said, "Pat and Scott are setting fire to the interior. Scott may be a little ahead. They're working off of each other's smoke so they can get the intensity they want. Pat can tell where Scott is and what his fire's doing by the color of the smoke. The darker the smoke, the more intense the fire." Whiter smoke indicated a backing fire.

To escape the heat and follow the progress of the burn, Pam, Little Ross, and I got into the truck and drove north about a hundred yards. "Scott and Pat have a really great synergy going," Pam said. "Pat writes a budget for the stands he wants to burn. Scott puts in firebreaks and does the prep work.

Recently Scott has Bush Hogged paths through the stands, which is a tremendous help where you have thick briers, especially Rubus or blackberry patches where it's impossible to walk."

Over the radio I heard Pat say again that the wind was "getting a little shifty." Blue-gray smoke rose into the air, and black and white ashes floated among the loblollies.

We parked and exited the truck. Pam's radio crackled again. "I'll be ready for some more fuel in a minute," said Scott.

Flames exploded in a blackberry thicket near where we stood. The heat was fierce. We stepped back a few paces. "We're getting some convection," Pam informed me. "As the lines of fire come together, they create their own little micro-weather." When lines of flames meet before the fuel burns out, "that's where you can get intense fire."

Despite the high flames, most of the pines were faring well. Their trunks were scorched black, but their bark was not on fire. A fifteen-foot sweetgum, however, was. "The bark of that hardwood is a lot thinner," Pam explained. "It's a finer fuel, more like paper. The sap in the cambium is boiling." Within minutes the fire had eaten like acid through the bole of the sweetgum, and it toppled.

"Pines," said Pam, "are better insulated against the flames." A thick layer of bark protects the cambium. At least one young twenty-foot pine, though, would not make it. We watched as flames leaped into its crown. Pam explained that Pat and Scott were trying to replicate the "natural process of thinning out smaller trees to get a parklike effect. It's what the forest would have looked like on old-fashioned quail hunts, with horses and wagons traveling through the woods."

I was thinking of Little Ross and how great it would be to grow up in a land of white-fenced pastures, thoroughbreds, southern forests, and wild game when Pat's voice came loud and urgent over the radio. "We have a spot over!" Seconds later Mike roared up on the ATV and skidded to a stop. Pam threw open the truck's tailgate. Mike flung two water bladders onto his four-wheeler, lashed them to the rack, wheeled around, and sped off toward the firebreak. Pam was filling another drip torch when Pat barked over the radio, "I need you here now!" She grabbed the drip torch and jumped into the truck as Pat shouted again over the radio, "I need more fuel! C'mon!"

I took Little Ross's hand, and we backed away from the truck.

"What they doo-ing?" he asked.

"They have a wildfire," I told him. I was going to ask Pam if there was something I could do, then decided I'd better stay put with Little Ross. She threw the truck into reverse and backed a hundred yards to the firebreak with Pat calling over the radio again, "C'mon! Where are you?"

The wind had kicked up markedly. Little Ross and I stood on the road and watched a white wall of smoke twice as high as the trees move slowly north, marking the progress of the burn. Deep in the woods monster flames jumped and roared.

Though the zone across from us and south toward the firebreak was still smoky, as far as I could see that part of the burn was subsiding. "It's dying out pretty quickly," I said to Little Ross. After several minutes I decided it might be safe for us to walk back to the firebreak and see the spotover.

On the burn side of the firebreak, the fuel was gone and the ground was black. On the spotover side, Pam was raking fuel along the irregular edge of the fire. Mark was farther down the slope, squirting out fire with a water bladder. The flames were only a foot or so high and not racing wildly, but the area of the spotover was perhaps two thousand square feet, and clearly the wildfire was not yet contained. Still, because the land sloped down to a bog, the situation seemed safe enough for Little Ross as long as we stayed on the firebreak.

The real action was still in the north end of the burn. There flames were twenty feet high. Heavy, swirling, green-black smoke obscured the trees. Even at this distance I could hear the fire's roar. I glanced at Pam, who had stopped raking momentarily to watch the burn, and I thought she looked concerned. I was.

Little Ross sat down in the firebreak, removed his sandals, shook out some loose dirt, painstakingly strapped them back onto the wrong feet, then corrected the problem.

I heard Scott's voice over Pam's radio. "I just saw some quail fly out of a burning bush."

As Pam worked, I asked how the spotover had started. She guessed that a wind shift had carried embers into the top of a twenty-foot snag—in this case a hollow, dead sweetgum. After the top of the snag had caught fire, embers dropped onto the ground, igniting the grass and leaf litter. Now the snag was aflame at the base too, and the top was smoking like a chimney. "The good thing is," she said, "if the flames reach the bog, there'll be too much moisture to carry the fire."

Moving quickly, Pat emerged from the burn and strode across the firebreak toward us. He first asked if we were all right and then said, "Scott and I are gonna wrap this burn up. We'll be done in fifteen minutes. Afterward we'll deal with this snag."

I was impressed with his surety that the burn would be over quickly. To me, the fire and smoke at the other end of the zone looked like a seething cauldron. I cleared my throat and said, "The fire there is looking pretty hot."

Pat nodded. "Yes, we did what we wanted to do out there." He took a drink of water and gestured to the spotover. "But it doesn't matter how much you think you know. You can't be cocky or complacent because a lawsuit will kill you. You have to patrol. I mean, we're lucky to be in a controlled environment on this property. Spotovers take energy and manpower away from the task at hand. You've got to stop igniting and jump into suppression mode."

Little Ross was safe in the firebreak, so I asked if I could help. Pat told me to get a shovel out of the truck, pointed to a burning log that lay in the spotover, and asked me to bury the log with dirt. Then he headed back to finish the burn with Scott.

I got the shovel. Because the ground in the spotover was root-bound, I was thankful for the soft, disked dirt of the firebreak. It made shoveling easy. Before tackling the log, I pitched dirt onto flames that were flaring up everywhere. Then I carried shovelful after shovelful of dirt across the spotover to bury the log, keeping an eye on the nearby snag in case it started to fall. When I was done, the twelve-foot log was interred in a mound.

"We'll be done in about three minutes," Scott said over Pam's radio. Right on schedule he emerged from the smoldering woods carrying his drip torch. He walked to the back of the truck, opened a cooler, and dug through the ice for a cold bottle of water.

Pat arrived. The lines of his face were grimed in smoke. Behind him ashes drifted like snowflakes. The ground was barely smoking. Now that the flames had subsided, the scene was quiet.

Pat and Scott joined us to quell the spotover. The snag finally fell, snapping off about two feet above the ground. Blue smoke rolled off the log. There was fire inside and along the trunk, which now lay in some duff. Scott attacked the log with a big yellow bladder of water. Later he and Pat tied a rope around the snag and pulled it back toward the firebreak.

WE HAD THREE MORE SPOTOVERS that day, all along the firebreak. None was as bad as the first. I continued to pitch in. At the second spotover, Pam introduced me to a council rake, a tool with four sharp triangular teeth or blades. "If you keep the blades sharp, they will chop through roots. It's really quite functional. Of course, it can't replace a shovel or a Pulaski."

I worked the edge of the spotover, raking fuel away from the fire. I was happy the teeth of the council rake were sharp because the ground was a mat of shallow roots. Hacking through briers and raking down to bare soil, however, was slow going. Since I was not wearing Nomex pants, I was careful where I stepped.

Working the same spotover, Pat paused to correct my technique. "Rake the leaves back into the ring of fire. Otherwise you might rake embers into new fuel and spread the flames."

We worked side by side and talked as we worked. "We've been burning out here quite a while, and these are the worst spotovers we've had." On average, fire jumps the break about one in ten times, but this spring had been unusually dry. "An ember can blow over and sit in the bushes for an hour before it catches. When it does, fire spreads out in a teardrop shape," he said, explaining the method for extinguishing a spotover. "You need to start on the back and the sides, pinch it out at the top, and contain it. Once it burns the available fuel, it calms down."

"The area we've edged is still smoldering," I said. "Are you worried that if the wind picks up tonight, it'll start another fire?"

"Tonight the humidity will increase so that if a fire does rekindle, it'll just creep along. Still, Scott and Mike will keep an eye on it. We're creating a firebreak around it now down to mineral soil so it can't creep out."

He stopped work to answer his cell phone. "Yes. We're finishing up right now. Yep. Out shortly. You're welcome, ma'am." He turned to me. "That was county dispatch. Somebody saw the smoke, rode by, and saw the flames. They were concerned, so they called 911. They're doing the right thing," he added. "On a Category 5 day like today," he continued, "you have the best conditions for a burn."

"And the most risky?"

"It can be. I've been burning with Scott so long, we kind of know what each other is doing. If I'm working with a new crew and on a Category 3 day or above, I'm looking for the fire to spotover."

"If the spotover had gotten out of control, what would have burned?"

"If the fire had burned into that drain," he said, gazing at the bog, "it would have petered out. It's pretty wet down there."

"What if we had not been able to extinguish a spotover?"

"If we couldn't have contained it, I would have called 911. I'm not that proud."

"If you call 911, what are the consequences? Do they bill you?"

Pat said that when he submitted a burn plan, he could ask the Forestry Commission to attend the burn and stand by in case something went wrong, "but they charge you for that. If a ranger is not at the burn and the fire gets out of control, I call 911. The fire department comes and puts the fire out. There's no cost." No cost, that is, except to Pat's reputation and livelihood.

"One bad thing about calling them," Pam added, "is that they won't suppress it by hand as we did" with bladders of water and shovels and minimal damage to the landscape. "They'll come in and plow around it," creating a firebreak but also uprooting trees and disturbing the soil.

"I have a good relationship with the county fire marshal," Pat said. "I've had outreach with them and had some of their volunteers come out and stand by with a brush truck," a four-wheel drive fire engine with firefighting equipment and a two-hundred-gallon water tank. "I get the benefit of their services, and since they mostly deal with structural fires and don't know why we do prescribed burns, they get a free education. It's a win-win situation."

In response to the concerned citizen's call to 911, Mac McLeod, a warden with the Fire Commission, pulled up in a big ten-wheel International truck towing a bulldozer on a flatbed just as we were squelching the last spotover.

We shook hands as Pat introduced us. "Mac lives right around the corner, not even a mile away. He's a local farmer and one of our county rangers."

Mac was affable and not visibly concerned. Wearing a purple tennis shirt and khaki slacks, he appeared dressed more for a round of golf. "A neighbor called me," he said. "The guy was worried that the fire was coming his way. I called dispatch and asked what tract was burning. When she told me, I said, 'That's Pat Ferral's burn, but I'll go over and check.'" Turning to me, he said, "I don't worry too much about these guys, but if I hadn't come and something happened, that would be bad. We have trouble sometimes when people are doing controlled burns along a property line where they don't own the land next to them. Here, if fire does spotover, it isn't likely to hurt anybody else's property. Even under the best conditions, though, we might be here with four bulldozers and the fire could still get away from us."

"It happens," Pat said. "We had a handful today. Embers were landing up in snags, finding dead spots, catching fire, and dropping to the ground. There was about an hour-and-a-half lag before the spotover got going. The fire behavior in the spotovers wasn't that bad, though. An ember would land in fuel and flare up, but the fire would just creep along. It didn't take ten minutes to get this one contained. I wouldn't conduct a burn on a Category 5 day if I didn't know the land well," he added.

I joked that I was hoping to get some kind of certification so Pat would have to pay me.

"That takes six or eight fires," Mac laughed. "Before that you gotta give him free labor."

Pat thanked Mac for coming. We loaded our tools into the back of Pat's truck, and I said goodbye to Scott, Mike, and Little Ross.

It was still early afternoon, and the day was sunny. Pat and Pam gave me a lift back to the Citgo station and my Jeep. On the way, Pat talked about job satisfaction. "It's good to have repeat clients. I get to come back, burn subsequent times, and see the change in the landscape. I don't feel like a hired gun. I feel some ownership. This is my work. As a wildlife biologist, I'm making a difference in the quail and wild turkey population. It makes me feel good."

NOTES

1. William F. Jacobs, "The Dixie Crusade," *American Forests* 84 (December 1978), 18.

2. Cecil Frost, "History and Future of the Longleaf Pine Ecosystem," in *The Longleaf Pine Ecosystem: Ecology, Silviculture, and Restoration*, ed. Shibu Jose, Eric J. Jokela, and Deborah L. Miller (New York: Springer, 2006), 30.

3. Ibid., 14–15.

4. Ibid., 13.

5. Charles C. Mann, *1491: New Revelations of the Americas Before Columbus* (New York: Knopf, 2005), 249.

6. Frost, "History and Future of the Longleaf Pine Ecosystem," 15.

7. Mann, *1491*, 250–51.

8. Aldo Leopold, "'Piute Forestry' vs. Forest Fire Prevention," http://www.nps.gov/seki/naturescience/upload/leopold20.pdf (accessed September 26, 2012).

9. Curt Meine, *Aldo Leopold: His Life and Work* (Madison: University of Wisconsin Press, 1991), 217.

10. Frost, "History and Future of the Longleaf Pine Ecosystem," 34–35.

11. See http://www.state.sc.us/forest/bfaq.htm#11 (accessed October 25, 2008).

12. Adam Latham, "South Carolina State Forest Policy," unpublished manuscript, 2003.

13. Margaret Katherine Trani, "Key Findings in 'Terra-1: Terrestrial Ecosystems,'" http://www.srs.fs.usda.gov/sustain/draft/terra1/terra1.htm (accessed October 25, 2008).

14. "Smoke Management Guidelines for Vegetative Debris Burning for Forestry, Agriculture, and Wildlife Purposes in the State of South Carolina," http://www.state.sc.us/forest/smg05.pdf (accessed October 25, 2008).

15. "How to Have a Firewise Home," www.state.sc.us/forest/hthafh.htm (accessed October 25, 2008).

Quail in a Longleaf Pine Habitat

"Look at a longleaf savanna that's seventy or eighty years old.
In my mind, there's nothing prettier."

Barclay McFadden, landowner

IT WAS JANUARY 29, and South Carolina was in the first cold snap of the winter. At 7:00 A.M. it was six degrees below freezing and windy when I stepped out of the house for a long drive to Scotswood Plantation. There I would meet Judy Barnes, wildlife biologist with South Carolina's Department of Natural Resource's Small Game Project, and Craig McFadden, manager of Scotswood, a 3,250-acre tract in the lowcountry.

The sky was wintry blue. Ditches along Route 401 were etched with ice, and power lines glistened orange in the sun. Two hours and one cup of gas station cappuccino later, I neared Lane, South Carolina. On either side of the road, loblollies grew in crop rows. The healthier stands were open and showed signs of prescribed burns. The less well-tended were weedy and suffocating, the typical snarl of roadside thickets we often see on drives in the country.

I drove over several flat concrete bridges across wetlands and swamps. Several miles outside of Lane, a white fence and two brick pillars announced the entrance to Scotswood. Atop each pillar was a cement Labrador retriever.

The drive to the house was gravel and bordered with magnolias and live oaks, some young and newly planted, others old with sprawling, massive limbs. Little resurrection ferns grew on the lower limbs. It must have rained recently; the ferns were green. On the right lay a clear-cut field. The ground was wet and muddy. Farther off stood some pines. A network of deep, water-filled ditches drained the property. As the drive curved past a horse pasture and approached the main house, the oaks became even larger and more ancient.

I parked in the shade of a live oak near some white pickup trucks, an old sway-roofed shed, and a small house that appeared to be under construction,

Quail thrive in the longleaf ecosystem. Prescribed fire helps maintain an early successional habitat on the forest floor in the midst of a mature forest. Photograph courtesy of Dr. William Alexander.

perhaps as a future guest or caretaker's house. Wind rattled the shed. Nearby was a green pond with a little cement alligator at the water's edge.

Beyond a vined archway, azaleas, camellias, and lawn stood the main house, single-story, white, and built of wood and brick. Five or more chimneys rose from its green metal roof. The main structure appeared to have been added on to more than once. A circular saw whined. Carpenters were at work remodeling the house. Because of the young live oaks and magnolias and the carpenters, the whole place had the feeling of regeneration, of a plantation being remade.

I was early for my meeting. I stepped outside of my Jeep and into the biting wind, shivered, and downed what was left of my coffee before the wind sucked all the heat out of it. After a few minutes a workman exited the house and walked toward a truck. I approached and said that I was there to meet Craig McFadden. He told me that Craig might be at a barn down the road, adding that Craig drove a white truck.

After climbing back into my Jeep, I drove down the dirt road, past a fenced pasture where a roan and a gray mare grazed, to several buildings that sheltered tractors, tools, fuel, bags of grass seed, farm equipment, four-wheelers, a bass boat, a horse trailer, and hoppers. Outside the buildings a white truck was parked. No one was around.

A couple of deer antlers lay on a bench. One was an eight-point, a rack I would have been proud to hang on my wall. A clutter of more antlers lay on a low-sloping roof. All were sun-bleached. I wondered whether the deer had been shot or had died of natural causes and someone had found the antlers in fields.

Behind the sheds was a silo. Hung like a necklace around it were forty gourds drilled with holes for purple martins. Purple martins, believed to be mosquito eaters, more often feed on beetles, butterflies, grasshoppers, and dragonflies. Because I hate mosquitoes, I love dragonflies. Once, camped on the beach at Shired Island in Florida, my wife and I were happy to see scores of dragonflies feasting on mosquitoes at the edge of the maritime forest.

At the edge of Scotswood's meadow sat more trailers, tillers, and equipment. The other side of the road had been Bush Hogged. All that remained of the brush were short sharp stems that stabbed out of the ground like Punji stakes.

I waited. After a minute a white truck whizzed by. A black Labrador with a red collar stood on a tool chest in the bed of the truck. Despite the truck's speed and the bumps in the road, the Lab never lost its footing. I waved, but the driver seemed in a hurry.

I got back into my Jeep and returned to the house just as a white truck arrived. In the truck was wildlife biologist Meg McElveen. Two years earlier I had met both Meg and Judy Barnes at a meeting of the S.C. Prescribed Fire Council.

Soon Judy drove up in a green DNR Chevy Blazer. A moment later Craig McFadden walked up with Barclay McFadden, the plantation's owner. Though Barclay and Craig shared the surname, they weren't related, except in their commitment to restoring longleaf pines. At Barclay's heels was a German shorthaired pointer. We all shook hands and walked toward the home's brick patio. I was especially glad to meet Barclay—I had not known that he would be at the outing.

Outside the doorway to the house, a basket brimmed with more antlers and big longleaf pinecones. The door knocker was a brass boar's head. Barclay invited us inside. The interior was ranch-style: wood floors, spacious kitchen, ample windows. On the wall of the entrance hall hung two framed shipping documents from the early 1930s when George H. McFadden and Brothers had been cotton brokers in Philadelphia.

In the living room hung a life-size portrait of Barclay reclining in a leather easy chair, a yellow Labrador at his side. Behind him in the painting, a big window looked out over a white-fenced pasture and horses. Next to the chair a small table was stacked with books, the largest entitled *Bobwhite Quail.*

Off the entrance hall was a small room painted hunter's green. In one corner a stone fireplace; in another, a Browning gun safe. Above the door, the head of a red fox. On the back wall, a bobcat taxidermically caught in a snarling leap. Under a gun table, a dog bed. On the mantel above the fireplace, small bottles of seeds—beggarweed and bicolor. Also on the mantel, a stuffed quail, one foot held breast high, palm up, with the middle toe extended—a shot bird shooting a bird. On the wall above the gun table, a map of Scotswood was stuck with colored pins that fixed the known locations of coveys of quail.

Standing at the map Judy, Barclay, and Craig debated the efficacy of game maps and call counts. To locate and estimate quail populations, call counts may be conducted in the spring, when males vie for mates, or in the autumn, when the birds form coveys.

"A lot of landowners do call counts," said Barclay. "We don't, but during the fall shuffle when the birds covey-up after breeding season, we get to know most every covey on Scotswood, and we peg these locations on the map. If we see a covey at one end of a field one week and a covey at the other end the next week, it's quite possibly the same covey. On the map we wouldn't peg those as two coveys unless we saw them on the same day. Each covey has an area it hangs around and an escape cover it runs to when a hawk or a hunter approaches. Unless you're between the birds and their cover, they fly pretty much in the same direction, so you know when a covey is going to fly north, south, east, or west."

Judy agreed that mapping the locations of coveys was a good idea. "Having a map of where you see coveys, marking down how many birds you see that day and where you see them in a given year—over time, that really helps. It also helps to note the habitat they're in. That habitat might be extended throughout the property."

Leaving the warmth of the house, the five of us stepped out into the wind and cold and got inside Judy's SUV. Judy drove, Barclay rode shotgun and gave directions, and Craig, Meg, and I sat in the back.

Barclay loved mature longleaf forests, and he intended to reestablish one. But he also loved to hunt quail, and quail need early successional habitats. Fortunately these were not rival affections. Frequent prescribed burning is one way to achieve an early successional habitat on the ground within a maturing forest. The seeming paradox of an old-growth forest towering above a young-growth habitat that supports many species reminded me of a poem by Gary Snyder:

> A virgin
> Forest
> Is ancient; many-
> Breasted. . . .[1]

"Turn left here," said Barclay as we drove down a dirt road into the plantation and past a stand of longleaf saplings. We stopped at a field. "Our plan is to return everything to longleaf savanna. We work on reducing the hardwoods, on harvesting the loblolly. Thirteen years ago we clear-cut this field and flipped the sod over with a bulldozer" to suppress weed competition. "Then we planted longleafs."

Barclay looked at the woods with pride, and he had a right to be proud. "The longleafs in this field have the highest survival rate we've ever seen, maybe 90 percent with bare root," that is, with seedlings bought with exposed roots.

Historically, writes James P. Barnett, "longleaf pine was often not chosen for reforestation because high mortality showed it to be very difficult to establish using bare-root seedlings and, even if survival was acceptable, many seedlings remained in the grass stage for extended periods. More recently, longleaf has been shown to survive well and begin height growth quite rapidly if seedlings are planted properly. Successful regeneration with bare-root seedlings requires healthy, fresh planting stock and precision planting on a well-prepared site."[2]

"My goodness," remarked Barclay, "we'll have to go back in and thin the longleafs."

"How many times have you burned here?" asked Meg.

"Close to every year. We need to thin some hardwoods out of here too. Sweetgums are probably our number one enemy."

"They are," said Judy.

"Everywhere," Meg agreed.

"We spent a good part of last summer spraying," said Barclay. "We're not just getting rid of sweetgums but also post oaks, blackjack oaks, hickory"—any hardwoods that might form a midstory to threaten the longleaf habitat. "We usually leave the cypress in the bottomlands," said Barclay, "because Jane, my wife, likes the way they look."

"Of course," said Judy, "the goal is not to eliminate every hardwood. If deer and wild turkeys interest you, mast producers are essential."

Barclay commented that the lowcountry was "overrun with deer." Meg acknowledged that "Williamsburg County is crawling with deer," and they both agreed that the population needed to be culled. With this in mind, Barclay had leased his land to a hunting club, hoping it would harvest a hundred does per year.

I wondered about the impact of deer on quail populations.

"Deer eat everything that quail eat," said Judy. "Take sunflowers—deer won't let the plant get to the flowering stage. When sunflowers sprout, deer graze them down. You'll see just stems up and down the rows. I'm excited that Barclay tries to take out a hundred deer per year."

According to Barclay, the trouble is that most hunters want only trophy bucks.

I said that I hunted for meat first, then remembered I hadn't put any venison on the table the past hunting season. My time would have been better spent foraging for roots and berries.

Judy asked how much of Scotswood had been converted from loblolly to longleaf.

"Sixty percent," said Barclay.

Forests of loblolly, shortleaf, and slash pine all support quail, but longleaf "is better suited for quail management." Because mature longleafs have "sparse crowns," more sunlight hits the forest floor, which means more herbaceous ground cover. Longleafs are also less prone than other southern pines to disease, insect blight, and windthrow; and their seeds are nutrient-rich and "highly preferred by quail."[3]

We turned down another dirt road and drove past a flock of wild turkeys in a meadow. Barclay looked back over the seat. "There were forty turkeys on that corner yesterday, Craig. They all took off at once."

"That is so great," said Judy. "I tell the landowners I work with, 'If you manage for quail, you benefit all wildlife. Rabbits, songbirds, deer, turkeys—they all love early successional habitat."

Next we drove past a tract of dense, gnarled woods on our left, the kind of woods you often see along a country road, a woods untouched by burns and choked with understory, a woods where little sunlight penetrates to the floor. These woods were owned by a neighbor. "In thick stands like this," said Judy, "there's no green vegetation and nowhere for quail to nest. That's one reason for their decline over the past sixty years: the elimination of nesting and brood-rearing habitat."

I recalled wildlife biologist Laura Housh's assertion that probably "every endangered species is endangered because of habitat loss." According to the South Carolina DNR and the USFWS, quail populations are falling as much as 4 percent per year. Possible reasons are the use of pesticides and herbicides; the planting of close-growing, single-species pine plantations; the sowing of pasture grasses, which form carpets; the loss of native, warm-season grasses such as Indian grass, bluestem, and broomsedge, which grow in bunches; the loss of farmland to development; the conversion of small farms to mega farms; and the "resulting loss of 'edge' habitat such as field borders" and fence rows.[4] In addition fire ants prey on ground-nesting chicks.

A red-tailed hawk soared over the pines.

"I haven't seen many red-tails lately," remarked Craig.

Judy commented that red-tailed hawks are not a major threat to quail. "It's really the cooper's or sharp-shinned hawks that hunt quail. I'm not saying a red-tailed hawk doesn't take quail, but they can't maneuver like a sharp-shinned, which can fly through a pine stand like a little jet. Quail, however, are prey species. Predators eat them from the egg up to the adult. To secure a quail population, people put in food plots and lespedeza strips, but that's not sufficient. Quail nesting habitats have to be relatively safe. They don't like to nest where they're vulnerable."

Barclay mentioned that hardwood habitats encourage predators such as snakes and birds of prey. Judy agreed that "hardwoods do harbor black rat snakes and hawks," and both hunt quail. But cats—feral cats or house cats from homes nearby—can be a greater threat. "A hawk will kill a quail and eat it. That's what hawks do. But a cat will kill six, walk away, and leave them."

Urban development and wildland loss go hand in hand, and more houses mean more house cats. "Scientific studies actually show that each year, cats kill hundreds of millions of migratory songbirds." One American ornithologist, Dr. Stanley Temple, "estimates that 20–150 million songbirds are killed each year by rural cats" in Wisconsin alone.[5]

Before we drove on, Judy looked again at the dark, impenetrable woods on the left. Even though the sun was climbing and the day bright, little light sifted onto the floor, which was a tangled mess of brown needles, leaves, branches, and fallen logs—an underworld of perpetual dusk. Even in summer there would be no grasses, no forbs, nothing green on the ground. "Deer would have trouble getting through there," she said, then added, "There's not much food at all."

On our right beyond a ditch and a bank of switchgrass, Barclay's forest was regenerating. Hundreds of longleaf pines were in the grass and sapling stages; and though the taller pines were not four feet in diameter or three hundred years old, the grassy, open pine savanna gave a hint of the old longleaf forests of the South.

Barclay said that "this is a mixture of planted and volunteer longleaf," volunteers being those seedlings that were not planted. At first glance the pine woods looked like prime quail habitat—tall grass interspersed with pines. "It should be a gorgeous woods for quail, but we don't have many birds back here," he lamented.

We parked and got out. "This is an area of Indian grass, bluestem, and broomsedge," said Judy. "To us, it may look good, but we need to walk through the grass and see what it looks like at ground level. What does a chick see, a chick that stands two inches tall? When chicks hatch, hens want to take them to a place with a lot of grasshoppers and crickets. If the grass is thick, will the chicks be able to maneuver through it?"

Judy knelt to examine the grass. "Native bunchgrasses are sparse at ground level but thick at the top." The sparseness allows chicks to forage and flee. The overhanging thickness provides cover from predators. "But grasses can grow together," reducing ground-level openness. Over time the bunchgrasses here had grown thick and now provided few open areas for ground birds to forage or flee from predators. "Kind of thick in here," she concluded, standing. "Running a fire through here will knock the grass back, but sometimes you might have to disk, clean it out, and make the ground bare. When you burn and disk at the right time of year, you stimulate the growth of new vegetation," creating, even in a mature forest, the early successional understory that quail favor.

Craig agreed and said that to "knock back the grass" he sometimes pulled a drag or harrow behind a skidder through the woods. "It does a pretty good job."

"Just make sure you disk between late November and early March," said Judy. "That way you'll keep out a lot of plants you don't want, noxious plants such as sicklepod, rattlebox, coffeeweed, and chocolateweed, which don't benefit wildlife. Disking in November and December will give you legumes. Disking in February and March will give you grasses. Most of the time when you disk, you'll have broomsedge first. If you're lucky, you'll get the other grasses and legumes because their seeds are in the soil."

I remembered that the Red-cockaded Woodpecker Recovery Plan of the U.S. Fish and Wildlife Service recommended a basal area of forty to sixty square feet per acre. For trees, basal area is defined as "the area of the cross section" measured at breast height "of a single tree, or of all trees in a stand."[6] I wondered what the basal area of this open acre of forest might be.

"Maybe a forty- or fifty-square-foot basal area," Judy guessed.

I asked if that ratio was good for quail as well as red-cockaded woodpeckers.

"Oh yeah," she said.

For good quail habitat, added Craig, "you need 50 percent of the sunlight to hit the forest floor."

"If you're only after timber," said Judy, "your basal area has to be higher; and for some landowners, timber revenue is very important. But in a forest with an 80- to 120-square-foot basal area, you won't have much wildlife. You won't have quail. A compromise for timber production and improved quail and wildlife habitat would be a 60- to 75-square-foot basal area."

We got back in Judy's vehicle, glad to be out of the icy wind if even for a minute. I wondered about Scotswood's quail population, about the yearly covey counts that Barclay and Craig conducted.

"In 1992," said Barclay, "we had 25 to 30 coveys." A typical covey has from 8 to 20 birds. "Since then we've had as high as 130 coveys," possibly 1,820 birds. "This year we're close to 100."

"You have to feel good about that," I said.

"Yeah," he laughed, "but we want more."

"The range of a covey is usually 40 acres," said Judy, "but the range can be much smaller if the birds have everything they need. The size of the range depends on how far they have to go to nest, to take their brood for a high protein diet, and to find protection. Many times landowners consider only what birds need during hunting season. But Mr. McFadden is providing year-round habitat, which is critical. If you provide that, the home range can be much smaller."

I asked how many coveys a well-managed forty-acre range might support.

"We've gotten away from numbers," replied Judy. "So much depends on soil and management. People used to focus on planting food plots or strips of bicolor," a lespedeza in the pea family. Although quail eat the bicolor seed, the plant does not attract insects or provide nesting habitat. "People would worry, 'I should have X number of coveys. Why don't I?' You can't hang success on one thing, for example, food plots," she advised. "Focus on the habitat."

"Judy doesn't want to talk about numbers," Barclay said, smiling, "but we're probably at .6 or .7 birds per acre. One year we had almost one bird per acre. Sometimes we were finding three coveys per hour."

I asked if quail were ever translocated to increase their population.

"The only way DNR would get involved in translocating quail," said Judy, "is if we knew for a fact—if we had been out to look at a landowner's property—that there had been a real effort to create habitat." An absence of wild birds may demonstrate "that there are components missing in the habitat." A translocation would be doomed.

We drove past a recently burned section of woods where the grass was more quail-friendly and not so thick, then stopped at an area of mixed longleaf and scrub oak. Barclay pointed to young post oaks. "This is one area we desperately need to spray. The logging operation knocked down a lot of the scrub oaks, but they're coming back. The area is rife with small hardwoods."

I recalled the observation of Dr. Van Lear of Clemson University that scrub oaks are "tenacious sprouters."

We motored past a dome of mature oaks and stopped at a nine-acre section that looked like a prairie of grass and longleaf. Barclay commented that they had harvested pulpwood from the area. "Got all the loblolly out, most of the hardwoods."

"Sprayed it with Garlon and Chopper to control the sweetgums," Craig added.

"We're trying to control the sweetgums with fire," said Barclay. "Our goal is to burn half to two-thirds of Scotswood every year so we can keep our ground cover checkerboarded. But if we don't use fire and herbicides each year to control the sweetgums, they get out of control and we have to cut them down, which is ridiculously expensive. If all Scotswood looked like this," he added, "we'd be pretty happy."

Judy agreed. "This is what you want it to look like."

"Yeah," said Craig. "It is real pretty when you're looking west and the sun's setting and all you can see is pines and grass."

"I know we have at least two coveys in here, possibly three," said Barclay. "In years past we've had three. And the briers have arrived too."

I asked if quail like blackberries.

"Yes," said Judy, "blackberry and plum thickets are good when quail are nesting. You don't want three thousand acres of briers, but scattered thickets. That's usually where the birds will try to nest. Hens get an energy boost from sugar in the berries and then go back and sit on their nests all afternoon."

Meg agreed. "Berries are an excellent source of carbohydrates."

As is ragweed. Barclay said that Jerald Sholar, a wildlife biologist with Tall Timbers Research Station in Tallahassee, had toured Scotswood earlier. "When Sholar visited, he asked, 'Where's your ragweed?' We planted about 150, 200 acres of it, and we'll be up to—how much ragweed this year, Craig?"

"Around 250 acres."

"Excellent," said Judy.

"Last August Craig phoned me from the field and said, 'There are so many quail calling out here we can't hear ourselves talk.' In part, I think it was because of the ragweed explosion. Then one afternoon during nesting season, we got four inches of rain. I don't know if Craig cried, but—"

Craig laughed and shook his head.

"—it flooded everything. Every nest drowned out." Barclay estimated that Scotswood lost over half of its quail population in that storm. Still, he believed that the quail calls before the flood proved that ragweed is a bonanza for them.

Ragweed seems designed for quail. "One great thing about it is its structure," said Judy. The stiff stalks leave the ground open for foraging. The leafy canopy conceals chicks from hawks. Ragweed is a good source of winter seeds. What's more, it attracts insects, essential protein for the covey.[7] "Planting native vegetation—" mused Judy. "I'm really excited about the ragweed."

We continued driving along a deep ditch, then parked at a dirt crossroads near the corner of adjacent fields. Barclay recalled that the ditches paralleling the roads had not always been so deep. "When we first bought Scotswood, there were wonderful hedge rows by the ditches, but the ditches had all filled in. We had to cut away the trees and clean out the ditches with a track hoe."

The terrain of Scotswood, Craig said, is low and often wet. Keeping drainage open is difficult. "When the ditches get real trashy, we Bush Hog. Then we burn them, try to knock back the sweetgum and persimmon."

Scotswood, Barclay said, had joined the USDA's Conservation Reserve Program, which works to reduce soil erosion, promote the production of food and fiber, improve water quality and wildlife habitat, plant native grasses and trees, and create filter strips and riparian buffers.

"First we planted filter strips that were 99 feet wide" along the ditches, "but we didn't get the quail we wanted on the strips. We expanded them to 150 feet wide," Barclay said and then turned to Craig. "How many miles of these filter strips do we have?"

"Seven or eight."

"We have miles and miles of what should be wonderful quail habitat, but quail are not happy here."

"Well," said Craig, "they're not happy here when we want them here. Summertime I can ride these roads and see little chicks. The quail may be happy here in the summer, but when we come to hunt, we might find one covey down each ditch bank. I actually saw a quail making a nest last spring," he added. "I was disking a strip and I saw the bird fly out. I went to the nest.

She was just getting it built. I guess I was so anxious and went to the nest so much over the next several days to see when she would lay eggs that she abandoned it."

"The key is nesting habitat," Judy said as we stepped out of the SUV again into the frigid wind. "You can put food out here, but if the quail don't build nests and have young, it won't matter." She led us to the corner of a field, where she knelt by some broomsedge and brushed away debris from under a bunch of grass. "This is how they build nests. They dig all this out at the base, then bend the stems over. What quail prefer is the old and the new, the brown and the green, a little camouflage."

Meg noted the presence of foxtail, another seed plant on the quail menu.

To make the quail happy and restore Scotswood's longleaf pine ecosystem, Barclay and Craig have sown native, warm-season grasses. "Last year," Barclay told Judy, "we disked a strip through here and planted bluestem, but we can't tell if it is coming up. Maybe it takes more than a year."

"It does," said Judy. "Bluestem takes two years, minimum. Maybe three. It's like longleaf. You have to baby it, be patient. But once it gets here, you won't have to worry about a drought. One man who planted bluestem kept telling me, 'Judy, it's not growing. I guess I'll disk it under.' I said, 'Please wait,' and after three years he had the most beautiful field of bluestem."

Barclay asked if the bluestem would "spread out into the field and the ditch bank, push out the broomsedge."

Judy answered that it would expand, but "if it did outcompete the broomsedge, you haven't lost anything. For quail habitat, bluestem is as good or better than broomsedge. Still, bluestem is not that competitive. It also grows well with Indian grass. What's so great about these native plants—ragweed, beggarweed, partridge pea, bluestem, Indian grass—is that regardless of how cold it gets, regardless of drought, they keep coming back. They may not be as succulent, they may not be as thick, but they hang on."

"And you can broadcast Indian grass," said Meg. "Marion County rents a seed drill that plants seeds one quarter of an inch deep, which is the deepest you want to plant. Usually a combination of bluestem, Indian grass, and switchgrass does well, along with a legume such as partridge pea or beggarweed."

"The USDA, Natural Resources Conservation Service, and Farm Service Agency have a number of cost-share programs that are useful in improving habitat," Judy informed me. "That's why Meg is here. She is a DNR wildlife biologist working out of an NRCS office, and she provides technical assistance to landowners. The state DNR has a number of habitat programs. Lots of landowners are involved. Meg can help, and by assisting you she's assisting wildlife."

We climbed back in Judy's vehicle and drove past a pine woods.

"This is all natural longleaf through here," said Barclay. "We thinned it out two summers ago. For Scotswood, this is relatively high ground. It's a pretty woods," he reflected, adding, "We have an RCW colony in there."

Craig pointed to a red-cockaded woodpecker cavity tree, marked by a ring of white paint.

Judy asked how many RCW clusters Scotswood had.

"Five," said Barclay. "We put in some artificial cavities, but I don't think any were successful. We may have lost a cluster. We haven't had any recruitment."

I said I knew a man who hunted his own land and who told me that if he saw an RCW on his property, he'd kill it.

"That was the mind-set of many landowners for years," Judy replied, "because they felt they couldn't sell their timber. Landowners did not want to report RCWs. They did not want anyone to see clusters" and did not want new nest cavities to be excavated. "But after Hurricane Hugo, we lost so many RCWs. The DNR had to do something to save the birds, so they implemented the Safe Harbor program."

Safe Harbor "features legal assurances that land management restrictions will not be imposed on private landowners should those landowners partake in conservation measures designed to help an endangered species."[8] Judy and Barclay explained the application of Safe Harbor with respect to endangered red-cockaded woodpeckers. "A landowner can choose how many clusters or RCW families he wants on his property," said Judy. "Say he has zero and doesn't want any. If an RCW comes in, we remove it."

"For example," Barclay said, "if I've agreed to have three RCWs but a fourth comes in and I want to cut timber around it, I call DNR and they remove it. They save the birds, and I haven't lost the timber income."

Of course, conserving habitats for red-cockaded woodpeckers improves living conditions for quail, wild turkeys, deer, and dozens of other species. "I think South Carolina was one of the first states to have Safe Harbor," said Judy. "It's a model for other states, and it's a win-win for landowners."

As we drove away from that section of woods, Craig noted that the grass there was getting thick. "If we don't burn, it's gonna get thicker. The quail won't have anywhere to nest or run. And if we don't burn on a two-year rotation, we end up with a bunch of briers and loblollies we have to fight."

Because Craig had mentioned Garlon and Chopper earlier, I asked Judy if there was any advantage to using chemical or mechanical treatments instead of fire.

"We prefer fire," Judy answered, "but we understand that, as time goes on, we may have to use more chemicals because we won't be able to burn."

I asked if she was referring to the threat of smoke in urban areas.

"Yes. People don't understand burning. They don't know the advantages of fire. Some people are scared of it. But fire is a great management tool, and I hate that we're losing it."

"Sooner or later a woods is going to burn," said Barclay, reiterating the belief of many foresters. "It's just a question of when and how hot."

I asked Judy if she really believed that fire was being lost as a tool for managing forests.

"Definitely, definitely. I'm excited about the South Carolina Prescribed Fire Council. I think they'll make a difference. But it gets harder and harder to conduct burns. A lot of people are moving to South Carolina. They don't want smoke on their houses, in their yards. We don't want smoke on the highways."

It's the old dilemma. The more we alter an environment, the more we live in a world that we create, the less it resembles its former self. Rampant logging of longleaf forests and the suppression of healthy fires throughout most of the twentieth century resulted in the loss of native grasses and forbs and the intrusion of hardwood midstories. As urban areas expand, as prescribed burns diminish, as species-rich forests are traded for the botanical desert of loblollies grown in rows, we surrender the natural history of our landscape. If a settler or Native American were transported from the 1700s and plopped down in a contemporary southern landscape—or many New England, midwestern, or western ones—the place would likely be unrecognizable to him. Likewise when we travel, even through a remote, unpeopled region, we move through a landscape so altered that it takes a studied imagination to guess what it once might have looked like. After listening to Judy, I thought about forest restoration and wondered if a variation of the old traveler's joke was true, wondered if you can ever get back there from here. It was a depressing thought, and it made me respect the McFaddens' work all the more.

JUDY DROPPED US OFF at our vehicles. Before departing I shook hands with Barclay and asked why he cared about longleafs and quail.

"I love to hunt, love the experience of being out with bird dogs and riding horseback. I don't even need to shoot. I just like watching the dogs, watching my friends and family. More than that, it's a matter of aesthetics. Of finding a piece of property that's been damaged and returning it to what it was to begin with—in this case a longleaf broomsedge savanna. You've seen pictures of those old savannas. We don't have any of those original forests left in South Carolina, but look at a longleaf savanna that's seventy or eighty years old. In my mind, there's nothing prettier."

As I drove home, I thought of Barclay and Craig's work, and my mind flew north to the Midwest, back to the 1940s and Aldo Leopold's farm: "On this sand farm in Wisconsin, first worn out and then abandoned . . . we try to rebuild, with shovel and ax, what we are losing elsewhere."[9]

NOTES

1. Gary Snyder, "Toward Climax," in Snyder, *Turtle Island* (New York: New Directions, 1974), 82.

2. James P. Barnett cited by Dale G. Brockway, Kenneth W. Outcalt, and William D. Boyer, "Longleaf Pine Regeneration Ecology and Methods," in *The Longleaf Pine Ecosystem: Ecology, Silviculture, and Restoration*, ed. Shibu Jose, Eric J. Jokela, and Deborah L. Miller (New York: Springer, 2006), 114.

3. "Georgia's Stewardship Forests: Managing for Quail in Forested Habitats," http:/www.gfc.state.ga.us/Resources/Publications/ForestManagement/ManagingforQuail.pdf (accessed October 25, 2008).

4. See http://www.dnr.sc.gov/news/Yr2007/feb5/feb5_quail.html (accessed October 25, 2008).

5. See http://library.fws.gov/Bird_Publications/songbird.html (accessed February 21, 2009).

6. See http://www.arcticatlas.org/glossary/index (accessed October 25, 2008).

7. See http://www.quailrestoration.com/sneezeweed.html (accessed October 25, 2008).

8. Ben Ikenson, "Sanctuary for the Houston Toad," *U.S. Fish and Wildlife Service News* (Summer 2008): 22.

9. Aldo Leopold, *A Sand County Almanac* (New York: Oxford University Press, 1989), viii.

In Search of the Elusive White Wicky

"[It] is in these frequently burned ecotones that most
of the unusual species are found."

A Guide to the Wildflowers of South Carolina

LOST FORESTS. ENDANGERED SPECIES. When I first met Scott Lanier, manager of the Carolina Sandhills National Wildlife Refuge, I asked why we should care if longleaf pines disappeared or red-cockaded woodpeckers went extinct. "Why not let nature take its course?" The premise underlying the question, of course, is that human destruction of a natural habitat is a natural act. Not so. It's one thing when dinosaurs die off after an asteroid strikes Earth. It's another when the ice in Glacier National Park melts from petrochemically altered global weather.

We don't have to travel thousands of miles to find a species hanging on by slender roots or nature on the ropes. One warm spring morning, I rode with forester Clay Ware through the Carolina Sandhills NWR to a pocosin to hunt white wicky (*Kalmia cuneata*), an endangered flowering plant. A month earlier I'd tagged along with Clay on another foray to find the same plant. The wicky hadn't been in bloom, and we'd failed in the attempt.

Clay is fit and tanned, with a salt-and-pepper goatee and steady brown eyes. As we stepped out of his white truck, biting yellow flies swarmed us. I sprayed my neck and arms with Deep Woods Off!, which made me smelly and sticky. Clay went DEET-less. He must have known the flies would stay at the truck and not follow us into the pocosin.

"Pocosin" is an Algonquian word for a shrub bog or an upland swamp. In the Sandhills, pocosins are often spring-fed or stream-head depressions where dry, sandy pine forests give way to bowls of thick vegetation—difficult for humans to traverse but great places for whitetails to bed down. From the ridge I looked down into a green tangle of shrubs. The ground was a spongy peat carpeted with moss.

White wicky is an endangered flowering plant found only in a handful of counties in the coastal plain of the Carolinas. Like longleaf pine, wiregrass, switch cane, pitcher plants, and numerous other flora of the longleaf ecosystem, white wicky requires fire to survive. Photograph courtesy of Clay Ware.

"Beneath these rolling hills," said Clay, "are layers of clay." Even on sloping ground, the stratum of clay helps to keep water from draining into underground aquifers.

"Although we're on the ridge of the pocosin," he said, "the water level is still high. Most of our pocosins are spring fed, so there's a lot of seepage. Because the ground stays pretty wet all of the time, the organic matter in the ground doesn't decompose." Hence the peat.

"You get a different ecosystem along the edge of pocosins," Clay continued, pointing to a rare Atlantic white cedar and the dense understory of switch cane, inkberry, titi, red bay, gallberry, peatberry, sweet pepperbush, and blueberry—"*Vaccinium crassifolium.* We don't usually get much of it on the refuge. It's more of a coastal plant."

The fire crew had burned the pocosin a year ago. Already you couldn't cross it without a machete.

"During prescribed burns, we run fire down into the stream heads," he said. "You see how thick this is now. If you burn to set the other plants back, white wicky will keep on sprouting. If we don't burn, it will get choked out by all of the holly and red bay. White wicky requires fire. It puts the plants on equal footing and enables white wicky to survive."

According to *A Guide to the Wildflowers of South Carolina*, fire "often does burn into [a pocosin's] upland margins, and it is in these frequently burned ecotones that most of the unusual species are found."[1]

White wicky is found only in pocosins, "particularly stream-fed pocosins. In fact, white wicky exists only in Carolina Sandhill pocosins and is found in just two counties in South Carolina—Chesterfield and Darlington. We know of three sites on the refuge where it grows," said Clay.

As Clay searched for the flower, I asked if white wicky could be cultivated.

"From what I understand, people have tried, but it doesn't work out. White wicky's niche is usually on the high edge of pocosins. It's hard to maintain the moisture levels and soil type." A few feet higher or lower, the ground might be either too dry or too wet. "Also the plant blooms for such a short time, it doesn't appeal to people who want flowers in their gardens."

A few feet down into the pocosin, Clay showed me a small tree, a bluejack oak. "*Quercus incana.* Typically it's an indicator of a wetter site," he said, continuing to search the flora. "We're on the upper edge of the pocosin. This is where we'll find the white wicky, which occupies this ecotone. An ecotone is a transitional area between two different habitats," he explained. In this case the ecotone was between upland forest and stream-head pocosin.

He bent to show me some swamp azalea. "It has a whorled branch pattern similar to white wicky. Some people call it swamp honeysuckle." It did have a fragrance resembling honeysuckle's. "There's a lot of it here. Initially I thought it might be white wicky until I saw the bloom."

This was a rich ecotone. In contrast to the open, sandy, dryer upland, the pocosin was a vibrant green with waist-high vegetation. I noted that cinnamon ferns and sweet pepperbush certainly weren't endangered. "Sweet pepperbush comes on strong in the spring," Clay said. "It's deciduous. It'll die back in the winter." Still looking for white wicky, Clay pointed out sweet bay magnolia, its buds white and almost ready to bloom, as well as red bay and highbush blueberry. We ate a few of the berries. "Not much flavor to them," Clay remarked.

"Not bad," I said. "Tart."

Birds chirped overhead, maybe fretful that we were pillaging their pantry. I saw male-berry (*Lyonia ligustrina*), fetter-bush (*Lyonia lucida*), bracken fern, and smilax. "A very competitive zone," I said.

"A ton of different plants in here," Clay agreed. "I wish I knew 'em all."

"That was one of Adam's first jobs," I remarked, "to name each living thing." It occurred to me that Clay was aptly named, since "Adam" means "man of clay."

"Here's the white wicky," he said, stooping. "All of this right here." It was almost an undramatic moment. I had expected, I don't know, a billboard or something to announce it. Had I been passing by (unlikely because pocosins are not great hiking spots), I would hardly have noticed the diminutive, low-stemmed blossoms. But there they were, white penny-size flowers with thin red rings around their centers.

"No kidding," I said, then realized I was standing next to the three-foot-tall, slender woody stem of one of the more endangered plants on the planet. I was afraid I might step on it, trip, roll down the pocosin, and seriously damage the species's chance of surviving an encounter with clumsy me.

A bee as big as the flowers was working the blossoms. "Bees don't get this flavor often," said Clay. I wondered how white wicky honey would taste.

We were standing about four feet down the slope. There was a good crop of the plant here, scores of blossoms. Looking down into the pocosin, we could see that the vegetation grew even denser. "You won't find white wicky deeper in the pocosin," Clay said. "It needs water, but not too much. This is where it likes to be—on the upper edge."

On the edge. The phrase described the precariousness of white wicky's chances. Which is why it is important to protect stream-head pocosins and Carolina bays. Why it is important, as poet Gary Snyder said, to know the names of the plants where we live, to know what the soil and water do. And what the fire does too.

NOTE

1. Richard Dwight Porcher and Douglas Alan Rayner, *A Guide to the Wildflowers of South Carolina* (Columbia: University of South Carolina Press, 2001), 88.

Snake Cruising II

"Close your eyes and grab."

Kevin Messenger, herpetologist

IT WAS AN ODDLY COOL DAY for mid-May. The air was heavy and damp, and the sunset glowered a weird orange. I was motoring along Over-Flow Drive, a dirt back road to the Carolina Sandhills National Wildlife Refuge, for a second snake hunt with Kevin Messenger. This time members of the North Carolina State University Herpetology Club were joining us.

The wind whipped past as the sun set behind the woods. It felt good to be riding up to the refuge again with the rag top off my Jeep, and it would be good to ride with Kevin in his open Jeep too, talking and cruising into the night.

It had been a dry spring, with many days red-flagged for wildfire alerts by the S.C. Forestry Commission. Legions of leafy, breast-high turkey oaks swarmed some tracts of longleaf pine. One recently burned tract, however, smelled smoky and fragrant, like the bowl of my great-grandfather's pipe.

Entering the refuge and zipping along Wildlife Drive, I caught up with a compact sedan. A hand reached out of the open passenger window and waved. I followed the car a couple of miles to Kevin's house, the one on loan from the refuge. We parked, and Kevin and his friends Mike, Adrian, and Liani, carrying sandwiches and soft drinks from the Subway in McBee, piled out of their car. Nate, a fourth member of the team, soon arrived in a second car.

They kindly offered to share supper. I told them I'd eaten.

"You have to see inside the house," Kevin said. "The place doesn't look the same."

"You cleaned up?" I joked.

We stepped inside and were met by Adrian's dog. Remarkably the interior of the house was more of a wreck than it had been, and not just from Kevin's housekeeping. The refuge was remodeling. The carpet in the living room had been torn up, exposing more dingy gray linoleum. The walls were new, unpainted Sheetrock. Dust was everywhere.

If a home expresses the character of its tenant, this was no exception. The house was in transition, and so was Kevin. He'd taken his finals at N.C. State. In a week, three days after he graduated, he would board a plane to central China and the Shennongjia National Forest Reserve, where for four months he would survey snakes for Dr. Craig Stanford and the University of Southern California and for Dr. Li Yiming and the Zoology Institute and Chinese Academy of Sciences.

A couple of metal chairs stood with their backs to the kitchen wall. There must have been a kitchen table too, but everything was so stacked and cluttered with backpacks, camping gear, books, clothes, bottles, cans, and the detritus of college undergraduacy that I didn't see one. Although Kevin had not been accepted yet into grad school, he hoped to use his research in China for his master's thesis. Thumbtacked to a wall was an impressive poster outlining his research at the Carolina Sandhills NWR. The poster was a bare-bones draft of his future Ph.D. dissertation, he said.

I gifted him two of my favorite reads of late—Archie Carr's *The Windward Road* and Mark Plotkin's *Tales of Shaman's Apprentice*—books to leaf through on his trip to China. I laid them on a stack of other books next to an SOG sheath knife and a small Tupperware bowl. Sealed in the bowl was a single fang of a canebrake rattlesnake.

"I took it from a big roadkill. It's huge," Kevin said, popping off the lid and handing me the bowl.

The fang was beautiful, about three-quarters of an inch long. It looked like a tiny scimitar carved from ivory. I imagined that venom might still be lurking on it and handed the bowl back.

"Last September I came across a baby canebrake DOR [dead on the road] near the south end of Wildlife Drive," Kevin said. "I kept on driving. Six minutes later there was a fresh hit, a forty-nine-inch DOR canebrake. I pulled out one of the fangs to see how big it was."

While the others wolfed down their subs, Kevin delivered a minilecture on canebrake venom. "The tricky thing about canebrakes is that there are three venom types. Type A is the worst. Take Mojave rattlesnakes; they live out west and give one of the worst bites. While most pit vipers are only hemotoxic, Mojaves have a mix of hemotoxic and neurotoxic venom. Neurotoxic venom is what cobras and coral snakes have. The venom of a Type A canebrake is roughly 35 percent neurotoxin and 65 percent hemotoxin."

Kevin mentioned a man in the lowcountry of South Carolina who had been bitten by a canebrake but refused treatment. "He died in forty-five minutes. Probably a Type A canebrake." Unfortunately there's no visual way to tell what type of canebrake you may stumble across. "No physical clues. You can't tell until you take a venom sample and analyze it. We don't know if the type is controlled by genetics or by locality, although in some parts of South Carolina, you can have all three types. A Type B is your average canebrake, which still has a pretty bad bite. A Type C is less venomous than a copperhead."

Kevin took a big bite of his sandwich, then said, "I have something else to show you." From a back room he retrieved a pillowcase, knotted at the neck, and a pan and lid. He set the pan on the floor, removed the lid, untied the pillowcase, and dropped a cottonmouth into the pan. "We'll release her and hunt for more cottonmouths tonight." The snake wasn't large, maybe twenty inches, but it had everyone's attention and wasted no time breaching the pot's wall and serpentining across the floor. In my direction.

"I left my camera in my Jeep," I said, thinking this a convenient excuse to retreat. Wielding the lid like a shield, Kevin corralled the snake, which coiled enough for him to trap it under the lid.

By the time I reentered the kitchen, camera in hand, Kevin had coaxed the snake to crawl halfway up a transparent plastic snake tube. Kevin had snake tubes that ranged from the tiny diameter of a pygmy rattlesnake to that of a diamondback. This tube was a tight fit, but the snake had obliged, perhaps imagining the tube to be an escape route. With the business end of the snake inside the tube, Kevin could now measure, weigh, examine, and mark the snake without fear of retribution. This snake was a recapture, female cottonmouth number 26.

"I've caught her eleven times," said Kevin, standing in the light of the kitchen window. "The same night I bagged her, I caught another cottonmouth that I'd previously captured in 2002."

That night Kevin would also release two other cottonmouths, a pregnant four-foot brown water snake, a forty-two-inch copperhead, and some pigmy rattlers. He would divvy up these snakes for release among our three teams: Adrian and Liani, Mike and Nate, and Kevin and me.

Because Kevin usually worked alone, I mentioned that I was concerned for his safety that night. "You have a lot of people here. Do you feel we might be a distraction?"

"No, I give talks while I'm handling cottonmouths."

I added that I didn't want him to get snake-bit just before leaving for China. He agreed that would be bad. Adrian said that he didn't want Kevin to get bit in China either. Kevin agreed that would be worse.

THE SUN HAD SET. Outside Kevin divided up the pillowcased snakes and gave instructions on where to release them. We split up into the three cars. One team turned left out of the drive. The other turned right. Kevin and I waited a few minutes to get some distance between us and the car we would follow.

I noticed a GPS on the console between the seats of his Jeep. He said it was a new purchase that he would take to China. "Every time I find a snake, I'll note its GPS coordinates," then post its species and location on the Internet. Interested parties, using Google Earth, would be able to pinpoint the capture on a 3-D image of the terrain, which was rugged and mountainous.

From past experience I knew that Kevin was exact in the recording of his data. If he captured a snake at 8:59 P.M., he recorded it as such, not as 9:00 P.M. I asked how the addition of two more crews tonight might affect his data.

"This hunt happens only once a year," he said. "It's the N.C. State Herp Club hunt. We'll probably find a lot of snakes. Datawise the hunt won't be as valid, but it's gonna be fun. I can sacrifice one day out of the year for everybody to have fun."

I asked how he felt about the other teams capturing venomous snakes.

"Everybody's fully trained. Adrian is just as much of a herpetologist as I am, knows how to handle and respect snakes. Mike and Nate learned from Adrian and me. Liani is Adrian's fiancée."

"She has a vested interest in his safety, then."

Kevin started the Jeep, and we headed off to a lake where he would release the brown water snake. "Water snakes are the most predictable. You'll find other species of snakes throughout the night; but about 70 percent of water snakes, you'll find within thirty minutes of sunset. Sunset tonight was 8:08."

"Any speculation why their behavior is predictable?"

"Fish. Fishermen know the best times to fish are dusk and dawn. Snakes know that too."

Spying a sliver of white in the road, Kevin performed his usual skid to a stop, saying, "Pygmy." Well rehearsed, I tossed him a flashlight as he jumped from the Jeep. He knelt by the snake and asked me to bring him a pillowcase. When I did, he balled it up and placed it on top of the diminutive rattlesnake, which he then turned over to examine for cauterization. "Pygmy 242," he said, noting the marks. "It was probably born in August of last year."

I asked how he knew.

"Because of the size," which helped him make an educated guess, although he couldn't be certain. "Also the snake has only one button on his tail, so he's shed only once, maybe twice, in his life." Caching the snake in the pillowcase, Kevin placed it in the back of the Wrangler, and we drove toward the pond to release the brown water snake. After we'd arrived and parked, Kevin unbagged the brown water snake. It was big, pregnant, and irritable. Kevin stood in the tall grass of the bank at the pond's edge, one hand gripping the snake several inches behind the head, the other hand cradling the thick, writhing length nearer the tail. He said that last year, one brown water snake he captured had given birth in captivity to thirty-six babies. "Every now and then, if I catch a pregnant snake—copperhead, pygmy, whatever—in late July or early August, I'll keep it just to make sure it doesn't get hit by a car before it gives birth." Such a roadkill might result in thirty-seven deaths. "That would be a huge loss to the population." After the birth, he would release the mother and babies at the site of capture.

Because the brown water snake Kevin was releasing tonight was aggressive and could give a nasty bite, he treated it with nearly as much deference as he would a venomous snake, holding it at arm's length longer than he cared to while I snapped a photo. Then he knelt and placed it at the water's edge. It disappeared into the grass.

We got back into the Jeep. "I love the Sandhills because they're so isolated," he said. "You can be by yourself out here. You don't have all the traffic of Charlotte or Raleigh. I'm not a fan of big cities. And the snakes are incredible. I just love it. I like spending every hour down here. That's one reason I'm sad to go to China. I'll miss the Sandhills."

Taking out his infrared thermometer, he checked the air temperature. "Right now the temp is 69." The high today had been in the upper 70s; the predicted low was 65. He aimed the thermometer at the pavement and said, "The temp of the road isn't so hot either. Seventy-five degrees. Kinda cool."

A chuck-will's-widow crooned from the dark woods. I glanced above the trees to the sky. The moon was round. I asked about its phase.

"Ninety-six percent full."

"Ow," I said, remembering that in years past his data had indicated that snakes, perhaps fearing predation, traveled less during a full moon. This, coupled with the cooler-than-average temperatures, might affect the night's hunt.

Mike and Nate's headlights approached. We parked side by side and climbed out of our vehicles to compare inventories. Mike had released a pygmy and already captured two banded water snakes. Last month, Kevin said, Mike had scored the first documented red-bellied water snake on the refuge.

As we stood and talked, a truck arrived and parked on the shoulder by the pond. Two fishermen got out. After hellos, Mike showed everyone the water snakes. Kevin reminisced that "back in 2002 when I found 134 cottonmouths, I found only 5 or 7 percent on the road, and two of those cottonmouths were dead."

Spooked, the fishermen nervously eyed the tall grass, hoping to avoid what the N.C. State teams hotly pursued. Before the fishermen got out their poles and tackle boxes, they checked under their truck like kids looking for monsters beneath their beds.

Our teams parted, heading off in separate directions. It wasn't long before Kevin skidded to a stop, grabbed the flashlight, and jumped out. Taking his comp book from the glove box, I followed. Another pygmy. Kevin wondered aloud if this was the snake that Adrian or Mike had just released. He decided it was not.

"How can you tell?" I asked.

"His tail is less yellow, his stripe is bolder, and he looks slightly bigger." Walking back to his Jeep, Kevin said over his shoulder, "I'm going to grab a pillowcase. If you'll make sure he doesn't move—"

"And if he does, what then?"

"Stand in front of him."

"Stand in front of him," I repeated. Staring down at the little viper, I took half a step back.

Kevin returned and handed me the flashlight. "Shine the beam here." He wrapped the upper body of the snake in the pillowcase and checked the tail for cauterized scales. "No, he's not a recapture. He's new."

Headlights approached, and Adrian and Liani's car pulled up. Kevin asked if they had released their snakes. Adrian said yes through his open window. Eager to be on the hunt, they motored off again.

I handed Kevin his comp book. He took a pen from his pocket and asked me to retrieve the GPS from the Jeep. He entered the time, 8:48 P.M.; the species; the GPS way point; the direction the snake was headed, west; the air temperature, 68.5 degrees; the road temperature, 80.5 degrees; the location, just north of the "coachwhip parking lot"—so named, he said, because he had photographed a fifty-five-inch coachwhip there. "Just as I laid the camera down, the snake latched onto my nose."

I mentioned that the pavement was warmer here. Kevin said that farther down the road the temperature might be five degrees cooler, depending on factors such as sunlight and wind.

He pillowcased the snake, and we drove off. No more than a quarter of a mile away, we nabbed a third pygmy. When Kevin bagged this one, I noticed that he reached into his pocket and dropped three pennies into the pillowcase with the snake. "Back in 2004," he explained, "I caught eleven pygmies in one night. If I don't mark which bag is which, it's hard to remember, for example, which snake was the seventh or eighth capture." He recorded this pygmy's data in the comp book, and we drove off again.

It wasn't long before we saw the headlights of Mike and Nate's car. Mike slowed and rolled down his window. As he taxied past, he told Kevin that they'd captured a copperhead and a scarlet king snake.

As we accelerated, I asked Kevin if snakes often escaped his clutches when he saw them on the road.

"Maybe three or four a year. In an average year, I catch around 450 snakes."

I wondered if I could catch a snake, a nonvenomous one, on the road. After all, I had ridden with a good teacher. Kevin was as skilled a herpetologist as any I'd seen on TV. But could I, in the heat of the moment, identify a snake as nonvenomous? I didn't mind handling nonvenomous snakes, I told myself—the smaller ones. They didn't creep me out, although I wouldn't want to tangle with an aggressive brown water snake.

Our next capture was a mud snake. The Jeep did the customary skid. Kevin leaped out. I followed.

The snake, oily black with pink-red markings on its sides, lay in a loose coil on the road. "It looks like maybe thirty-six inches," he said. "That's your average size male. The biggest female I caught was fifty-nine inches. I'll get a bag. You keep an eye on him."

"What if it tries to escape or moves toward me?" I asked.

"Grab him."

"What if it bites?"

"I'll give you a thousand dollars," Kevin said, walking back to the Jeep. "Mud snakes never bite anybody." He later confessed that he had, in fact, been bitten by one. "A fifty-nine-inch female on April 28, 2002. She was lying by Pool G at the refuge. She was so big that when I passed her, she looked like a black oil spill. When I approached, she didn't budge. I gently picked her up by the 'neck' area about a fifth of the way down her body. She immediately swung around and bit me on the hand that was supporting her. I looked down and said, 'Hey, you're not supposed to do that!' It was a quick bite. Then she flicked out her tongue, and after catching my scent, she went into a defensive posture and started musking all over the place. The fact that she bit me, combined with her delayed defensive behavior, makes me almost positive that the bite was simply a feeding response. One of a mud snake's techniques is to lie still until something, say a frog or siren, bumps into her. Then she goes after it. I am the only person I know who's been bitten by a mud snake."

As if on cue, this mud snake, hardly believing its good luck that the snake master had left a rookie in charge, began slithering away. Let it be known, I trusted Kevin indubitably. But not instinctively. When I reached down to pluck the snake by the tail, it struck back at my hand, and I recoiled as though I'd touched a live wire. The snake never hit me. I knew it was bluffing. It knew it was bluffing. But its instinct got the better of my instinct. I couldn't make myself touch it.

Kevin returned with the pillowcase. He picked up the snake and handed it to me. It felt limp and harmless. Embarrassed, I laughed at myself.

"Mud snakes are awesome," he said and gave me some advice on picking up harmless snakes. "Next time close your eyes and grab."

The following July, when Kevin was in China, he e-mailed me lengthy instructions on how to handle nonvenomous snakes. He disapproves of pinning or restraining them by the head. A flailing snake can suffer serious vertebral injury or death, which was why Kevin had cradled the big brown water snake with one hand several inches behind the head and the other hand farther down the body. If the snake is nonvenomous, he wrote, "what's the worst that can happen?" If it "makes contact, when you jerk back . . . your flinching could cause some teeth to get ripped out of the snake's mouth and become further embedded in your skin. So this reaction is likely to end up hurting the snake." Like other wildlife biologists and veterinarians I've met, he put the subject's welfare first.

He cached the mud snake in the back of the Jeep, and we climbed in. "Tonight," he said, turning to me before we drove off, "you've already seen something a lot of herpetologists never see—a pygmy rattlesnake and a mud snake in the wild." He smiled. "The Sandhills have spoiled me."

Next we headed to the cottonmouth sluice. So far that year Kevin had bagged three cottonmouths. "Two of the three were at the sluice near Pool G. I found the other at Twin Lakes."

Recalling the murky spookiness of the cottonmouth sluice, I realized that I had forgotten to bring a bigger flashlight. I hoped that Kevin had brought his huge spotlight and asked his preference regarding flashlights.

"Back in 2001 and 2002 I used a big Maglite with four D batteries. I would chew through those in a month or two, and D batteries are expensive. Then my dad bought me a one-million-candle rechargeable spotlight. It was exceptionally bright, and I saved a lot of money. I used it for a year, but after recharging it so many times, it lost its beam. Now I have this one," he said. He parked on the side of the road, reached over the back of his seat, and hoisted up a black spotlight the size of a small cannon. "This one is a rechargeable ten-million-candle spotlight." To demonstrate its ability, he illuminated a cypress one hundred yards across the lake. The tree lit up like it was on fire.

I asked if such a tactical nuclear device had any effect on the snakes he was hunting.

He suspected that the snakes at the cottonmouth site knew him by his light. "If I shine it on one I've caught before, he runs. As for the snakes on the road, no, it doesn't have any impact."

We got out of the Jeep, and Kevin, carrying the big light, walked to the rear. He handed me an empty pillowcase, donned knee-high rubber wading boots, then picked up long-handled snake tongs and a lumpy pillowcase that contained the cottonmouth to be released.

I asked if there was a danger in getting too used to handling venomous snakes.

"Yeah. I haven't gotten that way yet. I still give them a bunch of respect. The first two years I was around them, whenever I had to pin a venomous snake, I was nervous as hell. I wouldn't say I'm careless now, but I'm extremely cautious. The more you work with snakes, the better you can read their behavior and body language."

We hiked down a bank of high grass and down the same steep overgrown trail to the creek. I tagged closely behind. At the end of the trail, the ground flattened into a leaf-strewn bottom. It was spring, earlier in the year than my last hunt, and the large, orb-weaving spiders of autumn were absent. We were serenaded by a chorus of frogs, the *pe-tunk pe-tunk* of carpenter frogs and the rapid *gick gick* of cricket frogs. They sounded like crickets with frogs stuck in their throats.

Kevin laid the pillowcased cottonmouth on the ground. "The majority of the cottonmouths I find are half in, half out of the water," he said, spotlighting a brush pile on the other side of the creek. "There's one."

"Where?" I squinted, running my eyes along the creek's edge.

"Right there," he pointed. "See him?"

"No. Oh, there he is, at the foot of the tree."

"I know this one by sight," Kevin said, like a man recognizing an acquaintance on the street. He waded into the calf-deep creek toward the snake. Fleeing, it dove under the water's thick brown scum. Kevin hurried to the bank, scanned the water with his beam, pushed branches aside, and poked around with his snake tongs. "The likelihood of finding him is pretty slim," he finally said. He gave up that chase and returned to my side of the creek, where he soon located a second snake not far downstream.

Herding that one with his snake tongs away from the creek and onto the leafy ground, he carefully pinned the snake's head under the sole of his rubber boot.

"You got the bag?" he asked.

I handed it to him. "Now that is a cottonmouth, right?"

"Yes. Is it not beautiful?" he asked, but the question was more of a statement.

The snake was not smoky black or muted brown but had yellow markings separated by black bands that resembled lightning bolts. I agreed it was beautiful.

"I'll check what number he is." Still pinning the snake's head, Kevin bent down, took the snake's body in his fingers, and turned the tail over. Locating the cloaca, he began counting up to the cauterized scales. "One two three four five six. . . . Would you shine that light over here?"

"Sorry," I said. Without realizing, I had been scanning the creek for other snakes.

"Looks like cottonmouth number 48," he concluded. He let go of the snake's body. It writhed in the leaves. Removing his foot from the snake's head, he lifted the reptile with the tongs near midbody and placed it in the pillowcase, tying the bag shut.

Then, picking up the bag that contained the snake to be released, he waded back into the middle of the creek. The tea-colored current pressed against his rubber boots. Standing in the middle, facing downstream, he unknotted the pillowcase and poured the cottonmouth into the stream. The snake took a moment to get its bearings, then turned to swim upstream, circling around Kevin's right leg as if it were a cypress tree. Perhaps the boots, I thought, kept the cottonmouth from sensing Kevin's mammalian heat. In any event, for Kevin, the drama was uneventful. For the snake, who knows what weird tales of alien abduction it could tell of being pinned under a monster's heel, imprisoned in a dark sack, stuck up a plastic tube, measured, weighed, burned and marked, only to be plunked down the next night into the same familiar creek.

For me, it was a watershed moment. Somewhere in the sluice I made the transition from looking for snakes not to step on to looking for snakes to catch. Well, for Kevin to catch.

As we climbed the bank up to the Jeep, I felt the let-down of an adrenaline spike. I took a deep breath. "The crews that do prescribed burns—they get excited, get pumped up, get a rush. Do you get the same thing?"

"Oh yeah. The most exciting times are when I'm cruising along and way in the distance I see what looks like a big log on the road. I automatically know what it is—a four-foot canebrake rattlesnake with ten or twelve rattles. Sometimes canebrakes are mean as can be, sometimes they're laid back, but every time I find a canebrake that big, yeah, it's a huge rush. I mean, a pygmy is exciting, but you don't have that same level of danger. A canebrake that size is incredibly dangerous. Its bite would be very bad, so you're super careful and give it a huge berth when you're trying to bag it. That's exciting."

Not far down Wildlife Drive, we found the other teams' cars parked on the roadside. Standing on the pavement, Adrian, Liani, Mark, and Nate were having a powwow over a pygmy.

We parked. Kevin walked over, took one look at the snake, and said with a sigh, "This is one that they released earlier tonight, and, ah, they captured it again."

"Poor little bastard," I said.

"It was in the middle of the road," Liani laughed. "He's really small."

"Guess we'll release him again," said Mike, who returned the snake to the woods.

Nate showed us a corn snake they had captured. On the off chance of catching more water snakes, we all drove to a smaller creek, parked, and walked through a meadow of wiregrass, broomsedge, grass-stage longleafs, saplings, pinecones, and ferns. Stepping across a ditch, we came to a creek that was little more than a ditch itself.

Again there was a chorus of cricket frogs. Adrian, on his hands and knees, caught one, holding it between thumb and forefinger. The frog was less than an inch long. Adrian showed me the tiny warts on the back of its rump. "If they're small, it's a southern cricket frog. If they're bigger, it's a northern." Turning to Liani, he asked, "Do you remember what the warts are called?"

"Tubercles?"

"Yeah, something like that."

WE FOUND NO SNAKES at the creek. The next time we drove by the house, Kevin dropped me off at my car. We bid adieu. I wouldn't see him again until he returned from China in the fall.

Cruising alone along Wildlife Drive, eyes trained, I felt lucky. I had at least a few miles of refuge road to cover before I reached Highway 1. Odds were good that I'd see a snake. As a junior snake scout, I was eager to contribute to the hunt. I was almost to Kevin's coachwhip parking lot when I sighted one. It was reddish brown and about the size of our mud snake. I stood on the brakes, did a skid to a stop. I had no pillowcase or snake hook and knew I wouldn't have the guts to pick up the snake, but I hoped I could detain it long enough for Kevin, who was trailing me, to arrive. I prayed I hadn't run it over, threw the Jeep into neutral, grabbed my little flashlight, and jumped out, all too slow, too slow. The snake was gone. I immediately began searching the pavement under the Jeep, then searching the roadside grass and ditch.

I was still searching when Kevin pulled up. Together we combed the bank and grass, to no avail. We said goodbye again. As I wheeled off, I glanced up at the sky. The clouds looked scaly and ghostly, and from their midst the moon shone down like a cold reptilian eye.

Wild Turkeys

"Our biggest shortcoming in land management in South Carolina is that we're not putting enough fire on the ground."

Mark Hatfield of the National Wild Turkey Federation

IN THE EARLY TWENTIETH CENTURY Bernard Baruch, owner of Hobcaw Barony near Georgetown, South Carolina, wrote that wild turkeys were so numerous they caused traffic jams. By 1990 the turkey population at the barony had fallen, it's rumored, to a single bird. The causes for the decline, according to Lee Brockington, senior interpreter for the Belle Baruch Foundation, were twofold: 1) the loss of habitat due to fire suppression; and 2) an increase in the population of feral pigs, an "invasive, omnivorous, and ubiquitous blight." It's important to note that hogs, introduced to North America by Spanish explorers, are not members of our native fauna.

The Hobcaw Barony, home to the Belle W. Baruch Foundation, covers 27.4 square miles and encompasses every environment found in South Carolina's coastal plain. In the 1970s the barony was designated a wildlife refuge and hunting ceased. The population of feral pigs erupted to an estimated two thousand. The pigs wreaked environmental havoc.

Hogs are a ravenous lot. Favorite entrees on their menu, said Lee, are the eggs of loggerhead turtles and ground-nesting birds and the "starchy and sweet taproots of longleaf pines." The pigs also root up native grasses that help feed wild turkeys and foster insects for browsing. It's no coincidence that the last hunts of Belle Baruch, Bernard's daughter, were for feral pigs.

The fate of wild turkeys at the barony brightened with the introduction of prescribed burns to open the understory and bring back native plants and

"Wild Turkeys" first appeared in the March–April 2008 edition of *South Carolina Wildlife* magazine.

Wild turkeys fan their wings in a winter field at the Carolina Sandhills National Wildlife Refuge. Turkeys benefit from prescribed burns, which open the understory and encourage the growth of native plants for browsing. Photograph courtesy of USFWS.

with the trapping and killing of the hogs, in accordance with state law. The fall and rise of the turkey population there form a microcosm of the fortune of those birds nationwide.

During the Great Depression, the number of wild turkeys in the nation plummeted to under thirty thousand—a decline caused by overhunting, clear-cutting, and poor management of wildlife and timber. By 1973, the year the National Wild Turkey Federation (NWTF) was formed, the U.S. turkey population had rebounded to about 1.3 million, in part because of federally mandated wildlife restoration. Now the NWTF, which has five hundred thousand members, estimates the population of turkeys to be 7 million nationwide. That's one member for every fourteen birds.

A century ago, when the population of Easter wild turkeys (*Meleagris gallapavo silvestris*) had bottomed out, South Carolina's Georgetown County remained a repository for that species's "ancestral stock," explained Charles Ruth, S.C. Department of Natural Resources Deer and Turkey Project leader. "From 1750 to 1900, essentially all the woods in South Carolina—other than river swamps in the coastal plain, which weren't suitable for agriculture—had been cleared and stumped for farming. Cotton was king. Wildlife habitat disappeared. There was unrestricted hunting, as well as commercial market hunting. All of this kept the number of turkeys down."

Charles recalled an aerial photograph, circa 1920, from his graduate days at Clemson University. "The photo was taken above Clemson and looked toward Anderson, about fourteen miles away. You can see the rolling hills, but other than a shade tree or an old fence row, there were no trees in the photo. It looked like it had snowed, but it was not snow. It was cotton as far as the eye could see."

Despite the dearth of wildlife habitat, pockets of turkeys survived in the Francis Marion National Forest, the Savannah River basin, and some private plantations.

Enter the boll weevil, a bio-event that unexpectedly reforested much of South Carolina. "When the pest arrived from Mexico via the Gulf Coast states, cotton production began to fail," said Charles. "We also experienced a major drought in the 1920s, which further suppressed farming." As people walked away from their farms, forests began to regenerate.

Taking advantage of this reforestation, from 1951 to 1958 the state's DNR trapped 328 wild turkeys in the Francis Marion Hunt Unit and relocated them to Wildlife Management Areas in the Piedmont. "In state, from the mid-1970s until the early 2000s, we moved about 3,500 birds," said Charles. "Now we have birds in all counties, and all counties are open to hunting. If hunters and landowners can't find turkeys, they either have a habitat problem or they should be patient. There are turkeys around."

Also taking advantage of the reforestation, the forest industry began harvesting the state's naturally regenerated pine-hardwood forests in the 1970s and 1980s. At first this wasn't all bad for wildlife. The early successional habitat that resulted from clear-cutting, said Charles, "was good for our deer and turkey populations, which really took off." The downside of the timber boom was that these clear-cuts were often replanted with loblolly pine. "Once the rows of pines grow up and start shading out, there's no understory, only pine straw."

Fortunately for their breed, "turkeys are extremely omnivorous," said Charles. "They eat a broad range of foods—hard mast like acorns; soft mast like pokeberries, blackberries, persimmons, and crab apples; the seeds of grass, ragweed, and legumes; pine nuts, snakes, lizards, frogs, and insects." But the fact remains that as crop-pines grow, after ten or twelve years the canopy closes. Little sunlight hits the forest floor, so there is little food or cover for wildlife.

Recently, said Charles, wild turkey reproduction in South Carolina has been falling. The hunt-harvest of turkeys is also decreasing. "I'm not criticizing the commercial pine industry. That's business and many people's livelihoods. But a lot of the decrease is caused by habitat change."

Charles argued that it is possible to manage for both timber and wildlife, "but you have to decide how intense the forestry practices will be and how they relate to wildlife." A number of strategies, such as tree spacing, prescribed burning, and buffer strips, balance wildlife and timber. "You won't reap the full potential of a commercial pine plantation. It's a trade-off for a landowner." Maximizing profits must be weighed against providing habitat for wildlife.

Wild turkeys require a variety of habitats, explained biologist Mark Hatfield. Mark heads the NWTF's North American Wild Turkey Management Plan and, in 2007, chaired the South Carolina Prescribed Fire Council, an organization that encourages professionalism in those who conduct burns and promotes burning to conserve habitat and national resources. Mark is also an avid hunter. "My 2007 hunt went well," he said. "Heard lots of birds. Good companionship and camaraderie, which is more important. Killed two birds, one in Georgia and one in Kansas. And I got educated by several.

"Turkeys need early successional habitats with native warm season grasses. They need mature forests and the transitional areas between the two. They adapt to hardwood ridges, bottoms, and upland sites." During summer they nest and browse in overgrown fields and forest edges. "During fall and winter, when acorns are available, they shift to a hardwood environment. Turkeys are generalists in their approach to food, and their choice of habitat varies with the season." Because turkeys need a varied habitat, their home range is large—about a square mile, or 640 acres. "They travel plus or minus that distance in a year, based on their needs."

Prescribed burns are critical to maintaining wild turkey habitat, Mark said. Fire opens the understory, gives turkeys clear lines of sight and escape, and encourages new plant and insect growth for foraging.

"Occasionally," Mark said, "I get calls from people who say, 'Hey, I just bought a hundred acres. I'm not gonna do anything to it but give it to wildlife.' But Mother Nature is dynamic. Change is never-ending, and fire is a disturbance that's needed. Fire brings a greater diversity of plants and insects, which the poults [young turkeys] need for protein."

The NWTF believes that prescribed burns pose little danger to wild turkeys, in part, said Mark, because burns are often conducted in woods that are "too dense with sweetgums" to accommodate turkeys. "Remove a midstory of sweetgums and their leaf litter, and kill their root system with herbicides or fire, especially during the spring.

"Turkeys are big birds with big wings and feet. A mature hen weighs eight to eleven pounds; a mature tom, eighteen to thirty pounds. He can stand three and a half feet tall." The old bird is, as hunters say, as smart as a fox. He has the eyes of a goose and can fly like a wild duck and run like a horse.

"In a sprint," said Charles, "turkeys can outrun a galloping horse." Though running is their usual mode of escape, "turkeys can fly distances of more than a mile, sometimes at speeds of 55 miles per hour."

"Because their avoidance of predators is based on sight and hearing," said Mark, "they avoid a dense understory and won't select such a habitat for nesting."

Ground-nesting birds, "turkeys often nest in the crowns of fallen trees" for camouflage. "A nest is a scratched-out bowl about eighteen inches wide. The average clutch is ten to twelve eggs. Hens lay one egg per day. The eggs incubate from twenty-seven to twenty-nine days." In South Carolina the nesting season ranges from around March 15 till the end of May, although the season varies from the lowcountry to the upstate. "Hens typically lay one clutch per season and roost on the ground the entire time, nearly forty days."

Although hens occasionally leave their nests to feed, said Mark, "primarily they're on the nest, so they have a higher mortality rate" than that of gobblers, which roost in trees to avoid predation. If the nest is destroyed, a hen may renest, but with a lower yield of eggs. "If you average a survival rate of three poults per hen per year, odds are that the turkey population will be sustained or increase. But that's a crude estimate.

"A cold, wet spring is one impediment to an expanding population. Wet poults may succumb to hypothermia. They are on the ground ten to fourteen days before their feathers develop and they can fly. Two weeks of good weather are important to their survival.

"A cool, wet spring not only decreases poult survival, it decreases hen survival. Scent carries a lot better in cool, wet weather. Ground predators are more successful at finding nests. Think about it: when you hunt quail on cool, wet days as opposed to windy, dry ones, the dogs point a lot quicker."

A late spring freeze can also adversely affect the year's production of acorns, a favorite turkey food. Fortunately for wildlife, "Mother Nature doesn't put all of her eggs in one basket," said Charles. "For example, white oak species pollinate and produce fruit the same year. Red oaks, on the other hand—scrubs oaks such as turkey, blackjack, and bluejack—pollinate one year and produce the next."

While loss of habitat and bad weather affect the wild turkey population, Charles and Mark agreed that predation poses no significant threat. "People think that coyotes are the biggest threat" to the turkey population, Mark continued. They are not, despite the growing number of coyotes in the state. Hawks and owls hunt turkeys; and foxes, skunks, and coyotes prey on nests opportunistically. "A great horned owl will kill a mature turkey on the roost at night." The biggest predatory threat "probably comes from raccoons," but predation, Mark argued, does not have a significant impact on the wild turkey population. Once a turkey reaches full size, the rate of predation decreases.

Nor are hunters decimating our turkey flocks—despite an army of forty-five thousand turkey hunters in the state and despite the rule that hunters may bag five birds per season in most counties.

"You have to remember that turkey hunting, by and large, is an unsuccessful endeavor," observed Charles. "We're looking at roughly a 33 percent success rate among hunters." Only about fifteen thousand hunters bag one or more birds each. Charles estimated the current population of turkeys in South Carolina to be about one hundred thousand birds, which he believed is a healthy number.

The most significant threat to the bird's future, Mark said, is loss of habitat due to the suppression of fire. Charles agreed. "A lot of folks don't understand that historically a large percentage of our state's forests were controlled by fire," he said. "The Indians were well-versed in the uses of fire to change forest types and stimulate early successional vegetation."

Across the South, Mark said, prescribed burns are "not applied as often as needed. Our biggest shortcoming in land management in South Carolina is that we're not putting enough fire on the ground." If, on the other hand, we continue to provide "adequate, suitable habitat, the population of wild turkeys will continue to rise."

"When conditions are right," said Charles, "turkeys can produce a lot of offspring."

Evidence of this can be found at Hobcaw Barony, where the introduction of prescribed burns and the removal of feral pigs have reversed the fate of the resident wild turkey population. By 2007 the number of pigs had fallen by half to about one thousand. The turkey population had rebounded to about five hundred—a testimony to the resilience of these great birds when given a fighting chance.

Translocation

"We got a bird, we got a bird. Stand by for band number."

Greg Boling, biological science technician

IT WAS 5:30 P.M. ON SEPTEMBER 29. I was standing outside a Carolina Sandhills National Wildlife Refuge office next to forester Clay Ware and eight others: five from the refuge; two, Neal Humke and Bryan Watts, from the Nature Conservancy; and Sergio Harding, from the Virginia Department of Game and Inland Fisheries. Neal, Bryan, and Sergio had driven down from TNC's Piney Grove Plantation in Virginia for the event, an attempt to translocate six red-cockaded woodpeckers from the Sandhills to Piney Grove. This was, said Bryan, "a collaborative project."

The others from the refuge were Scott Lanier, manager; Laura Housh, wildlife biologist; Mike Housh, fire management officer; Mark Parker, forest technician; and Greg Boling, biological science tech. Clay would leave later that night in a U.S. Fish and Wildlife Service truck to haul a camper 750 miles to New Orleans, where it would house an employee whose home had been destroyed by Hurricane Katrina.

A year earlier Clay had told me that "it's all about the RCWs," the "it" being the preservation and restoration of longleaf pine forests. Protect red-cockaded woodpeckers and you restore a piece of southern history and promote an entire ecosystem, not only plants but a catalog of birds, mammals, reptiles, amphibians, and insects that take up housekeeping in the woodpeckers' abandoned cavities.

The early autumn had been hot, as usual, but that day a cold front had blown through, lowering the daytime temperature to the mid-80s, the nights to the low 60s. Not much of a cold front, but in South Carolina it would do. A few gnats sang around my ears, but thankfully no mosquitoes. The dryness of the Sandhills didn't support a large population of the latter.

Wildlife biology technician Greg Boling installs an artificial cavity nest insert for red-cockaded woodpeckers at the Carolina Sandhills National Wildlife Refuge. Photograph courtesy of USFWS.

Waiting for dusk, we made small talk. I asked Mark if he'd seen any excitement, any wildfires.

He shook his head. "There's one down in Texas."

"And one in southern California," I said.

"Saw that. It's about time. So-Cal's always the last to go."

Standing nearby was Neal, a tall, red-haired, bespectacled, energetic young man dressed in green jeans, a Nature Conservancy T-shirt, and a Nature Conservancy ball cap. A green Bushnell spotting scope with a shoulder stock was slung from his shoulder. He was excited. With luck he would meet his first RCW. If all went according to plan, he, Bryan, and Sergio would drive five hours through the night back to Virginia with six captured birds in time to release them to new clusters at dawn.

A successful translocation doesn't begin or end with shipping birds. The Nature Conservancy had been preparing for this event for two years. According to the U.S. Fish and Wildlife Service, "recipient populations must also have rigorous habitat programs in place to receive birds, including four suitable cavities per recruitment cluster, two recruitment clusters available for each pair of birds received, and an aggressive prescribed burning program."[1]

The Carolina Sandhills refuge had agreed to donate up to 10 red-cockaded woodpeckers per year to the Nature Conservancy for a period of ten years. Laura was in charge of this stage of the translocation, the capturing of sub-adult RCWs. And not just any RCWs, but the right combination: two males and four females. Laura was a balance of sweetness and professionalism but today had ratcheted up the tension. Preparation for this event had started at the refuge last spring with the banding and identification of 164 newborn RCW chicks.

At dusk tonight each bird would bed down in its own cavity, cozily ignorant of the U.S. Fish and Wildlife Red-cockaded Recovery Act of 1985, which mandated translocation; chirpily unaware that come nightfall it might be stalked, startled from its sleep, frightened from its nest, netted, bagged, boxed, and shipped to become part of a different colony in a different state and thereby participate in a gambit for its species's survival. The birds would be stressed. Laura was stressed too, although I would not have known it if she had not hinted to me how much was riding on this day.

"Laura likes satisfied customers," smiled Scott, nodding toward the men from the Nature Conservancy. More than that, Laura knew that one does not take lightly the capture and transportation of endangered animals protected by the federal government.

To organize the hunt, Laura divided the ten of us into three teams, briefed us, and reminded each team of her expectations: "Go to the roost and wait five or ten minutes after dark. It's important that you definitely know the sex of each bird you capture. If you're not a trained handler, don't handle the birds." She joked that Scott would be "the data management specialist."

"I like that title," he said.

I would be with Laura's team, observing and staying out of the way. She cautioned me not to take any flash pictures. "The birds will be stressed," she repeated.

With the gathering dusk, we split up into several trucks and headed off into far corners of the forty-five thousand–acre refuge. According to Laura's plan, the first destination for our team was Compartment 18. I rode with Scott. We followed Laura and Neal in her truck across a meadow, past a trailer and a shed, and along a twisted, bumpy firebreak that was more footpath than road.

When we finally parked, it was barely daylight. Longleaf forest was on both sides of the firebreak. Turkey oaks, head-high and leafy and green, crowded under the pines. For every twenty or so pines, there were one hundred or more young oaks. Curiously the spindly trunk of each new oak grew up around a second slender, blackened trunk with brittle branches that reminded me of a skeleton—evidence of a burn a few years ago. After that burn, Scott said, the oaks had resprouted from their roots, spending precious stored nutrients. He added that another burn would "really set the oaks back" and prevent them from threatening the pines and RCWs with a hardwood midstory. Beneath the oaks were clumps of wiregrass sprinkled with orange pine needles, ample fuel to kindle another burn.

"Mike and Mark must salivate when they see these oaks," I said, remembering what Mike Housh had said about his work, that his favorite jobs were starting fires and putting them out.

As we waited, Laura walked back to our truck. "The birds haven't roosted yet," she said. "We'll have to be patient."

A shin-high longleaf seedling stood by our truck's tire. Ankle-high huckleberry, its leaves turning rusty, grew abundantly on the sand.

"Hear that?" Scott asked me. "An RCW peeping. It sounds like a squeak toy, a rubber ducky."

I strained but heard nothing. Save for a jet passing overhead, the silence in the forest was so deafening that my ears rang.

"They're not gonna roost for a while," said Laura. "They're still pecking on the trees."

"Foraging," I asked, "or opening up resin wells?"

"Foraging," she said, "because they're not on their cavity trees."

Suddenly the woods sang with a shrill metallic whirring.

"Cicadas. Now the birds will roost," said Laura.

"Little-known folklore from Laura the biologist," Scott laughed.

"Don't quote me," she said. After returning to the bed of her truck, she shouldered a long, telescoping pole. A two-foot square wire frame was attached to one end of the pole. Nylon mesh was stretched tightly across the frame. In the center of the mesh, a hole four inches in diameter emptied into a four-foot camouflage sock that hung from the frame. The trick was to approach the nest stealthily without disturbing the RCW, position the hole in the mesh over the entrance to the cavity, and scratch or knock on the bark to startle the bird from the nest and into the sock.

Laura and Neal hiked down the firebreak toward tree 18-4. Unsure of whether I should stay or accompany them, I trailed several yards behind until Laura, looking over her shoulder, motioned me to remain behind. I went back to our trucks and borrowed Scott's binoculars. Cavity tree 18-4 was about one hundred yards off, and with the onset of night it became hard, even with the binoculars, for me to see Laura and Neal. The cavity (a natural one) was surprisingly low, about head high. Laura raised the pole, and Neal scraped the bark. I thought I might have missed the capture, it happened so quickly. Then she lowered the net. Empty. The bird had either failed to roost or escaped. Abandoning that site, she and Neal threaded their way through the woods and down a slope toward a second cavity tree. Though it was increasingly difficult to make them out through the turkey oaks and darkness, I watched as Laura raised the net to this cavity and Neal scraped the bark again, with no apparent success. They doubled back toward the first tree to try again.

By now the cicadas had ceased buzzing. Scott's radio broke the silence as the other teams called in from their sites. The birds had failed to roost; everyone was empty-handed. Clearly this was harder than I had expected.

Several minutes later Laura and Neal walked back to Scott's truck. "Got away from us, Scott," she said. Disappointment was evident in her voice. "The cavity in the first tree was so low, I think the bird heard us walking up. I couldn't get the net up in time."

"You saw it go, then?" I asked Neal.

"Yeah, saw it flying off. That's why we have backups," he said, referring to the other teams.

Scott told them the news, that the other teams had not bagged a bird.

"Really?" said Neal.

Without speaking, he and Laura stowed their gear in the bed of her truck.

"Scott, what does this mean?" I asked.

"Usually enough birds have roosted so we can pick other sites. When you run one out of a cavity, it may return or it may free-roost," that is, roost on a branch. "Capturing RCWs is not an easy job," he added, "but in the past Laura's been real successful."

A man's voice came over Laura's and Scott's radios. "The bird's not wantin' to budge out of its nest," the voice said, but I couldn't make out the rest of the communication.

"That's Greg," Scott told me, identifying the speaker. "They have one that stuck its head out of the hole, saw the net, saw them, and went back in. Won't come out."

I heard Laura say, "You have a ladder. Can you climb the tree?"

"Yeah, we're working on it," Greg replied. "Just wanted to keep you updated."

"Thanks. Good luck."

I asked Scott how the ladder would help.

"The bird will think, 'Something is coming up the tree closer to my hole.' Greg's crew will have a better chance of scaring it out."

Soon Mike's voice came over the radio. It was our first break. "OK, Laura, we got one," he said. He relayed the sequence of the bird's colored bands and the number stamped on the aluminum one, a litany that would become a ritual as the hunt continued. "We got bird number 9489246."

Retrieving a data sheet from her truck, Laura checked the bird's colors and ID number in the light of our truck cab. "Bird male," she said.

"Could you repeat the number?" Scott asked Mike.

Mike gave the bird number again. Laura compared the data, then said, "Confirmed male."

Scott showed me his copy of the data sheet. On it were listed nearly thirty cavity trees. Hopefully each had a roosting bird that was a candidate for translocation. Some trees had been highlighted in yellow. "Those are our team's choices," he said.

I asked about the process of "roosting" birds.

In late spring or early summer, he explained, Laura and her crew located and banded each RCW chick soon after it hatched. Each chick had three colored bands on one leg and one colored and one numbered aluminum band on the other. Each sequence and combination of colored bands was unique to each bird. Then in early fall Laura, her staff, and volunteers spent hours sitting near clusters of cavity nest trees at dusk waiting for the birds to roost. Using spotting scopes, they identified each bird by its colored bands, attempted to determine its sex by looking for that elusive red-cockade of feathers, and noted the tree it roosted in. "That's the preparation, the hard work," said Scott. "Tonight is the gravy."

"How many translocations will you try this year?"

"Just one. This is it."

"What if you don't get the six birds you're after tonight? Do you try again?"

"We can. It's up to the Nature Conservancy, how much they want to pursue it. They can't stay till tomorrow to try again, though, because the birds they catch they have to take to Virginia tonight."

Laura and Neal got into their truck. We trailed them through a labyrinth of weedy firebreaks and dirt roads to the next compartment. I rolled my window down. The sky was dark and starry, the night windy. Heat lightning flashed in the distance. It would be easy to get lost out here, I thought. Terrain always looks alien after dark. I recalled Scott saying that it took months for new employees to learn the bewildering passel of unmarked truck trails.

We parked on a road near the next cluster. "If we trap one, I'll flash my flashlight," Laura said. Then she and Neal, carrying the pole and net, trekked off toward a cavity tree. If Laura flashed her light, I was to bring the transport box, which was wrapped in a dark blue pillowcase in the back of the truck. I wondered what biologists and herpetologists would do if pillowcases had not been invented.

Waiting in our truck, Scott and I talked about the other national wildlife refuges he had worked at—Chincoteague in Virginia, Pea Island and Alligator River in North Carolina, Tensas River in Louisiana, and Wheeler in Alabama. I thought how great it would be to camp here in the quiet of the dark pines away from the sounds and lights and roofs and walls of town. I asked what he liked about the Sandhills.

"I like the openness of a longleaf forest. It's visually attractive. I like the history of longleaf pines, the culture and lifestyle that developed around them, the naval stores industry that was prominent in North and South Carolina. Not many people know about that now. I like the biological diversity of longleaf forests. It's sad to think that these forests were predominant in the Southeast but now only a small fraction remains."

Laura's light flashed, and Scott and I jumped from the cab. I grabbed the dark cloth bag containing the transport box and hurried after Scott across a ditch and into the woods.

The transport box, a cage for ferrying the bird to its new location, was about fifteen inches high by eight inches square. Two walls were wood. They were carpeted to give the bird a surface on which to cling. Two walls were wire mesh for ventilation and for feeding waxworms, mealworms, or crickets to the bird in transit. The lid was hinged. Attached to the inside of the box was a black sleeve that allowed the captor to reach into the box, release the captive, and extract his or her hand without giving the bird much chance to escape.

As we approached, Laura was kneeling at the trunk of the cavity tree holding the frightened bird. "The toes of one of its feet are snagged in the net," she told me. Neal held the flashlight in one hand and the data sheet in the other as Laura noted the colored bands on the free leg. "White, white, mauve." She then asked Neal to grasp the bird so that she could free its other leg and read the number of the aluminum band.

This was a dramatic moment. Not only might the RCW escape as it changed hands, but also it was the first time Neal would hold one of the endangered birds. He handed me the flashlight.

"If you would put your hand around my hand . . ." Laura said to Neal, then cooed, "Let go, buddy, let go" to the bird while she gently untangled its foot.

As Neal grasped the RCW, I shined the flashlight so that Laura could verify the number on the aluminum band. "Ah, the flashlight's shining right in his eye," she said.

"Oh," I said and shifted the beam, suddenly aware that the light had no doubt intensified the bird's fright. Laura, like other skilled and compassionate biologists and veterinarians I've known, had the ability, despite the pressure of the job and the push of time, to focus first and last on the animal, to feel its emotions and intuit its discomfort.

"White, white, mauve, aluminum, purple. Band number 9515035," she said.

Neal, checking the colors and number against the spreadsheet, gave a series of "uh-huhs."

"Male," she said. "You can see it's losing its red patch on the top of its head. That's why it's hard to identify a male in the field."

Laura asked Scott to verify the colors and number again, which he did. A second confirmed male. Then she removed the transport box from its cloth bag, unclasped and raised the lid, and opened the black sleeve. Neal, bird in hand, reached inside the neck of the sleeve and deposited his charge. As he withdrew his arm, Laura gathered the sleeve close against his wrist and hand to prevent the bird's escape. Then she tucked the sleeve into the box, closed the lid, placed the box in the bag, and tied it shut.

"Your first RCW," Laura said to Neal. I congratulated him. Laura asked Scott to take the bird back to her office, then she and Scott arranged to meet, after we had dropped off the bird, at a three-way stop on the way to the next cluster. "Den, you can hold the box in your lap."

Back at our trucks Laura radioed the other crews to tell them we had the males we needed. "Focus on females," she said and wished them luck.

Another voice, perhaps Greg's, answered. His crew had captured a third RCW. "Blue, aluminum, white, white, light green," he said and gave the number. Checking her sheet, Laura repeated the colors and number. "Confirmed female," she said. "The first of the night. Is the bird already in the box?"

"Affirmative."

"We're halfway there," Laura said, "but we need three more females. I've got to look at the map." She rifled through her sheets and scanned her list of candidates and back-up sites. "Male, male, male. There's another female," she said and directed Greg's crew to proceed to the back-up site.

"Copy that," Greg said.

Scott turned the truck around and drove the few miles back to the office. Not a peep from the bird on the way. We entered the darkened building, and

I followed Scott through the lobby and down a hallway to Laura's office. He opened the door, and I carefully placed the bagged box on the carpet in under her desk and quietly closed the office door behind me. We headed back to meet Laura and Neal.

I had been worried, with the shaky start, that the translocation might fail. But things were beginning to roll. Just as we pulled up to Laura and Neal at the three-way stop, Greg came over the radio again. "We got another female. We got two boxed now."

Scott and I stepped out of our truck and walked to Laura as she was asking Greg for the second female's vital info.

"Purple, purple, mauve. Band number 94192268."

"OK," said Laura. "Confirmed female. Go ahead and take the birds back to the office. Let me know when you get there."

"Affirmative."

"Greg," she added, "we still need another female. We might run back to 18-4 and see if that one has rerooosted. As a last resort, you may need to go up to 3-1 to trap a female. Clay roosted that tree, so he might be able to give you some tips on that cavity before he leaves for Louisiana."

"Copy that. I roosted it also, so we oughta be able to do something with it."

Mike's voice broke in. "We're over here at 21-3," he said. "Got a bird that's holed up and refuses to exit."

"Don't take your net off the cavity entrance," Laura instructed. "Did you climb the tree?"

"We're gonna need a ladder and a belt."

"Copy that. Greg has a ladder and belt. I'll call and see if he can run them up to you." Laura whispered to herself, "Boy, we really don't have a spare female," then asked Greg over the radio to take a ladder and a belt to Mike and Mark at 21-3.

The radio fell silent. For a moment the only sound was the chirping of crickets. "How critical is it that we get four females?" I asked.

"Four females is optimal," said Scott. "It won't be a huge tragedy if we don't, but it's the best-case scenario."

"Two of the females," Laura explained, "will be going to solitary males," that is, males that were already established in clusters at the Nature Conservancy refuge.

"All of our translocations are unrelated subadults," Laura continued. "We grab a male and a female who are unrelated and move them as a pair to a new location" that already has artificial cavities.

"It would be good to send up two pairs," Neal said.

The pairs would be potential breeders. I wondered about the efficacy of matchmaking.

"Often," Laura observed, "a female doesn't stay with the male that the translocators pick."

I pondered the possible U-turns and dead ends of romance, how sad it was that our efforts at translocation and the regeneration of a species, pursued with the most noble intent, might end, in part, with a broken male heart or two. Still, the world must be birded.

At 10:30 P.M. Greg's voice came over the radio. "We got a bird, we got a bird. Stand by for band number." There was a pause. "Aluminum over mauve. Mauve, Mauve, white." There was another pause.

"Is that a female?" Laura asked, and there was another long pause. The only sound was the crackle of radio static.

"That's a female," Greg finally said, breaking the silence. "Stand by for the number."

The number matched that of a female on Laura's list. "Confirmed female," she said. "Bring the bird into the office."

"Copy that."

"Greg is a female magnet," I said.

Despite Mark's and Mike's use of Greg's ladder, the bird they attempted to net never left its cavity. Greg's was the last RCW captured that night.

All in all, the crews had captured two males and three females, one female shy of the goal. It was time for the Nature Conservancy crew to depart for Piney Grove so they could release the translocated woodpeckers at dawn.

There had been two cases of mistaken identity. Once Mike radioed that his crew had "trapped a bird" which, according to the roosting data, should have been a female, "but it was a male."

A second time, at a resin-coated pine by the side of a dirt road, Laura and Neal signaled to Scott and me. They had a bird. Unfortunately that RCW had also been erroneously identified by a volunteer as a female. Holding the bird in one hand, Laura brushed back the black feathers of its cap to show us the male's little red cockade. "Look at that," she said. "You can just see a couple of red feathers. That's why the sex is so difficult to identify in the field."

Mike and Laura had released the two birds.

BACK AT THE HEADQUARTERS, Laura and Neal invited me to watch them "verify the birds" one last time. "I'm going to ask you to sit very quietly in the corner," Laura told me, "because the birds are going to be very stressed."

The office door creaked as Laura opened it. The room was dark. She switched on the fluorescent lights. Five boxes in cloth bags were huddled under her desk. Inside the boxes the birds were pecking loudly now like miners trapped in black caves testing the walls with pickaxes for the best routes of escape, or like prisoners tapping Morse code and planning a breakout—"where are we now, how many of us are here, how do we get out?"

Neal and Laura knelt and crawled across the carpet on their hands and knees. They untied the cloth bag of the first box, unclasped the lid, and loosened the inner black sleeve.

Crouching, Neal reached inside the sleeve. A brief, panicked high-pitched squeaking. In response, a sympathetic cessation of pecking from the other birds. A moment of silence and suspense as Neal felt blindly inside the box and Laura whispered instructions on the proper way to grasp the bird gently but firmly with its head between the index and middle fingers. A quick muffled beating of frightened wings. Then a louder angry screeching and more determined hammerings from the other jailed birds. Neal extracted the RCW, which alternately panted and peeped as Laura confirmed its number and the color of its bands with her data sheet. That verification done, Neal returned the bird to its box, clasped the lid, put the box back into its pillowcase, and cinched the bag shut.

As he reached for the next, Laura breathed a deep sigh of relief. She had cinched the translocation. Months of patience, planning, and work had paid off. That night three *Homo sapiens* motored off into the darkness with five *Picoides borealis* in an effort to save one of the most resourceful and feisty little birds on the planet. RCWs were in peril due to habitat destruction. Laura and her crew had found them some new homes.

NOTE

1. Ralph Costa and Roy S. DeLotelle, "Reintroduction of Fauna to Longleaf Pine Ecosystems: Opportunities and Challenges," in *The Longleaf Pine Ecosystem: Ecology, Silviculture, and Restoration*, ed. Shibu Jose, Eric J. Jokela, and Deborah L. Miller (New York: Springer, 2006), 346.

The Francis Marion

"We're trying to restore a botanically diverse native system, one that's pretty close to being lost."

Bill Twomey, fire management officer

"THERE IS A GOOD CHANCE that we may be burning tomorrow," e-mailed Bill Twomey, acting fire management officer at the Francis Marion National Forest. "If you can make it, let me know." When I called to ask the odds, he said the weather forecast looked good and that he was "about 90 percent sure." Because of its proximity to major urban centers, the Francis Marion, as it's known, is smack dab in a wildland-urban interface (WUI) and squarely in the middle of the debate over burns.

The burn season in the coastal plain was coming to an end, so I jumped at the chance. Wrapping up my work and chores, I made the long drive to Charleston, where I spent the night. Early the next morning, I drove to Mount Pleasant across the Cooper River Bridge. Beneath lay Charleston Harbor, Patriots' Point, and the USS *Yorktown*, a World War II aircraft carrier. Runners jogged on the pedestrian path. Mothers pushed baby carriages. Above it all were fluffy clouds, a blue sky, and the gold sun. A wonderful day for a burn, I thought.

Despite the lagging national economy, the city of Mount Pleasant and its visitor center, shopping malls, banks, and building supply stores appeared to be booming. New motels were under construction. The sounds of power tools and hammers rang in the air. The traffic north out of town was heavy, but that headed to Charleston was bumper-to-bumper. I was glad I'd left early. I wanted to make the fire crew's briefing before the burn.

Escaping the city, I turned left onto Highway 41, crossed the Wando River, and entered a land of fields, marshes, horse ranches, black-water creeks, ranch-style homes, live oaks, old cemeteries, and double-wides painted peach or apricot. Highway 41 ran straight as a rod. Gravel lanes branched off.

Standing on a firebreak, a burn crew fills drip torches with slash fuel. Nearby is a brush truck equipped for firefighting. Photograph by the author.

Yellow flowers and toad flax grew alongside. An old couple sat in the shade of an oak.

Entering the Francis Marion, I missed my turn onto Copperhead Road and doubled back at the U.S. Forest Service Research Station. Across the road stood old brick columns and a locked iron gate that sported emblems of flying ducks and the inscription "Limerick 1707." This tract, part of the Santee Experimental Forest, included "parts of the oldest colonized land in the United States. King Charles II granted the land to Thomas Colleton in 1683." The upland was cleared for livestock and naval stores. Rice and indigo were grown in the bottomlands.[1] Beyond the gates a grassy dirt road stretched into a woods of huge live oaks. Resurrection ferns sprouted on the oaks' heavy limbs, which were garlanded with Spanish moss and ivy vines. I felt that if I walked down the road, I'd step into a forest older than the United States and European settlement and enter the ancient land of the Seewees and Wandos.

Turning around, I backtracked and turned left onto Copperhead Road. Dense forest bordered both sides of the road. On the right was evidence of a recent burn. Needles were scorched and trunks were blackened up to ten feet. On the left the forest was thick and impenetrable, not like the open woods I was used to walking through at the Carolina Sandhills National Wildlife Refuge.

I turned right onto Weatherbee Road and parked at the ranger station beside some green U.S. Department of Agriculture Forest Service trucks. Behind the office was a tall fire observation tower. On the front lawn a Smoky the Bear sign announced, "Fire Danger Moderate Today." A man in green Nomex pants and a yellow shirt was entering an office building. I followed.

Inside, the hall and offices were crammed with copy machines, desks, computers, and firefighters. Several aerosol cans of Repel Permanone—"Repels and Kills Ticks and Mosquitoes"—stood on a table.

In the hall I shook hands with Bill Twomey. I had met him the previous fall when he had addressed the South Carolina Prescribed Fire Council concerning burns on federal lands. Bill began his career with the Forest Service by fighting wildfires in San Bernardino, California. Tall, lean, and tanned, he appeared to be in his thirties but was in his mid-fifties and fast approaching retirement after thirty years with the Forest Service. I recalled the similar youthfulness of Dave Robinson, another retired forester.

The first thing Bill said was, "That 10 percent I told you about bit us." Due to predicted 30-mile-per-hour wind gusts, the day's burn had been scratched. "Yesterday the forecast was perfect," he added, "but that's what happens. We never really know if we'll burn till the morning of." He added, however, that he had some downtime and offered to drive me around the forest. I was disappointed at missing the burn but readjusted my expectations. This was a chance to see the Francis Marion with an expert guide.

We entered his office. More desks and computers. On a wall, a large photo of two men working with drip torches. On a table, Shibu Jose, Eric J. Jokela, and Deborah L. Miller's excellent tome, *The Longleaf Pine Ecosystem: Ecology, Silviculture, and Restoration.* Bill's window looked out into a green woods.

"Let me show you a plan of the burn we had in mind," he said, and then he spread out a map of the national forest. The Francis Marion National Forest, which stretches over 250,000 acres of pines, swamps, and bottomland hardwoods, is triangular in shape, like the state of South Carolina. The forest's northern boundary is the Santee River. The towns of Awendaw and McClellanville and the Cape Romain National Wildlife Refuge—one of my favorite places to kayak—lie to the east. Mount Pleasant and Charleston lie to the southeast. The forest's southwest boundary is a branch of the Cooper River.

"We also have a lot of in-holdings, or private property, in the national forest." On the map Bill pointed out Mepkin Abbey, a community of Roman Catholic monks on the banks of the Cooper River. "In the 1950s Claire Booth Luce—she and her husband published *Time* magazine—donated this land, about three thousand acres, to the Catholic Church. It's a beautiful site. The monks are restoring native plants and using private contractors to conduct prescribed burns on their land."

Next Bill rolled out this year's prescribed burn map. It was color-coded like the map that Mark Parker had shown me of the Carolina Sandhills NWR burn compartments. "The white areas are private properties," said Bill. "The orange are what we plan to burn. The black, about a third of the forest, are what we have already burned. We always hope to burn more than we think we can so we have flexibility."

The burn plan, said Bill, "is mostly driven by the red-cockaded woodpecker," one of several endangered species in longleaf forests. "We try to burn where we have concentrations of the woodpecker." Other factors influencing burns include weather, wind direction, the proximity of roads, and the wildland-urban interface. "Based on a day's weather forecast, we determine where we can burn. Today, for example, we intended to burn Compartment 81 because the forecast was for an east wind, which would blow smoke away from Highway 41. Unfortunately the forecast changed to 30-mile-per-hour gusts, which would make holding the fire really hard."

A year's burn plan is also determined by what was burned the year before. "We try to burn each area every two or three years. The last time Compartment 81 had fire in it was three years ago. We want to hit it again to mimic the natural fire cycle and keep the vegetation fresh. Historically fire burned the Southeast's longleaf ecosystem, which once stretched over about ninety million acres, every two to three years, perhaps every year, either through lightning strikes or aboriginal burning. We're trying to keep that cycle."

In the past, longleaf dominated the Francis Marion, Bill said, "but logging and fire suppression in the early twentieth century changed that. A lot of old-growth longleaf was cut. When the Forest Service acquired most of the Francis Marion in the 1930s, the discipline of forestry in the United States was in its infancy. Fire was seen as bad. We had inherited European philosophies of forest management. They believed that fire didn't promote regeneration. They excluded fire, suppressed any fires that occurred, and tried to get the locals to stop burning. During that period, loblolly pines invaded the Francis Marion."

I studied the burn map. Most of the black areas were in the interior of the Francis Marion. Little burning had been accomplished in the more densely populated areas of the WUI, for example, near McClellanville, Awendaw, or along Highway 17, which skirted the coast.

"Along the Highway 17 corridor," Bill said, "we have a hard time burning because of the wildland-urban interface, the risk of smoke on highways, and the danger to people who have respiratory illnesses." Closer to Mount Pleasant, "the traffic is horrendous. We burned that area last year and had to shut down Highway 41 for several nights and early mornings. The smoke was so thick, it was unsafe for driving."

I wondered how the shutting down of a highway was received by the locals.

"They were OK. We placed employees on the road all night long. We manned checkpoints to detour cars and to isolate the smoke-impacted highway so that no one got trapped. Highway 41 is a heavily used commuter route. Sometimes we get complaints from people who are trying to get to work. Many understand the importance of what we do, but when someone has worked an all-night shift or is late for his job or a doctor's appointment, his patience goes out the window. If he asks, 'Why are you burning?' and we answer, 'The red-cockaded woodpecker and the longleaf ecosystem,' it doesn't make sense to someone who is busy with his own life. The effort to restore an ecological community is far down his list of priorities.

"We've been struggling with this issue for fifteen years. There was a time in the early 1990s, after Hurricane Hugo had left a lot of residual fuel on the ground, when smoke on roads caused traffic accidents. We'd burn a unit, but the fuel would smolder at night. A smoke inversion would set in. Smoke couldn't lift. It would lie close to the ground and sock in the roads. I think there were six accidents in three years. Thank goodness, no one was seriously injured." There was only one lawsuit. "A motorist was driving too fast for conditions, and the court sided with the Forest Service, stating that we had posted signs and patrolled the road to slow down traffic."

The morning after a burn, Bill added, a road can still be "smoked in" from smoldering stump holes and logs. "If motorists get trapped, they can't see." I thought of how frightening it would be to drive in a smoking woods and not be able to see the road.

"Since 1996, whenever we burn a sensitive area, we set up checkpoints along the road to detour traffic," Bill told me. "An employee or private contractor staffs the checkpoint all night."

The Forest Service takes special precautions when burning in the WUI. "We notify adjacent residents and landowners. Because of night-time residual smoke, we cruise at night to manage the traffic. We burn less in the WUI, more in the forest's interior. I'm happy with burns in the interior, but even there we have interface areas with private landholdings. I'm frustrated with burns in the WUI. Every year there's more traffic on the roads, more parcels of land being subdivided, and more people building."

Smoke from burns can reach nearby metro areas, such as Mount Pleasant and Charleston. "To make sure we don't throw down a big plume of smoke, we burn when we have good wind direction and atmospheric dispersion. Once, back in the mid-1990s, we shut down the Charleston Airport for a few hours. The smoke got thick and hazy. We heard a lot of complaints. If we didn't mitigate public safety and people got hurt, we would have to curtail our burn program significantly."

Issues regarding burning, however, reach beyond forests, metropolises, and government agencies. In the long run, prescribed burns, by spurring below-ground carbon sequestration, may improve air quality, and not just locally.

"The Environmental Protection Agency recently declared carbon to be an air pollutant that must be regulated," Bill said. "That was a good decision. For us, the question is, how will this declaration affect prescribed burning? Will the carbon that we emit during a burn be regulated?

"Ever since oxygen became about 20 percent of the atmosphere, ever since there was lightning, ever since humans used fire in the landscape, there have been fires. But levels of carbon emissions from fire, a natural process, compete with levels of fossil fuel combustion from coal plants, automobiles—"

"And fossil fuel combustion is not a natural process," I said.

"Exactly. Add the burning of biomass to that of fossil fuels, and the question is, will carbon dioxide levels rise beyond what the biosphere can handle?

"When we burn, we emit a lot of carbon. A single one-thousand-acre burn on the Francis Marion may pulse tons of carbon into the atmosphere. However, the big difference between us and other carbon emitters is that the carbon we emit is current carbon, carbon that has been sequestered in the last several years, not several hundred million years. Consider all of the carbon sequestration after a burn. Green vegetation comes back. That sucks carbon out of the atmosphere. By the end of the growing season, the areas we've burned will be green and lush.

"Much of the carbon that these plants take in gets down into the root system. The below-ground biomass is about seven times greater than the above-ground biomass consumed during a burn. If a longleaf forest, for example, is burned every few years, you'll emit carbon, but the total below-ground sequestration will be positive. When we burn, we don't release the majority of the carbon that's sequestered below ground. It's a carbon sink. If this is correct, when we burn we're restoring an endangered ecosystem, encouraging species diversity, and reducing climate change."

TO BETTER UNDERSTAND the health issues of smoke management in the wildland-urban interface, I had met earlier with Brian Barnes, environmental health manager with the South Carolina Department of Health and Environmental Control in Columbia. Brian is something of an interface himself, a liaison between those who burn and the Air Planning Section of the Bureau of Air Quality.

"I started with DHEC about twenty years ago," he told me. "I'd been on the job only a couple of years when I was invited to my first wildland-urban interface talk with the Forestry Commission. Early on they asked us to work on the WUI committee. We took our ideas to the S.C. Prescribed Fire Council and participated in their steering committee. Although we don't vote, we keep them mindful of the public health impact.

"We're advocates for prescribed burning when it's done right. Burning is important for forest regeneration and also for the controlled release of pollutants in ground litter. If you have a prescribed fire, know you're going to burn forty acres, know the mixing height and where your smoke plume is going, you can have a controlled release of pollutants. But with a wildfire, all bets are off. A wildfire doesn't care if it's a high-ozone or high-wind day. You have no control over the release."

At the national level, Brian explained, the Environmental Protection Agency, with input from a scientific advisory committee, "sets ambient air quality standards for public health. The position of DHEC is not to comment on what those standards should be. We leave that to EPA and their scientists. DHEC implements what the EPA decides." One difficulty in meeting the EPA's standards, however, "is that they reset the standards every five years. Most recently the acceptable ozone level was lowered in 2008."

To check for compliance, "South Carolina DHEC has a number of air monitoring stations around the state. We monitor air quality levels, compare them to the national standards, and implement policies to affect where we are in relation to those standards. If the state exceeds the standard," that is, violates the regulation, "we implement policies to get back within it."

Fire management officers, I said, are often concerned with the attainment and nonattainment of air quality standards. I asked Brian for some definitions.

"Attainment refers to the levels for ozone and particulate matter [PM] established by the EPA." Ozone and PM are two pollutants that affect air quality and attainment. Both pollutants result from prescribed burns as well as from the burning of fossil fuels for heating and transportation.

"Attainment is important for two reasons: public health and economic development," said Brian. "If the level for ozone is 0.075 ppm [parts per million] and we're at or below that level, we're in attainment. If we're above that level, we're in nonattainment.

"Primarily, nonattainment has an adverse impact on public health. Secondarily, it hinders economic development. If a county is trying to recruit industry, one of the first questions the industry will ask is, 'What is your air quality attainment status?' If the answer is, 'We're in nonattainment,' that industry will probably consider locating elsewhere.

"Ozone is a respirable lung irritant that occurs when oxides of nitrogen and volatile organic compounds," such as fuels, solvents, and refrigerants, "combine in sunlight. Ozone is a summertime pollutant. Here in the Southeast, we examine ozone levels between April and October. The ozone we're talking about is ground level, so most of our monitors are six to eight feet high. That's where we take our readings. The old standard for ozone was 0.08 ppm. The new standard is 0.075 ppm. We look at our statewide monitoring data and ask, 'Where have we exceeded the standard?' Then we implement policies to reduce emissions and pollutant loading from stationary sources, transportation planning, or, in some cases, outdoor burning.

"Particulate matter is a direct emission of internal combustion engines and industry from sources such as cars, power plants, boilers, road dust, and brake dust. DHEC is concerned with particulate matter that is 2.5 microns or less, the really small stuff. In the past the standard addressed PM of 10 microns, but health advisers said that it's the really fine PM that creates health issues, and the standard was lowered to 2.5 microns."

When humans talk about health issues, they usually focus on Homo sapiens. I wondered if the EPA considered the effects of ozone and PM standards on wildlife.

"Ozone, in fact, has two standards, a primary one and a secondary one. The primary standard relates to human health; the secondary, to impact on the environment, for example, on vegetation or even statuary. Ozone is a very reactive pollutant. It can deteriorate concrete walls and eat up the resin plastic furniture around your pool deck. When an automobile tire dry-rots, that's probably the result of ozone.

"Ozone is a lung irritant that is especially problematic for people who have asthma. Fortunately standards for ozone levels are getting tougher. Ground-level ozone is decreasing. Ten years ago we would monitor ozone levels, for example, of 0.090 ppm. Those levels have declined, largely because of stiffer regulations and reductions in NOX, that is, in oxides of nitrogen produced by power plants, cars and trucks, and heavy-duty construction.

"Particulate matter, on the other hand, can be inhaled deep within the lungs. These small particles can actually embed in the alveoli," tiny air sacks in the lungs. "They interfere with the exchange of oxygen and carbon dioxide in the blood. The American Heart Association attributes some heart attacks to the presence of PM in the lungs."

Foresters and fire management officers are often doubtful about the future of prescribed burns in South Carolina. Brian agrees. "South Carolina ranks as one of the five or six top states for land conversion from forest or agriculture to urban use. DHEC certainly understands the position of prescribed burners in our state. We are not here to impede their work. At the same time, we are charged to protect the public health. We agree with the sound principles in the smoke management guidelines and want everyone to abide by them."

BILL TWOMEY ROLLED UP the burn map on his desk at the Francis Marion National Forest. Like Brian Barnes, forester Pat Ferral, and wildlife biologist Judy Barnes, Bill is pessimistic about the future of prescribed burning. "It's really disheartening. We have only so many burn days. We can't exceed our burn prescriptions, which is why we're not burning today because of the predicted wind gusts. You don't ever want to burn out of prescription. If you do and something goes wrong, your liability protection goes out the window. You have to adhere to your prescription and burn plan to a tee, and we do. Unfortunately that reduces our opportunities. Because of public health and safety issues, because of smoke on highways or in houses, and because we have only one burn crew of about ten people, we burn only on days with really good atmospheric dispersion. So a lot of the forest is not getting the fire it needs."

We headed out to his truck. "I'll drive you through the core area we've been burning. You'll see a dramatic difference. Then we'll go up Halfway Creek. That area is beautiful."

Outside the sun was warm, but the day was breezy and would only get windier. First we drove to a compartment of forest, a low wet area that "was burned three years ago but before that had not seen fire in a decade." Tall pines, mostly loblolly, towered above charred shoots, green cinnamon ferns, leafy switch cane, fire-ant hills, and an understory that was fairly clean of debris. The midstory was rife with scrub oaks and "a lot of sweetgums too. You can tell the sweetgum," Bill added as we exited the truck, "by the corky growth of its bark."

I scanned the forest floor. "There are thousands of sweetgum shoots here," I said.

"That's what happens when you don't burn often. The sweetgum isn't totally dead because its roots are still alive. We only top-killed them. The sprouts are coming back. We burned this compartment again this year and hope to keep that rotation going to restore the longleaf."

A dragonfly flew past. I recalled Bill's speech to the S.C. Prescribed Fire Council and his remark that cogon (*Imperata cylindrica*), an invasive grass in the Francis Marion, is "pure evil." Cogon, also known as Japanese blood grass, is an exotic ornamental that often escapes from landscaping. I asked if the forest had trouble from other invasives.

"Yeah. We're getting eat up with Japanese climbing fern." Despite its name, the fern is not a "fire ladder" like wisteria. "It's easily killed by fire. We also get some wisteria in the bottomlands."

The compartment we were touring had been burned in February, a winter burn. "The proliferation of sweetgum shoots shows why it's important to keep the two- to three-year burn rotation consistent," Bill told me. "If we wait another five years to burn and knock the sweetgum back, it will be eight feet tall again. We'll have lost the open understory characteristic of a fire-maintained ecosystem."

He pointed to a cinnamon fern. "This is good. These ferns are native to fire-maintained ecosystems. Along with bracken fern and Virginia chain fern, cinnamon ferns are one of three fire-loving ferns in the forest. Switch cane also loves fire. There's a lot of diversity in the ground cover after a burn: netted chain fern, sweet pepperbush, cherry bark oak, winged sumac, blackberry, royal fern. When you don't burn—"

We were interrupted by a loud snap and crash nearby in the forest.

"Did you hear that?" Bill asked. "Probably a dead snag falling. Red maples are sprouting too," he continued. "As long as they're kept low, maples are OK. But if we don't burn, they grow up and shade out the diversity of the understory. Burns open the understory and allow plenty of sunlight to hit the ground. In the past this was longleaf forest," he reflected as we walked back to the truck, "but due to fire exclusion, loblollies seeded in naturally from the wetter areas. In the future we'll keep these stands thin."

In loblolly's early growth stages, it cannot tolerate fire. "All the seedlings will die in burns," Bill said, "and there will be no young loblollies to replace the big ones as they die out." But prescribed burns won't kill mature loblollies, which can withstand low-intensity fires. It would take decades to convert this stand to longleaf. I remarked that it looked as though the Forest Service would be managing loblolly for the next hundred years.

"We don't really want to take out all the loblollies," Bill said. "Within ten years a logging crew will selectively take out some to open up the stand. We'd like to convert it to longleaf, but we'll have to do that by artificial regeneration, by planting longleaf pines in the understory. In fifty or sixty years of fire regimen, the stand will open up through natural attrition. If we keep fire on the ground, plant some longleaf pines, and let the loblollies die out, we can slowly convert the stand to longleaf. That's what we plan to do in some areas of the forest."

"What if the public says, 'We don't like the burns, and we don't give a rip whether the forest is loblolly or longleaf?'"

Bill cleared his throat. "Longleaf can perpetuate itself with a two-year fire regimen. Compared to loblolly, longleaf seedlings are fire-resistant. They are even more fire-resistant when they mature. With repeated burnings—and I'm talking a century down the road—once longleaf seedlings are established and grow into mature trees, they provide a seed source. They are more resistant to insects, disease, and windthrow," a desirable trait in a hurricane-swept region. Longleaf pines are also much longer lived. The life span of a loblolly is little more than a century. A longleaf can live four hundred to five hundred years.

"All this deals with policy and politics," Bill mused. "Who knows what people will think in one hundred years? Twenty years ago the big emphasis in national forests was on timber production, commodities, and recreation. The emphasis now is on restoration of natural ecosystems."

"But if I live in Mount Pleasant and never set foot in the Francis Marion, why should I care what trees grow here?" I asked him.

"It probably won't matter to you. We can get into discussions about the interrelations of humans with the biosphere, which we depend on, and the long-term health of humans on the planet. There's a great concern that we're experiencing mass extinctions of species. We're trying to restore a botanically diverse native system, one that's pretty close to being lost."

What about the threat of wildfire to the public fifty years from now when Mount Pleasant, Awendaw, and the other communities have grown deeper into the WUI, I wondered.

"We saw in North Myrtle Beach what happens if you don't burn and manage the fuel on the ground," Bill said. There a wildfire in April 2009 torched almost twenty thousand acres and destroyed or damaged nearly 175 homes. "It's easier to maintain a longleaf forest."

This was an argument that even the ecologically challenged could love. A wildfire-resistant forest with little fuel on the ground is a safer WUI.

The North Myrtle Beach wildfire had thrown a wet blanket on spring burns at the Francis Marion. "That same day we had planned to burn, but the Forestry Commission issued a burning ban because all of their resources were headed to the wildfire. We didn't want to take any chances. If another fire in a different part of the state had gotten out of control, they'd have had no resources to fight it. When they lifted the burning ban, we were out of prescription," that is, the weather conditions were unsuitable—too dry, wet, or windy for a burn.

Bill had hoped to burn forty thousand acres that year, but "so far we've burned about thirty-five thousand. This late in the burning season, I doubt that we'll burn five thousand more."

We headed back to the truck and drove past a woods interspersed with loblolly and flattop longleaf pines.

"The flattops are probably ninety to one hundred years old. The loblollies are probably about forty. The flattops tell you that at one time this stand was probably dominated by longleafs before most were logged out. If we burn and keep the loblollies thinned out, longleafs will naturally reestablish seedlings in the understory."

Ruminating, Bill circled back to our earlier topic of restoration. "The importance of restoring longleaf habitats—that's a difficult thing to convince people of. What's the importance of biodiversity to our daily lives? We forget that we live in a biosphere. We think we're isolated from the natural world. The implications of our relationship to nature won't hit us until we see drastic changes in the climate or reductions in our food-growing capacity. At the Francis Marion, we're working on a small piece of the much larger puzzle. Since Hurricane Hugo, about ten or twelve thousand acres have been restored to longleaf through site preparation and planting. As for natural regeneration, a lot of areas are slowly reverting to longleaf through frequent fire."

We braked for a yellow rat snake to cross the dirt road, then drove through an experimental forest where a research station, the Southeastern Wetlands Lab, conducts watershed experiments. "See how thick these stands are?" he asked. "We're getting into bottomland. In a fire ecosystem, this is typically where loblollies reside, in wetter areas where fire doesn't often penetrate."

"Look at all the sweetgum," I remarked.

"Sweetgum, red oak, swamp gum, wax myrtle, and loblolly."

We stopped at a twelve-hundred-acre compartment of tall loblollies that had been recently burned. I could smell the char. The ground was a blanket of bluestem, panicum, dropseed, and toothache grass. Three wild turkeys hiked through the woods.

Bill pointed out some blackroot, used by Native Americans to alleviate menstrual cramps, and eupatorium, also known as boneset and used to treat fevers. "Here's some silver-leaved grass," he said, "another fire-dependent species. It's not really a grass. It's an aster with beautiful yellow flowers that butterflies love." The ground was lower and wetter than what I was accustomed to seeing in the Sandhills.

"We're in the outer Atlantic coastal plain," Bill explained. "The landscape is a lot flatter. This area was logged about forty years ago. We burned it two years ago and again this April to open up the midstory so sunlight gets down to the forest floor. If trees have room to grow, they are healthier and more resistant to disease and infestation." An open forest can also thwart an attack of southern pine beetles, "which like stands of stressed-out trees grown close together. Sunlight on the floor also means more biodiversity," which encourages wildlife.

Older loblollies had survived the burns unscathed except for blackened trunks, but I noted a scorched loblolly seedling. "That one won't be coming back," Bill observed. "Its roots are dead. A longleaf at that stage would definitely have survived."

We drove to a woods heavily damaged in 1989 by Hurricane Hugo. Fortunately several towering longleafs had survived. Before the storm, the Francis Marion was home to the second largest population of red-cockaded woodpeckers, the largest being in Florida's Apalachicola National Forest.

After the storm, 87 percent (1,536) of the Francis Marion's RCW trees had fallen. "Large, saw-timber pines were blown down," Bill told me. "These are our only big longleafs left standing after the hurricane. They're open, old, and large, and their crowns are big. They are some of the oldest longleafs that we have in the forest."

Some were ringed with white paint for identification as red-cockaded woodpecker trees. Some of the ringed trees contained artificial cavity inserts. The longleaf I stood next to was big, at least two feet in diameter at breast height. Despite these pines' good luck in surviving Hugo, the scarcity of other big trees in the area exposed them to violent weather. "If we get another hurricane," said Bill, "these will be more vulnerable to windthrow. If these larger trees do break, there are few if any favorable trees left for artificial RCW cavities."

To accommodate an artificial cavity, a tree should be at least fifteen inches in diameter at the height of the cavity insert. Nearby was a stand of longleafs that "were real young when the hurricane blew through," Bill continued, "which is why that stand is relatively intact." If the older longleafs fell to another storm, I doubted that any of the younger ones would be stout enough to fit the bill.

"That's a big concern if another hurricane rips through here," Bill agreed. "RCWs made a comeback in areas where we've been able to burn consistently, but in parts of the forest where we haven't burned because of interface issues, the woodpeckers are struggling."

He gazed around. "This area is typical of a native longleaf forest. Eventually the older trees will be replaced by the longleaf seedlings and saplings that grow in the openings. It's gorgeous through here. All we need to do is keep burning. We'll be in longleafs forever," he said happily.

"This is good habitat for Bachman's sparrows, which like open grassy understories, and for wild turkeys and deer. Here's dollar weed, another little legume that's common in burned forests," he pointed out, stooping. "Quail like the seed. Legumes are really important. They fix nitrogen back into the soil when it's been volatilized into the atmosphere after a burn. We have a healthy quail population—I hear them whistling a lot—and a healthy population of fox squirrels too. Their numbers are good in the areas we burn. I guess their coats," often black, gray, and white, "are camouflaged on the burnt trunks of longleaf pines."

I recognized an iris. "Blue flag iris," Bill said, turning his ear to the *sweet-sweet-sweet-sweet* of a prothonotary warbler deep in the woods. "A beautiful little yellow bird with gray wings. Here's some bull thistle," he showed me as we walked through the understory. "When it flowers, it's a good pollinating plant for butterflies."

Now that he had pointed out the thistle, I saw it everywhere. Beside it grew *Eryngium yuccifolium*, a flowering plant with saw-toothed, sharp-tipped leaves, hence the name "*yuccifolium*," though the plant is not in the genus *yucca*. Also known as rattlesnake master, it was used by Native Americans to treat rattlesnake bites. "It's in the carrot family. It'll bloom in June and July." Bill pointed to persimmon and milkweed, *Asclepius longifolia*. A host plant for monarch butterflies, milkweed is mentioned in one of Bill's favorite books, Sue Halpern's *Four Wings and a Prayer*, which chronicles the migration of monarchs.

The farther we walked, the more boggy the ground became. "More sweet-gum here," I said, "and look at those pitcher plants." I swatted at mosquitoes, which were out in force, and wistfully remembered the aerosol cans of Repel back at the HQ.

"Hooded pitcher plants. The soil here is poorly drained, fairly infertile. Pitcher plants have an interesting adaptation, a modified leaf that attracts insects into the nectary. Inside the plant, hairs point downward and prevent an insect from climbing up. It can go downward only. It dies, and the by-products of its decomposition are absorbed by the leaves."

"Doesn't that provide nitrogen?"

"Nitrogen and other minerals."

We were surrounded now by rotting logs, red maples, and ferns. "Virginia chain fern," Bill told me, "another fern that really likes fire; and here's sweet bay, which is in the magnolia family. Its white flowers are just opening up. Looks like one has been pollinated." Deeper in the bog were cypress knees, royal ferns, and pond pines. "Pond pines like to grow where cypress grows, in real wet areas." Despite its fondness for wetlands, pond pine is another fire-dependent species. "Their cones are held closed by resin. When fire melts the resin, the seeds drop."

We drove next to the most bizarre woods I'd ever seen. It reminded me of a forest that Dr. Seuss might have drawn. From a few feet above the ground, the longleaf pines, which were fairly young, were all bent in the same direction. Then they curved into *C*s like standing longbows, and finally straightened to grow vertically to their crowns.

"When Hugo hit, these were young saplings," Bill said. "They were bent over as much as 40 degrees. Then the terminal buds resumed growing skyward," and the trees righted themselves.

Near the stand was another pocosin of five or six hundred acres. "This area was burned real hot in mid-April," said Bill. He knelt by a shrub that was only knee high. "This is *Quercus pumila*, or runner oak, a real interesting plant. It sprouts from rhizomes, underground runners." Forming colonies of clones, runner oaks are common to sandy sites in the southeastern United States. "See how extensive it is? Runner oaks know they can't grow tall" in a fire-prone landscape. "Fire will knock them back down, so they spread out. They grow only a few feet tall, but they produce acorns as big as a live oak's. Runner oaks are a great source of mast for wildlife." Because this site was burned recently, however, "they won't have any acorns this fall. They need a fire-free year to produce. Next fall they'll be loaded with big acorns."

I commented on all of the ferns and switch cane.

"This pocosin is dominated by switch cane, chalky bluestem, a bunch-grass, cinnamon fern, red bay, sweet bay, fetter-bush, evergreen shrubs, and pond pines. These pond pines look like they're dead," he observed. "Anytime you burn a pocosin, the fire gets real intense."

"I guess because it's damp, it has to get hot to burn."

"A lot of the pond pines were killed, but the fire opened up their cones, which will release their seeds. So the pond pines will seed in and regenerate."

There were colic roots, used as a remedy to aid digestion; more runner oaks; goat's rue in bloom; and "either post oaks or southern red oaks," Bill told me. "They're hard to identify when they're young because the leaves are so variable. And here's dwarf chinquapin, *Castanea pumila*. By the fall, it will produce a burr with nice seeds for wildlife."

The seepage bog was a bouquet of trumpet, sweet, and hooded pitcher plants. Of the three, said Bill, "sweet pitcher plants are the rarest." Surrounding the pitcher plants were switch cane, huckleberry, ground blueberry, crow poison, and meadow beauty, "which produces beautiful blue flowers in June. Over here is an orchid, a grass-pink *Calopogon tuberosus*. At this site, subsurface drainage keeps the soil wet and provides a special habitat.

"Some years we can't get fire into the pocosin. It's too wet. But this year we had a good burn here, and I'm glad we did. Pitcher plants love fire. It keeps shrubs and hardwoods down so the pitcher plants can get plenty of sunlight. If we don't burn, the site gets overgrown and suppresses them."

I thought of the irony—another wetland species that, like pond pine and white wicky, needs fire.

"Here's another orchid, rose begonia," he said and cataloged some sights and sounds of the wildlife around us: a little wood satyr butterfly; the *wicket-wickety* of a common yellow-throat, "a little warbler with a black mask"; a blue-gray gnat catcher; a pileated woodpecker; more sweet bay "that got knocked back by the fire"; a great crested flycatcher that "probably has a nest near here; another prothonotary warbler; a white iberia; and barely two feet up the slope of the pocosin, a ridge of longleaf pines. "Pretty extensive ground blueberry. Next summer it'll have little white flowers and then berries," Bill said. "Aldo Leopold wrote that land is a fountain of energy flowing through soil, plants, and animals. There's a lot going on here."

We headed to Battery Trail, the last stop on our tour. "There's the remnant of a Confederate Civil War battery on the Santee River," Bill said as we stepped out of the truck and began hiking down the trail. Turkey buzzards and a swallow-tailed kite soared over the river. "The battery is one of our premier historic sites. We burned this area almost to the river. This all used to be longleaf, but due to fire exclusion and clear-cutting before the Forest Service acquired it, it converted to loblolly.

"About five or six years ago, we removed the loblollies from here but saved the hardwoods. Since then these oaks have undergone a tremendous amount of growth. We want that for wildlife habitat and acorn production. We burned here last February and burn every two years to keep it open. Essentially we're shooting for an oak savanna. It's looking really good. I like the openness of the hardwoods. It will be interesting to see how it looks through the years."

Knowing that fire is often considered a bane to hardwoods, I asked how burns benefit oak woodlands.

"We think that fire plays a critical role in reducing competition," in this case from loblollies, "and in helping acorns germinate. Fire in oak woodlands should not be as frequent as in longleaf forests. Oaks require some fire-free years for their seedlings to get established. Sometime we'll plan for regeneration so that hardwood saplings can grow into the canopy and replace these older oaks. That means we'll have to exclude fire from this site for a while."

To underscore this point, he strode across the crunchy dead shoots of sweetgum and sumac, competitive species that fire weeds out, to a hickory sapling. "See how fire top-killed this hickory? Its root system is still viable. We'll have to curtail burning to let the hickory sucker reach a size that can withstand low-intensity ground fires."

We continued hiking down to the river terrace. I was overwhelmed by the richness of the landscape: summer tanagers, the female yellow-orange, the male the only bird on the continent with all red feathers; coral bean, with bright red petals spanning out from a spiny stalk, "another legume that likes sandy soil"; blue flag iris; the *sweet-sweet-chew-chew-sweet-sweet* of an indigo bunting—like the tanagers, a tropical migrant; a yellow-throated vireo; the spiky white flowers of "blackroot, a member of the aster family *Asteraceae*"; pencil flower; beauty berry; a red-eyed vireo; and buckeye butterflies. We walked past an enormous poplar, "one of the few in the forest," Bill said. "Poplars aren't real fire-resistant, but this one is big enough to withstand low-intensity ground fires. You can see where a fire came through and blackened its trunk."

As we approached the steep bank of the wide Santee, the huge loblollies gave way to water oaks, pignut hickories, and cypress trees draped with Spanish moss. "Some young loblollies have seeded in. They'll replace their parents. Fire can't get down in here easily."

Below us rolled the olive green of the great river. "Lots of gators," Bill commented, though we saw none. To our right were earthen works and embrasures, mounds of dirt that once cradled Confederate cannons that "would have been aimed at the river to stop Union ships from sailing up to Jamestown."

The sky had turned stormy. Wind was gusting in the treetops. Bill had made the right call not to burn today, I thought. We turned away from the river and started back.

I stopped to examine a four-foot-tall longleaf sapling, its trunk charred to about three feet high. The longer needles were orange and dead, but "the rest is new growth," Bill said. The new needles were short, "but by the end of the growing season they'll be long. They contain a lot of moisture. During a fire, they cluster around the bud to act as a heat shield. Longleafs have all sorts of adaptations to survive fire, such as deep taproots and real thick terminal buds. Longleafs, in fact, are the only pines with white scales on their terminal buds. They're white to help reflect heat. If the bud survives a burn, the tree survives.

"Another longleaf adaptation is the sapling's thick bark, which protects the growing, living tissue of the cambium from heat." Rapid vertical growth is another survival strategy. "Unlike loblolly, there's very little side branching." Not far off was a seven-foot-tall longleaf sapling with only three branches. "A young longleaf puts all of its effort into growing upward quickly to get its terminal bud as high above flame lengths as possible. I think we burned this area about forty-five days ago. These young longleafs have already had a foot of growth."

Halfway up the trail, Bill stopped to kneel by two young saplings, one loblolly and one longleaf. It was a case study in fire management. The longleaf was only about a foot tall; the loblolly was head high.

"The loblolly's trunk is slender," Bill said.

"No thick bark on its trunk," I agreed.

"Here you can really see the difference between these pine species. The loblolly is almost six feet tall, but even at its base it's only an inch and a half in diameter." He twisted its needles between his fingers and thumb. "Its needles aren't succulent; they make poor heat shields. And its buds are small with dark scales. They absorb heat."

I looked around. Several loblolly saplings nearby had been fire-killed.

"See how the loblollies put a lot of energy into lateral branching?" Bill asked.

"A bad strategy," I replied.

He corrected me. "Not always. Historically loblollies were in wetter areas that didn't burn as often. If there's no fire, it's an acceptable strategy. For a wetter landscape, lateral growth is a great idea because loblollies compete with hardwoods. Because fire was excluded from this site for decades, loblollies marched up the hill from the river basin into an area where longleaf pines had dominated. But when we reintroduced fire, the loblollies' strategy failed. Fire is a powerful biological tool that filters out certain species. All we need to do is keep burning. Pretty soon these loblollies will die out. When I say 'soon,'" he added, "I'm talking about decades, of course."

Again I appreciated the mind-set of foresters who look back to aboriginal days before fire was suppressed and the great trees fell. I look forward to forests that may live decades or centuries after they, the foresters, are gone.

Bill turned to the longleaf sapling. "This little longleaf shows how they withstand fire. See how stout its trunk is?"

I got down on my hands and knees to look at the tree. "It's a stout little guy," I agreed. "Only a foot tall, but the diameter of its trunk is already at least two inches."

"I know," Bill said. "Isn't that amazing?" The longleaf's thick girth and corky bark are "adaptive mechanisms."

Careful not to damage any of its needles, I searched for its terminal bud and asked Bill if he could see it.

"Yeah, it's right there. It's really small."

"It would be interesting to know how deep the tree's taproot goes."

"Pretty deep, probably several feet."

The longleaf's root reached deep into the earth to store energy for the future. Its strategy for survival reached deep into the past. The numerous tactics that longleafs have evolved against environmental threats—deep taproots; white terminal buds; thick, corky bark to ward off heat; prodigious early growth to thrust their buds above ground fires; highly resinous needles that, when fallen, encourage fire to reduce competition; copious resin to push out pine beetles—make them the ideal trees to reign over a land of lightning strikes. The threat for which longleafs had no survival strategy, of course, was the Euro-American appetite for tar and heart of pine—that and our early ignorance of fire ecology.

The sky had darkened, wind was in the trees, and raindrops spattered around us. I was sorry the burn had been scratched but glad to have toured with Bill. I had knelt by a grass-stage longleaf, a youngster that carried in its DNA the wisdom of ages, and I was wiser for the meeting. I was happy too because soon I would travel to North Carolina to meet the Grandfather Pine, the oldest known living longleaf.

NOTE

1. See http://www.srs.fs.usda.gov/compass/issues5/expforests.htm (accessed May 24, 2009).

Wildland-Urban Interface

"This was a huge burn, not in terms of acreage but because of the heavy fuel load next to these houses. The woods had gone unburned so long because of its urban proximity. It had to be burned, but conditions had to be just right."

Bennet Tucker, manager of Hitchcock Woods

A SPRING EVENING, 8:00 P.M., and I was back at home with a killer sinus headache. Gray, blue, and yellow smoke swirled inside my sinuses. I wondered if the men I had been with on the day's burn had similar ailments. But I wasn't complaining. It had been a good fire. I was still excited.

The night before, Pat Ferral of Ferral Environmental Services, Inc., had called unexpectedly. Short notice, he said, but he was going to attempt the prescribed burn of a thirty-six-acre tract in the Hitchcock Woods of Aiken, South Carolina, and he invited me along.

This was the chance I had been waiting for. The question—to burn or not to burn—and the future of prescribed fire, at least in southeastern forest systems, did not depend on burns in remote, rural tracts where the only complaint might be smoke blowing across a little-traveled county road. The fate of prescribed fire and ultimately the fate of longleaf pine forests as well depended upon managing burns in the wildland-urban interface, the WUI, pronounced *wou-ee.*

Aiken, South Carolina, is a pretty town—rolling hills, wide wooded streets, and old mansions. More than a century ago, the polo player Thomas Hitchcock of Long Island, New York, wintered near the town on his three-thousand-acre estate and helped establish a "winter colony" centered on horses, polo, fox hunting, and steeplechases. He later bequeathed land to the foundation that bears his name and manages over two thousand acres of forest.

A historical marker outside one entrance proclaims Hitchcock Woods to be "one of the largest urban forests in the United States" and "the greatest

On an ATV, burn boss Mark Parker patrols a firebreak to search for spotovers during a prescribed burn. Photograph by the author.

equine playground in America." Nearby another sign, this one temporary, announced "Burning Today Hitchcock Woods." As I stood reading these signs, a white South Carolina Forestry Commission truck drove by towing a trailer and a Honda four-wheeler. Riding shotgun was a black Labrador retriever with a red collar.

I got back into my Jeep, drove through the entrance, and parked in a dirt lot near a shed and not far from the foundation office, a small green wood-frame house. Parked near the shed was a GMC Sierra dually with a City of Aiken Public Safety logo on the door and a water tank and pump in the bed. Next to it was a Hitchcock Woods Foundation 4 x 4 Nissan Frontier. Drip torches, yellow water bladders, rakes, and axes filled the truck bed.

I got out, careful not to step in the occasional ball of horse manure. A horse trail sloped down into the woods. At the trailhead, another sign welcomed pedestrians and horses but prohibited bicycles and motorized vehicles. I watched a man with a dog on a leash head down the trail and into the woods. At a kiosk yet another sign warned of "controlled burning in the woods this winter and spring." According to a map posted at the kiosk, this year's plan was to burn 463 acres.

The map's trails sported names such as Lovers Lane, Foxes Den, Rabbit Valley, Tea Cottage Path, and Calico Creek. Behind the kiosk and down one trail was a mix of pines and hardwoods, thick undergrowth, and "ladders" of drape fuel and wisteria that would quickly coax any fire up into the canopy. Pat had told me that the acreage he planned to burn today had not been burned for fifteen years. If that acreage looked anything like this, he would have his hands full.

A woodpecker knocked on a pine. A minute later Pat pulled up in his red F-150. Following him in the white S.C. Forestry Commission truck was Bennett Tucker, manager of Hitchcock Woods. Bennett, a tall young man, was dressed, like Pat, in green Nomex pants and a yellow shirt. "Bennett," Pat informed me, "has been on many burns with us." Accompanying Bennett was another young man, Brandon Heitkamp of the S.C. Forest Commission. Brandon, who had the Honda ATV, was the S.C. Forestry Commission's project forester for Aiken, Barnwell, Bamberg, and Allendale Counties—"all the way from here to the beach." Brandon was there at Pat's request. That day his job was to attack the fire if it jumped the line.

We shook hands as Pat mixed slash fuel for drip torches in a six-gallon can, three and a half gallons of diesel to two and a half gallons of gasoline. The diesel, he said, lowered the flash point of the gasoline.

Pat was smiling but seemed tense. Burning always pumped him up, and this burn especially. This was a bona fide WUI. A narrow dirt road, really a horse trail, was the only firebreak between the woods and a neighborhood of houses, corrals, and barns. It's an understatement to say that a lot was riding on the burn—not just Pat Ferral's good name and livelihood, but also a forest of mature longleaf pines, a row of million-dollar homes, and thoroughbreds as pricey as BMWs. I thought of old movies I'd seen of horses in burning barns and feared that the horses would panic if they smelled smoke.

Although Pat planned to burn only thirty-six acres, "This is a big one. We got a very heavy fuel load," he said. "It hasn't been burned in fifteen years, and it's right up against property lines. This is a wildland-urban interface, there's a lot of liability, and there's gonna be a lot of smoke. We have to take special precautions."

I knew that liability was on his mind. If plans went awry, if a house burned down, who would pay?

"A homeowner's insurance should cover it, but I'd get sued and the Hitchcock Woods Foundation would get sued. We tried to burn this unit a week ago, did some test fires, but despite a favorable forecast, the wind wasn't right and we stood down."

I asked what the test fires had indicated.

"Sporadic, gusty winds. Sometimes the National Weather Service gets the forecast wrong," he told me, shrugging. "I've already contacted Aiken County Public Safety that we're gonna burn today. Next I'll call the Forestry Commission and get a notification number. Then we're ready to roll."

Using the tailgate of his truck as a lunch counter and desktop, he unwrapped a Subway sandwich, opened a Gatorade, and showed me the prescription for the day's burn, the fire weather sheet, and a comparison of an adjacent unit that he had burned the year before. "It burned hot as hell."

"What was the flame length?" I asked.

"Twenty, thirty feet. There was a lot of mortality," he said, referring to the loss of trees, "about 20 or 30 percent. But it had to be burned."

I asked if he caught any flack for the trees that died.

"No, it's just part of it. We're trying to restore longleaf pine savannas, but the main thing," he said emphatically, "is hazard reduction, especially in the WUI."

As Pat wolfed down the sandwich, I looked over the weather sheet. Mild and cloudy; 30 percent chance of precipitation in the afternoon, .02 inches; high of 79 degrees; light variable wind from the southwest at 9 miles per hour; maximum humidity 46; a Haines index of 4, which indicated a low potential for wildfire; mixing height, 5,600 feet; transport wind, southwest at 16 miles per hour; ventilation rate, 89,600. Ventilation rate, an estimate of the atmosphere's ability to disperse smoke, is calculated by multiplying the mixing height times the transport wind.

I asked if the forecast of rain would affect the burn plans.

"It's supposed to start raining about the time we finish," Pat said. "I think we're gonna get this one today." Yesterday afternoon he had checked today's weather forecast "to get a rough idea," then contacted the Hitchcock Woods Foundation, the Forestry Commission, the Aiken Fire Department, and county dispatch about the impending burn. "The weather for the day usually comes out between 4:30 and 5:30 A.M. Short notice, and it takes a lot of planning." He drained his Gatorade and then lamented, "Wasted a day last week coming down here. Was all ready to get out in the woods and burn, then had to stand down. There's gonna be a lot of smoke today, but as long as we have a consistent wind . . ." Thinking back, he trailed off. "If we had burned last week, it would have been a disaster."

I asked how many were on his burn crew today.

"Me, Bennett Tucker, Namon Corley—he's the caretaker for the woods—and a forestry technician. We've requested two brush trucks from the Aiken Department of Public Safety, four individuals to work those trucks, and a dozer from the Forestry Commission. At the last minute I requested the second brush truck and a dozer from the Forestry Commission because of the high fuel load and the proximity of the houses. If we start and the fire's not doing what we want, we have to be able to plow it out. I like to call that 'staying inside the reservation.' I'm taking all the precautions I can. It's gonna burn hot."

He showed me a map of the Hitchcock Woods. Outlined on the map were several units marked for burning. Most had been scratched out with a pencil as already burned. "Here is the boundary line of the unit we'll burn. There are houses all along this dirt road." The road was labeled "Mr. Cooper's Ride."

Mr. Cooper's Ride, a homeowner later told me, is an easement on the landowners' property, "which was put in a long time ago. Mr. Hitchcock died in 1941. Probably Cooper's Ride has been here since the 1930s."

I remembered the man with the dog heading down the trail. "Do you worry about joggers, walkers, equestrians not knowing that you're burning?"

"We put signs out. Aiken Public Safety notifies people. Generally people support us. They understand the potential for wildfire, and they know why we're burning—hazard reduction. You know, if a wildfire kicked off in the woods with that heavy fuel load, it wouldn't stop till it hit Whiskey Road," a residential street about two blocks from Hitchcock Woods. "No telling what it would tear up on the way before Public Safety and the Fire Department could contain it."

I asked if he could quantify the fuel load.

"With experience you can estimate whether a load is light, medium, or heavy. A normal fuel load is five to eight tons per acre. This unit is ultra heavy, probably fifteen tons per acre. The unit is so close to the property lines—that's the reason it hasn't been burned."

Ultimately not a good reason, I thought. The longer prescribed burns were put off, the greater the risks of wildfire and property loss. Better to start a fire when the conditions could be chosen.

Pat discussed his strategy for this burn. Because of the high fuel load, he and Bennett would use three ignition methods. First they would lay down a black line with drip torches and back the fire into the wind. Next they would drip spot fires about five to ten feet in front of the flame line. These spot fires would flare out in all directions, consuming the fuel until they met other flames. Finally they would use "strip-head fires," that is, lay down a continuous line of fire upwind of the flaming front. Running with the wind, the head fire would gain intensity and race until it met the backing fire. "When they meet, that's where you can get some really high flame lengths. If we get lit off in an hour," he concluded, "we should finish up about 3:30, 4:00."

While Pat finished gearing up for the burn, I took the opportunity to talk with Doug Rabold, executive director of Hitchcock Woods, at the foundation office.

"Because the woods are surrounded by neighborhoods," Doug told me, "we're sensitive about when we burn." Even on days when a burn would be approved by the Forestry Commission, "we may not burn. We want to be conservative." The decision to burn is jointly made by the fire boss, Pat Ferral, and the woods superintendent, Bennett Tucker.

I asked how the foundation handled public relations, how they notified the neighbors and addressed their concerns.

"Every burn season, the local newspaper prints two articles explaining the reason for the burns and the precautions we take." This year the *Aiken Standard* published digital photos of a burn on their Internet page. "We want the community to support the burn program, and they have. We post signage; we publish a newsletter. Today I called four neighbors to advise them that we'd be burning behind their houses. We try to be totally transparent."

Was there opposition to the burns from the community?

"Occasionally in the past. We've had complaints about smoke, so last year we adopted a policy to minimize the smoke that's produced. We burn as early in the day as possible and stop burning a lot earlier than the law requires to avoid a late afternoon inversion that might bring smoke down into a neighborhood, even though, once the personnel and equipment are assembled, it would be more cost effective and efficient to burn more acres. Because we're conservative, we pay more."

They burn the Hitchcock Woods for several reasons: to reduce hazardous fuel load; to control hardwoods; to eliminate invasive, exotic plants, the seeds of which are carried by birds into the woods from neighboring gardens; to improve grazing and bedding conditions for wildlife; to foster the growth of wiregrass and herbaceous ground cover; to return nutrients to the soil; to create litter-free conditions for longleaf seeds, which need bare mineral soil to sprout. The Hitchcock Woods is aiming for an uneven-aged longleaf forest.

I thanked Doug and rejoined Pat, and we drove to the burn zone. On the way we passed a woods thick with "ladders," vines that clung to the trees, some of which were century-old longleafs. Pat glanced at the woods. "That area's not too bad," he said. If that wasn't "too bad," I worried what the burn site would look like.

We drove past a ridge called the Devil's Backbone. There were several stunted, brown-leaved water oaks amid the tall pines. I asked if a recent burn had killed the oaks.

"No, that's just top-kill. They'll come back. It's dry out here," he added. "It's dusty. Pretty soon it's gonna be smoky."

We passed a small canyon caused by storm-water runoff. Bumping along, we caught up with a small caravan of trucks wending through the forest on a roller coaster of narrow dirt roads. Pat had invited the Forestry Commission out for extra support. "This is a real high-profile area. A lot of landowners are concerned about the burn. They know it has to be done, but they're still scared. So I bring in the cavalry and try to allay their fears."

We arrived at the unit to be burned and parked on the corner of Mr. Cooper's Ride, which would serve as a firebreak, and a wide power line right-of-way, which would serve as another. Namon's blue Ford tractor was waiting, along with ATVs, two Aiken Fire Department brush trucks, two Forestry Commission trucks, and two bulldozers, one on the ground and one on a flatbed in tow. I guessed that these larger trucks had driven down the right-of-way and not the woods' trails. Facing the burn unit, all were lined up in the dusty wide right-of-way as reinforcements—Pat's cavalry. The dozers gave Pat "the capacity to plow out a fire" in case things go wrong.

"But I don't think we'll need it. You can have too many people on a burn," he reflected, "but most of the time there aren't enough. I stay on good terms with the county fire marshals, and I don't mind calling them and saying, 'Would you bring out the brush truck and stand by for me?'"

I looked down the horse trail that would serve as one firebreak. A homeowner in jeans, a ball cap, and a white T-shirt was hosing down his grass in the hope that if the fire jumped, the wet grass would stop it from spreading. Beyond him were more homes, fences, stables, and grazing horses.

The setting was beautiful, with a calm breeze, robin-egg blue sky, fine houses, dark thoroughbreds grazing in small green paddocks, and a pine woods. As we got out, Pat donned a hard hat and leather gloves. He nodded toward the homeowner who was hosing down his lawn and said, "I'm just trying to be as safe as I can. We're taking care of the forest and protecting their property at the same time."

Soon Pat and Bennett were out of sight in the woods. With drip torches, they had already started lighting the black line, which was creeping into the forest. Nearby Namon Corley, also dressed in Nomex, was working the fire line with a rake. The air was smoky. Flames were about two feet high.

I walked over to Namon and introduced myself. He had a deep voice and slow, rhythmic way of talking. The ground, I noticed, had been recently disked. I asked when.

"The other week, but we didn't get to burn. The wind wasn't right. It was blowing straight toward Fox Chase," an Aiken subdivision.

I remarked that Namon was an uncommon name.

He agreed. "I'll be in the church, and the preacher will be talking about patriarchs begettin' and namin', and the people will turn around and think he's talking about me."

I laughed and asked how long he had been caretaker of the Hitchcock Woods.

He leaned on his rake. He was seventy-one years old, married for fifty-four. "I been out here forty-eight years. I didn't know I was gonna be out here that long. Started when I was twenty-three. I take care of the woods out here. I'm retired but still working. I worked out here when there wasn't a house in Fox Chase, wasn't a house nowhere. It was just like this," he said, nodding toward the woods. "We backing the fire in now," he said as he resumed raking. "Long as it don't go toward those houses."

"When are you going to retire?"

"I feel all right," he chuckled. "Might work another year."

It was after noon, and the burn was progressing slowly. I thought of the late start and the acreage yet to be burned. I walked through the smoke to the end of the compartment, where another wide firebreak dog-legged to the left. The flames were anemic, a mere six or eight inches high, creeping along at about a foot per minute. There was practically no bunchgrass to keep the matted leaves and needles off the ground and feed oxygen to the flames, which was why the burn was tiptoeing. Farther up the burn and farther away from the houses, though, the black line had widened considerably. I caught up with Pat at the corner. I remarked that the fire line "wasn't exactly raging."

"We got a good day," he said. "I think we're going to pull it off. I strung the fire up this far to make sure it would do right. The wind's out of the southwest, but the eddy effect of the power line is causing the fire to flank a bit."

I followed as Pat walked on and dripped another strip of fire inside the black line.

"This is the most critical time in the burn," he explained. "You gotta be patient. You can see how heavy the fuel is in there." The forest floor was thick with branches, deadfalls, and a mat of leaves and pine needles. Indeed there were so many pine needles, Pat said, "it's like walking on a sponge. Watch yourself," he warned.

I asked what the next phase would be.

"We'll drop spots of fire in front of the flames. When I get up this hill, I'm going to help Bennett get his side blacked in a little more because we don't want a head fire. I'm excited," he said as he stepped across the black line and began pouring fire from his drip torch onto the fuel load and ladders, which were ten feet high in some places and even higher in the interior. Average flame lengths were three to four feet high, with flames occasionally jumping to fifteen feet. The ground was blackened. All that remained of pinecones were little piles of white ashes. Thick blue smoke stung my eyes and ate at the back of my throat. I walked back toward the trucks in the power line to chat with Brandon Heitkamp.

"In Aiken, because it's good horse country," Brandon said, "we have a lot of 'snowbirds,' people who have moved down from up north. They may not burn in New York, and when they move down here and have horses, they're deathly afraid of the burns. It's a public relations battle," he said, citing the destructive cycle of fire suppression, fuel accumulation, and catastrophic wildfire. "Part of our job is to educate people why we burn. This year we had a program on wildland-urban interface during Fire Prevention Week. Prescribed fire is the best, cheapest tool we have for controlling the woods and protecting people's homes, for limiting the risk of wildfire, for introducing more nutrients into the soil, and for killing undesirable plant species. Some people don't realize that if there was a fire without trained personnel on-site, it could take their homes or their horses. If too much fuel accumulates, even a bulldozer won't stop the fire."

I asked his opinion on the future of prescribed burning.

"It's up in the air. You gotta have a million-dollar insurance policy to burn, a two-million-dollar policy if you use a helicopter. That's our biggest problem."

There was the *ggrrr* of a John Deere Gator ATV with a water tank on its back. Its driver, the forestry technician, was prowling for spotovers. He parked and hosed down a horse jump built of pine logs and brush. The jump, which straddled a horse trail that served as a firebreak, looked as if it were begging to burn. Given half a chance, the jump would lead fire from the burn unit across the firebreak and into the woods. Bennett advanced with his drip torch, dropping more fire. He called to the forestry tech, "Douse that limb and pinecone," then said to me, "I'll be ready to see some rain tonight."

White ashes fell like snow. Smoke stung my eyes. I rubbed them. I was ready for some Visine. I checked my wristwatch. It was nearly 1:00 P.M. The flames here were just inches high, creeping along, it seemed, without much appetite. The wind was shifty but, all in all, calm. In the distance a homeowner was still watering his lawn. Suddenly the fire crackled into a big pile of brush. Happy to find something to eat, the flames leaped up eight feet. Hiking the black line, I found Pat at the other end. "Wind seems to be doing what you want it to," I said.

"Yeah." He pointed across the firebreak to a section of woods he had burned last year. "To get a feel for the conditions, we compared today's weather with the weather we had when we burned over there." Because of the heavy fuel load there, "it still got a little too damned hot," and some pines died. Pat walked across the smoking ground and through the low flames, dripping another strip of fire in front of the advancing black line.

Down Mr. Cooper's Ride, a horse whinnied. Upwind of the smoke, another horse grazed peacefully, head down, tail ruffled by the breeze, oblivious to the fire visibly licking the ground forty yards downwind. I stepped over the black line and through a low spot in the flames and walked into the woods. The flames' lengths were increasing, the fire quickening. Things were getting hot. I stood and studied a small longleaf that was about eighteen feet tall. Fire licked three feet up its trunk. Not finding an easy meal, the flames passed by, singeing the bark but not scorching the needles. Amazing how longleafs withstand this, I thought.

Despite their resistance to ground fire, longleafs don't always survive low-intensity burns. After a number of fireless years, accumulated duff at the bases of trees can create "donuts" of thick, matted fuel. Feeder roots can grow into the duff, which can smolder after a burn for hours or days, killing those roots and damaging the cambium as well. "This is especially true during a drought and in a stand of older age longleaf," Dave Robinson wrote in an October 11, 2011, e-mail. If this occurs, the stand of longleaf pines, living off its stored reserves, may look healthy for two years or more, but the damage is done. The pines are dying on their feet. Eventually the needles turn orange and the trees die. John McGuire, senior project manager with Westervelt Ecological Services, saw an entire stand die this way.[1]

"Fire must be a part of the restoration process, but must be reintroduced very carefully if it has been long excluded. Excessive fuel buildups can result in damaging or lethal fires, even in mature stands. . . . Long-term fire exclusion usually results in a woody mid- and understory. These fuels can feed hot fires, especially if needles draped on vines and shrubs and 'ladders' flame up into the canopy."[2]

When Pat walked back toward his truck to grab a second drip torch, I asked whether enough duff had accumulated to be a problem, whether it might keep smoldering and girdle and kill the pines. "Is that a concern here, since this hasn't been burned in fifteen years?"

"No. The duff here is not so bad. The trees are so thick, they can stand some mortality." He recalled a burn at Sandy Island, the largest undeveloped freshwater island in the eastern United States. "In some places duff out there around the big trees was a foot thick. The feeder roots will come up to the surface to get moisture. That's when a burn can kill a tree. Sometimes," he added, "you intentionally burn hot to kill some pines."

I observed that the wind was blowing away from the houses. "It's doing just what you want it to."

Pat got a lemon-lime Gatorade from a cooler in the bed of his truck. "It is today, thank God," he said as he headed back into the burn. Nearing the corner of the woods, he turned and began slinging fire from his drip torch back up the line.

The burn was heating up. The black line now was between ten and twenty feet wide. Flames sizzled and cracked, raced, and jumped into the crown of a fifteen-foot pine.

Every couple of feet, oaks mingled with the pines. Some oaks were young; some were big. In front of the edge of the flames, the forest was green and leafy. Behind, there was scorched earth and a blowing curtain of blue smoke. It was strange to watch this transformation.

I met Namon again, standing on Mr. Cooper's Ride. More than forty years ago, he had made this run. "A man laid it out," he said, "and I went behind with a tractor and cleared it out."

Pat emerged from the burn and walked toward us. He took a break, squatting on Mr. Cooper's Ride to wipe sweat and drink some Gatorade. Brandon and an Aiken fireman joined us.

"We got it right today," Pat said. "Won't have to bring in the cavalry. We would have had a disaster on our hands if we'd burned last week with the wind shifting all over the place and all these houses." He produced a large pickle from his pocket, unwrapped it, and bit into it.

"Pickles," I said. "Are they to prevent dehydration?"

"A lot of sodium, a lot of liquid," Brandon replied.

"I just grabbed one on the way out of the house this morning," Pat told us.

"You can see smoke all the way over on the bypass," said the fireman.

"Residual smoke is our biggest enemy today," Pat said. "It bothers a lot of the neighbors. It might blow over their property and get into their houses." He coughed. "In the evening if the wind dies and smoke settles in low areas, there can be poor smoke dispersion. Tonight smoke dispersion will be fair, especially with this weather front coming through. And today's mixing height," the height where smoke stops rising, "is well over three thousand feet."

I asked if he was concerned that the rain might come sooner than expected.

"No, it would be fine with me. It would lower the intensity of the flames, put out what was still burning where the fire had already passed." He stood and stretched, and I followed him back into the woods, where he dripped flames about twenty feet apart and in front of the advancing fire. By consuming fuel, this tactic would keep the burn from becoming too strong. "A big head fire would get into the crowns. We don't want that." Each circle of flame was yellow as it advanced, then turned orange and leaped momentarily higher when the circles met.

At least one tall longleaf would not survive. Its bole was about a foot and a half in diameter at breast height and had a collar of fire fifteen feet up. Flames never reached the crown, but the collar kept burning.

Still following Pat, I walked deeper into the woods parallel to the dotted line of fire he put down. Flames licked around the trees. The heat was getting intense. The flames were taller; the smoke, dark. A horse whinnied. Green grasshoppers flew out of the fire. Some younger pines would suffer needle scorch, but their branches were not burning. Nearby scrub oaks of the same height, unable to take the heat, were all aflame. Because of the heavy dark smoke, the forest seemed to descend into night, despite the brightness of the fire.

"The burn is going well," Pat said, "but I have to go slow. You can't just run across the woods with a string of fire. If you did, a head fire would get up in the crowns. Longleaf pine needles are very, very volatile."

We kicked our way through tufts of needles, leaves, and low brush. A sulfur butterfly flew past. Black smoke streamed from Pat's drip torch. I was surprised at the flame length, which was now twenty to twenty-five feet. Across Mr. Cooper's Ride, houses shimmered in the hot air. Several homes down, Dick and Diana Postles and Bobby, a neighborhood boy, stood by a rail fence watching. I headed over to talk with them.

"We came out to see what's happening," Diana laughed nervously.

I mentioned that this section of woods had not been burned in fifteen years.

"Well, we've been here ten, and it certainly hasn't been burned in our time," Dick said, taking a deep breath. "I understand the need for the burn, but I suspect that there are as many negatives as positives."

The flames were dramatic. Another large pine near the edge of the firebreak was on fire. It wouldn't survive.

"This is enervating," Dick said. A few seconds passed. "We live in a frame house. My roof shingles will burn, and if the crowns of these pines get going," he said, his voice turning serious, "that's the end of the ball game."

"But the wind is in a good direction," Diana said. "For a little bit the wind really picked up, but it's still blowing away from us."

I asked if they thought the burn crew had checked the wind forecast prior to the burn.

"Oh yeah," they nodded assuredly. "Bennett Tucker stopped by the other evening," Dick said, then trailed off. "The wind swirls here," he said, speculating that the eddy effect had something to do with the horse paths and local topography. "It's an extensive woods. Even this morning for a little while, the wind was coming out of the northwest," a direction that would have blown the fire toward their home.

They had no pasture, no stable. "You're not horse people?" I asked. They shook their heads. "Then what are you doing in Aiken?" I joked. "Didn't they tell you?"

"We came here from Philadelphia before most of the horse people. We've lived down here for twenty-five years. We've been in this house for ten. But it's nerve-racking when you have a frame house that's fifty feet from the edge of the fire."

I imagined all of the family heirlooms in their house, all the photographs hanging on the walls. "No doubt," I replied.

"I'm glad that the burn is being done as carefully as it is," said Diana. "They're doing a good job."

"Right," Dick agreed.

As if on cue, Pat and Brandon emerged from the smoke and trees.

"How's it going?" I shouted, hurrying to catch up with them.

"Going well," Pat said happily.

Flames exploded in some heavy fuel, and with a chimney-like effect of smoke, heat, and light, they flared fifty feet up into the crown of a longleaf. I stopped to watch, awestruck. Although this burn was on a comparatively small scale, I had never witnessed one this intense. Some pines will be lost, I thought. As if reading my thoughts, Pat intoned, "Casualties of war," and walked on.

"Thermal thinning. It was kind of tight in there anyway," said Brandon, who called the woods "dog-hair pine" because of the thickness of the trees. "You get less needle scorch at 11:00 in the morning than you do in the heat of the afternoon," he added, passing by.

What amazed me was not the sudden ferocity of the fire, but that the incident—the flames climbing a ladder of vines, shooting up the trunk and into the green crown to kill the tree—was over in far less than a minute. What's more, the flames did not jump from crown to crown as I feared. In perhaps thirty seconds, the fire had fallen back to the forest floor and to less threatening, man-size lengths.

I rejoined Pat on his next sweep through the woods. Trudging fast alongside as he worked with his drip torch, I said, "The flames jumped fifty feet into the crown—"

"That's the heavy drape fuel," he said, referring to the sparkleberry and the wisteria vines that were draped with fallen branches and highly flammable pine needles. The vines reached from the ground to the canopy. "That's why this woods is a fire hazard. There's no other way to burn it." Pat marched on, laying down a solid line of fire about twenty feet in front of the advancing flames.

A lapdog barked on a porch across the firebreak of Mr. Cooper's Ride. A gray-haired man stepped out onto the porch, apparently unconcerned with the goings-on, and told his dog to shut up.

Deep in the interior of the woods was another "chimney fire." Flames shot forty or fifty feet up a group of pines. The smoke was blue near the ground and white near the crowns. Yellow smoke billowed a couple of hundred feet above the trees. The sound of the roaring fire pulsed like the crashing of waves on a shore.

This is intense, I said to myself. If you did not know what was going on, it would scare the hell out of you. Along Mr. Cooper's Ride, a few onlookers stood with their arms crossed, watching the fire.

Another chimney fire, with flame lengths of sixty feet, enveloped a dozen more trees, their bark glowing all the way to the crowns. The *whooshing* of the fire was weird, like the sound of a storm in a furnace. As before, the event was over in half a minute, and the nearby trees escaped apparent damage. Occasionally these chimney fires were repeated throughout the burn. Still, the flames never leaped from crown to crown.

One young longleaf near the firebreak was not as lucky. Namon raked pine straw away from its trunk, but the bark had already ignited, and sap boiled in the cambium. Because the pine stood at the edge of Mr. Cooper's

Ride, a fireman arrived in a brush truck to hose the tree down and avert a potential spotover.

Then the flames had passed by, and with them the Postles' apprehensions. I walked past Dick Postles. He grinned and held up fists of victory, saying, "Yes, yes!"

Despite the late start and initially slow progress of the burn, once the flames hit ample ground fuel and ladders, the fire had raced through the woods. Now the burn was wrapping up. Pat retrieved his truck from the power line right-of-way and parked next to a brush truck and Namon's tractor at a dirt crossroads where the crew had gathered. The mood was like that in a locker room after your team had won—tired but exhilarated and full of talk. Brandon's dog summed it up, wagging and panting hard.

"I believe we done beat the rain," Namon commented.

"With all that sparkleberry in there," said Pat, referring to the drape fuel, "the fire was gonna explode." Despite sparkleberry's habit of holding fuel for fire, however, it's worth noting that the shrub, like wild azalea, red bud, dogwood, magnolia, and persimmon, is more fire-resistant.

An older fireman asked a younger one if he had learned anything today.

"Yeah. I learned I hope they keep this up."

"Why is that?"

"'Cause I'd sure as hell hate to be out here trying to put out a wildfire."

"This was a huge burn," said Bennett, "not in terms of acreage but because of the heavy fuel load next to these houses. The woods had gone unburned so long because of its urban proximity. It had to be burned, but conditions had to be just right."

The empty drip torches clanged as Pat stored them in the bed of his truck. He thanked Brandon, the Forestry Commission, and the firefighters from the Fire Division of Aiken Public Safety "for coming out today on a moment's notice. We had to do it at the last minute. But that's usually the way it goes. You never know. When I've got a woods to burn, I get up before dawn and I'm scared to look at the fire weather. The forecast may have totally changed." The drip torches clanged again. "But we got it right today. I'm happy."

"Done in time to go to church tonight for a revival," said Namon.

It was 3:45 P.M. The burned compartment looked like a battlefield. Smoke drifted, trunks were charred black, and little of the understory was left. A few flames flickered around the bases of trees.

Bennett shook hands with a firefighter and then drove off on the Gator ATV to patrol the perimeter and check for spotovers.

I climbed into Pat's truck for a ride back to my Jeep. Namon ate a bag of chips and drank a Gatorade. He waved goodbye from his tractor. "We got it today!"

"Yeah," Pat replied. "If not, it would have kicked our butts." He lit a cigarette and shook out the match. "And we'd be in the jailhouse."

NOTES

1. John McGuire, senior project manager with Westervelt Ecological Services' Southeast Regional Office, address to the South Carolina Prescribed Fire Council, Columbia, South Carolina, November 18, 2008.

2. Rhett Johnson and Dean Gjerstad, "Restoring the Overstory of Longleaf Pine Ecosystems," in *The Longleaf Pine Ecosystem: Ecology, Silviculture, and Restoration*, ed. Shibu Jose, Eric J. Jokela, and Deborah L. Miller (New York: Springer, 2006), 289–90.

The Grandfather Pine

"It is a very old pine who at last forgets which of his many candles is the most important, and thus flattens his crown against the sky."

Aldo Leopold

WHEN I FIRST VISITED Scott Lanier's office at the Carolina Sandhills National Wildlife Refuge, I was looking for a short topic—maybe coyotes or cottonmouths. When Scott asked me to write a news article to explain the importance of prescribed burns, I knew nothing of longleaf pines, wiregrass, or red-cockaded woodpeckers. Soon, with the help of new friends, I was discovering one of our planet's great ecosystems, one in peril, like so many others, but one with advocates, caretakers, and lovers. Several years later, I'm still discovering.

I would like to say that Earth is resilient and the forests are resurgent. I would like to be hopeful, despite the doubtful future of prescribed burning and therefore of longleaf forests. Old-growth forests, strong-limbed and green-crowned, offer some hope that with stewardship and restraint, wildlands will not only survive but prevail. Why save longleaf forests? "Because we are the reason they are in danger," Laura Housh would say, and because we can.

A few years back I rode with forester Clay Ware into the Carolina Sandhills National Wildlife Refuge to an old pit where clay had been dug and used to resurface the refuge roads. The pit looked like a crater, a moonscape. Eroded, hard-baked, pink-orange dirt sloped up to a ten-foot bank of exposed roots where, atop the bank, the woods began again. The pit was a barren spot, really ugly.

The winter before, Clay entertained a crazy dream to reclaim the place. "I had some leftover longleaf seedlings. People told me I was nuts to plant here, and maybe they had good reason. I kind of thought I was too but decided to give it a try. I know how tough those seedlings are. I stuck them in

Though not all grass-stage longleaf pines survive prescribed burns, they have strategies to help withstand fires: white terminal buds reflect heat; thick, corky bark protects the cambium; and succulent needles gather around the bud, emit moisture, and act as heat shields during fires. Photograph by the author.

the ground back in February, four months ago." Persimmons and slash pines grew in deeper, sandier soil around the perimeter of the wide depression. Clay had planted the longleaf pines, however, where "the ground is hard as a rock. But as you can see, most of them have made it so far."

I would have overlooked the little seedlings had Clay not pointed them out. Now that he had, I saw scores of them. Some of the seedlings grew on mounds the size of children's fists, as if the dull ground had tried to expel these upstarts. "Frost heaving," Clay said. "Sometimes when there's cold weather, moisture in the ground freezes, expands, and pushes the seedlings up."

There were faint, perfect circles scratched in the dirt around the seedlings. I asked what made them.

"Wind blowing the needles around."

He had planted nearly one hundred seedlings. "If they can survive the planting," he augured, "they may make it." He stooped to examine one seedling's needles. "This one looks like it tried to die, but there's new, fresh growth. That shows how tough these little guys are."

NOW I WAS ON THE ROAD to meet another survivor. The morning fog was lifting along Highway 15, magnolias bloomed, white-flowered lily pads floated on a black-water pond, and a wild turkey browsed in a long, level field of young green corn. I passed through Society Hill, South Carolina. A historical marker proclaimed that the town, the oldest in Darlington County, had been founded in 1736. Outside of town, traffic slowed: two escaped cows were grazing in roadside grass.

I crossed the state line and continued north toward Southern Pines, North Carolina, driving past clear-cuts, through soft, sandy hills, and past forests with open understories and evidence of recent burns. I rolled down the window and breathed in the sweet smells of the woods. The sky brightened to blue. It was a beautiful day.

I arrived at the office of North Carolina's Weymouth Woods Sandhills Nature Preserve, where I met Kim Hyre. Blonde and fair, she was dressed in a park ranger's uniform, as she had been while working for twenty-two years. We got into her truck and drove off to the Boyd Round Timber Estate.

I asked Kim why it was called the "Round Timber" Estate.

"Its trees have never been turpentined. Because there's been no slicing or angling into the sides of the trunks, the trees are round."

With 98 percent of America's longleaf forests lost to back turpentining practices, logging, development, and fire suppression, why, I wondered, had these longleafs survived unscathed?

In the early 1900s, Kim explained, "the Boyd family secured the tract and protected it with a vengeance." Even then not all of the tract was old growth. Only a smaller parcel of about 120 acres had escaped. "I don't know if the Boyds knew the value of what they were preserving, but they did not like the decimation" of the landscape that surrounded Southern Pines. After the unbridled clear-cutting of the early twentieth century, "there was little left here but sand and a railroad." I had seen old photographs of this unimaginable barrenness—all the trees gone, nothing but sand as far as the eye could see.

A bluebird exited its house. "I've witnessed changes here," Kim said as we skirted a pocosin. "Twenty years ago," because of the undergrowth, "you could not see through here. Now the forest is more open."

"And the changes were wrought by—?"

"Fire. Some sections of this unit are burned annually." One field we drove past was rife with foot-high turkey oaks, wiregrass, broomsedge, and longleaf seedlings and saplings. "We also have some gigantic yellow pitcher plants. The wiregrass," she added, "is always ready to burn." She slowed and pointed. "See that fox squirrel?"

"Yeah. A big black body with a white tail. He's movin' fast too."

"He's gorgeous."

We entered the Boyd Round Timber Estate, descending, climbing, winding, and turning on rutted, sandy dirt roads. We drove through a unit of about 150 acres that had been burned a couple of years ago. The understory was open. "Look at the little longleafs sprouting up. Thousands of them!" I exclaimed.

"A winter burn," Kim said, pausing near a rolling hill of aged longleaf. At least five of the longleafs were flattops. "This is one of my favorite views. When the longleafs top out like this, you know that they are ancient."

I asked why she thought their tops flattened out. "Is it a survival strategy?"

"There's no advantage in this dry, sandy soil to growing any higher. If you flatten and don't grow as tall, competition for water is less intense." Also, in the lightning-prone Southeast, there's no advantage to being the tallest tree on the block. "If the tallest, straightest trees are more likely to be struck by lightning," she said, "then let the younger bucks take the hit. The growth rings in these old longleafs are incredibly tight and strong," Kim remarked. "We think of pine trees as having soft wood, but with longleaf, that is such a farce."

We drove on. I wondered if there were any active red-cockaded woodpecker cavity nests in the old flattops.

"No. There is an active RCW colony beyond this patch of hardwoods, and we have other active red-cockaded colonies on the preserve; but here the hardwood midstory has enveloped these old longleafs and chased the woodpeckers out." For decades fire in this unit had been suppressed. "The Boyds did not understand the concept of prescribed fire, and they restricted all burning on the property." Another consequence of fire suppression, she added, was that "you don't see any longleaf reproduction here."

Because of the resulting midstory of oaks, dogwoods, and hickories, burns were now out of the question: fire would easily leap into the crowns of the pines. To open up the forest again, Kim said, the brush and hardwood midstory "will have to be mechanically taken out."

After parking we exited the truck and started up a winding trail lined on both sides with old longleafs—tall, beautiful, straight-up trees. "Pretty by Hollywood standards," Kim commented. We hiked up a slope through hickory, turkey oak, sassafras, persimmon, and magnolia trees. A crow cawed. Soon we were in the midst of more than a dozen old flattops that were probably, Kim said, in the three- to four-hundred-year-old range.

"The understory is fairly open here," I remarked.

"Yeah. This is one of the areas we've mechanically cut" to reduce the threat of wildfire to the pines.

Then she introduced me to the oldest known living longleaf pine. It was not as big or tall as I had imagined, but it looked strong and healthy. "When I think about how long this old longleaf has been standing here," I said, "how deeply it's rooted, how much it's endured, how much of human history it's lived through . . ."

"And for years we didn't even know it was here," Kim said.

Why wasn't it marked, I asked, with a plaque?

"For protection." If these trees were easily identified, they might be poisoned or spiked with copper nails by vandals. "I've seen this done."

"And someone would do that because . . . ?"

"Evil," she answered, shrugging. "To kill something just to brag about it."

"There's a nice open sky above him."

"That may be one reason he's doing so well."

"He probably makes sure no other trees get too close—elbows them out of his way," I said, observing his strong limbs.

Nearby stood another old longleaf, larger than the Grandfather Pine and the second largest in North Carolina. "Look at the size of him," I remarked.

"Isn't he beautiful?" Kim told me of "a forester who was collecting the DNA of old-growth trees so that they could be reproduced in greenhouses. I showed him the oldest longleaf, and he just said, 'Hmmm, ok.' Then I showed him this longleaf, the second largest in our state"—a taller, straighter, more handsome pine "by Hollywood standards," as Kim would say. "The forester said, 'Wow! This is the one I want!' He wasn't impressed by the attractiveness of our oldest pine. Its trunk is crooked; its crown is not as big or impressive."

"Sometimes it's the gnarled, scarred trees that have more character," I said. I was going to say that I hoped I would look as good when I'm as old, then realized, not being as deeply rooted, I'd be lucky to see twenty more years.

"I wouldn't want to live as long," Kim told me, reading my thoughts.

"We're not built for it," I agreed. "But the older I get, the prettier this old pine will look." Its bark was scarred by fire. "Look how thick that bark is," I commented. "An inch and a half, two inches thick, like armor plating."

"Good protection. Prescribed burns wouldn't hurt it, but now we cut around the tree by hand to keep the understory open."

Four hundred and sixty-two years—that was the age of the Grandfather Pine. Its age, Kim said, "was discovered by accident three years ago. Jason Ortegren, a master's student at the University of North Carolina at Greensboro, was writing his thesis on the history of drought conditions. We gave him permission to core about thirty trees. He took the corings back to Greensboro, counted the rings, and realized he had found a longleaf that was two years older than the oldest longleaf on record." Later, after finishing his master's thesis, Jason told Kim, "I'm still known as the kid who discovered the oldest longleaf."

"Of course," Kim told me, "its record could be beaten at any time."

"That's right. It's not necessarily the oldest, just the oldest known. I thought that four hundred years was the edge of their life span."

"Five hundred is thought to be the edge. This is getting to the max." She showed me the little round scar where Ortegren had taken the core sample.

"It looks like a belly button," I said.

Nearby a younger sibling, which Ortegren had also cored, was 459 years old. The Grandfather Pine dated back to 1548; the younger, to 1551. These trees, I said, were born about the time that Europeans first arrived in the Carolinas and eyeballed the longleaf forests for a naval store. The tree was older, in fact. The Grandfather Pine had sprouted 36 years before English explorers reported to Sir Walter Raleigh that they had found enough tar and pitch in the New World's longleaf forests to make Britannia rule the waves.[1]

"I might have to measure him," I said, taking a tape measure from my pocket.

"Go for it. I hug him all the time." Wrapping her arms partway around the trunk, Kim helped me with the tape measure.

"Seven feet, ten inches in circumference," I noted, measuring at breast height, "and about thirty inches in diameter." Not as tall as a California redwood by a long shot, or as old as a bristlecone pine, or as large as a colony of quaking aspens, but there was nothing hoary, doddering, or decrepit about it. It was simply there, deeply rooted, green-topped, healthy looking under a blue sky. Its strength and age gave me some hope for its kind.

"Well," I said, "it looks strong. Do you suppose it has red heart fungus?"

"I expect so. Bees are flying in and out of that dead limb too. Probably a hive. That doesn't hurt the tree. It's just another home."

We grew quiet. Nearby a downy woodpecker knocked on a tree. The old flattops reminded me of Tolkien's Ents or of a stone henge I once chanced upon in England. But there was nothing grandiose in this setting. I might have walked by the trees a hundred times without an inkling of their age. They were not particularly huge. Yet they were older than the United States; they had weathered the "peculiar institution" of slavery, the Civil War, the Trail of Tears, the Great Depression, industrial and technological revolutions, the fall of the Twin Towers, and more. The Grandfather Pine was 188 years older than the town of Society Hill, but no bronze marker boasted its presence—no trumpets, no flags, no billboard. Only itself.

NOTE

1. Lawrence S. Earley, *Looking for Longleaf: The Fall and Rise of an American Forest* (Chapel Hill: University of North Carolina Press, 2004), 86.

INDEX